This
HOLY BIBLE FOR CHILDREN

is presented

to _____

by _____

for _____

date _____

MY FAMILY TREE

My Name _____

Date of Birth _____

Place of Birth _____

Brothers _____ Birthday _____

Brothers _____ Birthday _____

Sisters _____ Birthday _____

Sisters _____ Birthday _____

Mother's Name	Father's Name
Date of Birth	Date of Birth
Place of Birth	Place of Birth
Brothers	Brothers
Sisters	Sisters
Maternal Grandfather	Paternal Grandfather
Date of Birth	Date of Birth
Place of Birth	Place of Birth
Maternal Grandmother	Paternal Grandmother
Date of Birth	Date of Birth
Place of Birth	Place of Birth

MEMORIES

My church is _____

_____

My pastor is _____

My Sunday school teachers:

Name _____ Year _____

Name _____ Year _____

Name _____ Year _____

My favorite Bible story is _____

My favorite Bible character is _____

My favorite Bible verse is _____

_____

My best friends in Christ are:

Name _____ Age _____

Name _____ Age _____

Name _____ Age _____

Special Events in My Christian Life

_____

_____

_____

_____

_____

The Holy Bible
for Children

The Holy Bible for Children

A Simplified Version
of the Old and New Testaments

Edited by Allan Hart Jahsmann
Illustrations and Maps by Don Kueker

Publishing House
St. Louis

Concordia Publishing House, St. Louis, Missouri
Copyright © 1977 Concordia Publishing House

MANUFACTURED IN THE UNITED STATES OF AMERICA

Library of Congress Calaloging in Publication Data

Bible. Selections. English. Jahsmann. 1977.
    The Holy Bible for Children.

    SUMMARY: A simplified retelling, including maps and
pictures, of selected portions of each of the books of
the Bible.
    [1. Bible—Selections] I. Jahsmann, Allan Hart.
II. Title.
BS197.J27   220.9'505   77-3226
ISBN 0-570-03465-5

A Note to Parents and Teachers

Why another translation of the Bible? What's so different about this version? And why should anyone want to have this book if he or she already has a Bible and a Bible story book?

There are many available books of Bible stories—some well written, some wooden and very adult. Some wander carelessly away from the text, and some remain closer to the original text than others.

There are also books that claim to be the Bible for children. Some of these are an adult version of the Bible with a few pictures added. Others are Bible excerpts or readings for children from a standard translation. A few are a paraphrase, which means that the translator has treated the text rather freely and has often departed from it.

This version of the Bible is not just another translation or a paraphrase. Nor is it simply another Bible story book. It is a careful selection and a simplified retelling of those parts of the Bible that most children and youth can read and understand. By such reading they will grow into the Bible itself and be blessed by it; and that is the purpose of this book.

So this is a simplified version of the Bible, simplified through what has been selected, and simplified by the language through which the selections are presented. At the same time all the books of the Bible have been included—to give the young reader a feel of the entire Bible.

The very first book I wrote, almost 30 years ago, was titled *Leading Children into the Bible*. Today that challenge seems to be taken less seriously than it was then. But the need for some introduction of children to a personal use of the Bible continues.

This simplified version of the Bible is offered with the hope that it will lead young people into the reading of the most important book in the world—the Book of Life—the Word and revelation of God. By dealing with it directly and in a form they can understand, young readers will discover its saving and transforming power for themselves. That is my hope for them.

Allan Hart Jahsmann

A Word to the Young Reader

This is not a book of Bible stories written to entertain you. This is the Bible—shortened and put into present-day simple English. This makes it easier for you to read the Bible itself for yourself. By doing so you will begin to get acquainted with the most important book ever published—the Holy Scriptures, the Word of God.

The word Bible means *book,* but it is a book of books, a collection of 66 books. As you probably know, there are 39 books in what is called the Old Testament and 27 in the New Testament.

A part of every one of the 66 books is in this simplified Bible so you can start to get acquainted with all of them. Because the books were written to and for adults who lived thousands of years ago, some parts are too difficult for young readers. But we hope that by reading parts you can already understand, you will someday want to read a more complete Bible too.

Originally the Old Testament books were written mainly in Hebrew, the ancient language of the Jews. The New Testament books were written in the Greek language. Since then the Bible has been translated into more than a thousand languages, and many different English versions have been published.

In the Protestant churches in North America the most commonly used Bible translation today is the Revised Standard Version, the RSV. The Common Bible is a joint Roman Catholic-Protestant edition of the RSV.

Perhaps the most widely read version today is the Good News Bible published by the American Bible Society. The New Testament and the Old Testament are called the TEV, meaning the Today's English Version. Some people still prefer the KJV, meaning the King James Version that was published by order of King James I of England in 1611.

The Old Testament begins in Genesis with the story of God's creation of the world and how sin and evil came into existence. It then tells how God developed a nation of people called the children of Israel, the Jews, and how they were to be God's light and saving power in a dark world. But the Old Testament is the story of how even God's people often forgot him, his ways, and his plans for the world.

The New Testament is the story of how God sent his Son Jesus Christ to live in this world as a human being in order to save the world and its people. The New Testament begins with four books called the *gospels*. They are called gospels because they tell us the godspell, meaning *good news*. The good news is that God was in Jesus Christ.

Following the gospels is a book called the Acts of the Apostles. It tells how the Christian church began and spread. The text of the New Testament, except for the last book, is made up of letters written by some of the first church leaders, like Peter and Paul and John.

All of the writers of the Bible were inspired by the Spirit of God to write what they wrote. What they wrote, as you will see, is the wonderful message that through the love of Jesus we receive forgiveness and peace with God and a life that never ends. That's worth knowing.

Allan Hart Jahsmann

CONTENTS

Key to Pronunciation Helps

Some words in the Bible will be strange to you. You may wonder how to say them. To show you one way to pronounce the difficult names and places, such words are repeated and spelled the way they might sound. The syllable printed in capital letters receives the accent, as in AK-sent.

s<u>ay</u>, c<u>a</u>t, s<u>aw</u>, <u>ah</u>, s<u>ee</u>, m<u>e</u>t, s<u>i</u>t, h<u>igh</u>, <u>oh</u>, h<u>o</u>p, <u>uh</u>, sh<u>oo</u>t, b<u>u</u>tcher, si<u>ng</u>, c<u>ow</u>, b<u>oy</u>, <u>th</u>ick, <u>sh</u>op, <u>hw</u> as in <u>wh</u>y, <u>ch</u>op

Note: The words with an asterisk are in the Glossary.

The Names of the Books of the Bible Arranged Alphabetically

Acts (AKTS)
Amos (AY-muhs)
1 Chronicles (KRON-i-kuls)
2 Chronicles (KRON-i-kuls)
Colossians (Ko-LAH-shuhns)
1 Corinthians (Kor-IN-thee-uhns)
2 Corinthians (Kor-IN-thee-uhns)
Daniel (DAN-ee-el)
Deuteronomy (Doo-ter-ON-ah-mee)
Ecclesiastes (Ay-klee-zee-AS-tees)
Ephesians (Eh-FEE-shuhns)
Esther (ES-tur)
Exodus (EX-uh-duhs)
Ezekiel (E-ZEEK-ee-el)

Ezra (EZ-rah)
Galatians (Guh-LAY-shuhns)
Genesis (JEN-eh-sis)
Habakkuk (Hah-BAK-kuk)
Haggai (HAG-igh)
Hebrews (HEE-broos)
Hosea (Ho-ZAY-ah)
Isaiah (Igh-ZAY-ah)
James (JAYMZ)
Jeremiah (Jair-eh-MIGH-ah)
Job (JOHB)
Joel (JO-el)
John (JAHN)
1 John (JAHN)
2 John (JAHN)
3 John (JAHN)
Jonah (JO-nah)
Joshua (JAHSH-oo-ah)
Jude (JOOD)
Judges (JUHD-jehz)
1 Kings (KEENGS)
2 Kings (KEENGS)
Lamentations (La-men-TAY-shuhns)
Leviticus (Leh-VIT-ee-kuhs)
Luke (LUEK)
Malachi (MAL-ah-kigh)
Mark (MAHRK)
Matthew (MATH-yoo)
Micah (MIGH-kah)
Nahum (NAY-hum)
Nehemiah (Nee-heh-MIGH-ah)
Numbers (NUHM-bers)
Obadiah (Oh-bah-DIGH-ah)
1 Peter (PEE-ter)
2 Peter (PEE-ter)
Philemon (Figh-LEE-muhn)
Philippians (Fill-IP-pee-uhns)
Proverbs (PRAH-vurbs)
Psalms (SAHMZ)

Revelation (Rev-eh-LAY-shuhn)
Romans (ROH-muhns)
Ruth (ROOTH)
1 Samuel (SAM-yoo-el)
2 Samuel (SAM-yoo-el)
Song of Solomon (SAHL-ah-mahn)
1 Thessalonians (Thess-ah-LOH-nee-uhns)
2 Thessalonians (Thess-ah-LOH-nee-uhns)
1 Timothy (TIM-uh-thee)
2 Timothy (TIM-uh-thee)
Titus (TIGH-tuhs)
Zechariah (Zech-ah-RIGH-ah)
Zephaniah (Zef-ah-NIGH-ah)

List of Selections

OLD TESTAMENT

THE
OLD TESTAMENT

THE BOOK OF
Genesis*

The Beginnings of the World

In the beginning God made the heavens and the earth. . . . And God said, "Let there be light," and there was light. And God saw that the light was good. Then he separated the light from the darkness. He called the light *Day* and the darkness *Night*. That evening and morning were one day, the first day.

Then God said, "Let the watery stuff [which was the beginnings of the earth] separate into sky and water above and watery stuff below. . . ." That all happened on the second day.

And God said, "Let the waters beneath the sky gather into seas and oceans, and let dry land appear." And this happened. [Dry land appeared.] God called the dry land *Earth,* and the waters that had come together he called *Seas.* And God saw that what had happened was good.

And God said, "Let every kind of grass and seed-bearing plant start to grow on the earth, and fruit trees with their seeds inside the fruit. And let these seeds produce the kinds of plants and trees they came from. And God saw that this too was good. That was the third day.

Then God said, "Let there be lights in the sky to separate days from nights. Let them also make the season and days and years and give light to the earth." And so it was. God made two great lights, the larger one to rule in the daytime and the smaller one to rule at night. He also made the stars. . . . And God saw that all this was good. This was the fourth day.

Then God said, "Let the waters [of the seas] be filled with living creatures, and let birds fly across the skies above the earth." So God made the great sea animals and all the living creatures that live in the water and every kind of bird. And God saw that this was good. So God blessed the fish and birds and told them to multiply. And all this happened on the fifth day.

And [on the sixth day] God said, "Let the land also bring forth living creatures—cattle and creeping things and wildlife of every kind." And so it was. . . . And God saw that it was all good.

Then God said, "It's time to make people who will be like us. I will have them rule over the fish of the sea and over the birds of the air and over cattle and over everything else on the earth." So God made some human beings in his own image (IM-age).* Like himself he made them, both male and female.

And God blessed them and said to them, "Multiply and fill the earth and rule it. . . ." And God saw everything he had made: it was all very good. That was another evening and another morning, the sixth day.... And on the seventh day God rested from all the work he had done.

1:1—2:3

The First Two People

The Lord God made [the first] man out of . . . ground and breathed into him the breath of life. That's when the man became a living human being.

And the Lord God planted a garden in Eden, in the eastern part of the world, and there God put the man he had made. And out of the ground God made all kinds of trees grow, both trees that are beautiful and trees good for food. He also put *the tree of life* in the middle of the garden, and *the tree of knowledge of good and bad*.

Then the Lord God put the man in the garden of Eden to take care of it. And he gave him this order: "You may eat all you want from every tree in the garden except from the tree of the knowledge of good and bad. On the day that you eat from it, you will die."

Then the Lord God said, "It's not good for the man to be alone. I will make him a helper who will be just right for him." So out of the ground God made every kind of animal and bird and brought them to the man to see what he would call them. Whatever the man called a creature, that was its name.

The man [Adam] gave names to all the birds and animals, but he didn't find a mate for himself. So God made Adam fall into a deep sleep. While he was asleep, God took one of Adam's ribs out of his side and made a woman from it. When he brought her to Adam, Adam said, "This is my own flesh and bone. She will be called *woman* because she was taken out of man."

2:7-9, 15-23

The First Sin Against God

The most cunning creature the Lord God had made was a large snake. This snake said to the woman, "Did God tell you not to eat the fruit of any of the trees in the garden?" The woman answered, "We may eat the fruit of any tree except the one in the middle of the garden. For God said, 'You should not eat or touch this fruit or you will die.'"

"You will not die," said the snake. "God knows that when you eat of it your eyes will be opened and you will become like God. You will know what is good and what is bad."

So the woman looked at the tree and saw that it had good fruit. Because it looked so good and she thought it would make her wise, she took some of the fruit and ate it. She also gave some to her husband and he ate it.

Then the eyes of both of them really did open up, and they began to see things they hadn't noticed before. They noticed, for example, that they were naked. So they sewed fig leaves together and made themselves skirtlike coverings.

In the cool time of the day [the evening] the man and his wife heard the sound of the Lord God walking in the garden. At first they hid themselves from God among the trees in the garden.

But the Lord God called to the man, saying, "Where are you?" He said, "I heard the sound of you in the garden, and I was afraid, because I was naked. So I hid myself."

"Who told you that you were naked?" asked God. "Have you eaten fruit from the tree that I told you not even to touch?" The man said, "The woman you put here to be with me, she gave me fruit from that tree, and I ate it."

Then the Lord God said to the woman, "What is this you have done?" The woman said, "The snake tricked me and I ate it." The Lord God said to the snake, "Because you have done this, you will be cursed. . . . You will crawl on your belly and eat dust all the days of your life. And I will put an enemy between you and this woman and between your children and hers. He will crush your head, and you will wound him in the heel."

The Lord God said, "See, now the man is like one of us. He knows good from bad." Then the Lord God drove the man out of the garden of Eden so man would never be able to take fruit from the tree of life and live forever [as a sinner]. From then on he would have to work the ground from which he had been made.

3:1-15, 22-23

Sons of Adam

Adam and Eve had a son. They called him Cain. Eve said, "The Lord gave me this boy." Some time later she had another son. He was called Abel.

Now, Abel raised sheep and Cain grew crops. One day Cain brought some of the produce of his fields as an offering to the Lord. Abel brought one of the first and fattest lambs of his flock. And the Lord was pleased with Abel and his offering, but with Cain and his offering he was not pleased.

So Cain became very angry and he wouldn't look

up. . . . Then Cain said to his brother Abel, "Let's go out to the field." And when they were in the field, Cain attacked his brother Abel and killed him.

Then the Lord said to Cain, "Where is your brother Abel?" Cain answered, "I don't know. Am I my brother's keeper?" "What have you done?" said God to Cain. "The voice of your brother's blood is crying out to me from the ground. And the earth which opened to receive your brother's blood now curses you. From now on when you cultivate the ground, it will not give its strength to you. You will be an outlaw and a wanderer on earth."

Cain said to the Lord, "My punishment is more than I can stand." . . . But the Lord put a mark on Cain so that anyone finding him would not kill him. After that Cain went away . . . and lived in the land of Nod, to the east of Eden.

4:1-16

Noah (NO-ah) and His Ark

When people began to multiply on earth, . . . the Lord saw that they had become very wicked. All their thoughts and desires were evil. The Lord was sorry he had ever made people to live on the earth, and he felt very bad about it.

So the Lord said to himself, "I am going to destroy the people I have made, also the animals and creeping things and the birds of the air, because I am sorry I made them."

But there was a man named Noah who pleased God. . . . Noah walked with God. And Noah had three sons, Shem, Ham, and Japheth (JA-feth).

To Noah God said, "I have decided to put an end to all people on earth, for the earth is filled with wickedness through them. So I will destroy them along with the earth."

To Noah God also said, "Make yourself an ark (AHRK)* out of cypress (SIGH-press) wood. . . . For this is what I'm going to do: I am going to cause a great flood that will destroy everything that lives on the earth. But with you I will make a covenant (KUHV-eh-nuhnt),* and you and your sons and your wife and your sons' wives are to enter the ark."

God then told Noah, "You must take with you two of every living creature, a male and a female, to keep them alive with you.... Also take with you some of every kind of food that is eaten and store it up. It will be food for you and for the creatures with you."

And Noah did all that God told him to do. And he and his sons and his wife and his sons' wives went into the ark to escape the waters of the flood. After seven days the flood began, . . . and rain kept on falling for 40 days and 40 nights. . . . Soon the waters increased and lifted the ark so that it floated above the earth.

And every living thing on the earth—people and animals and creeping things and birds of the air—died. Only Noah and those with him in the ark remained alive. And the water covered the earth for 150 days.

6:1, 5-10, 13-22;
7:5, 7, 10, 18, 23, 24

Noah's Blessing

God remembered Noah and all the living creatures with him in the ark. He made a wind blow over the earth to dry up some of the water. At the end of 150 days, the waters had gone down. In the seventh month, on the 17th day of the month, the ark settled down on the mount of Ararat (AIR-ah-rat). And the water continued to decrease. . . .

At the end of 40 days Noah opened a window of the ark and sent out a black bird. It kept flying back and forth until the waters were dried up. He also sent out a dove to see if the water had dried up enough for ground to appear. But the dove could not find a place to rest, so it returned to the ark, for the water still covered the whole earth. So Noah put out his hand and took the dove back into the ark.

For seven more days Noah waited. Then he sent out

the dove again. That evening, when the dove came back to him, she was holding a fresh olive leaf in her mouth. By that Noah knew the waters were going down. After another seven days Noah sent the dove out again. This time the dove didn't come back.

Then Noah removed [a part of] the roof of the ark and looked out and saw that the ground was dry.... So Noah and his sons and his wife and his sons' wives went out from the ark; and with them went all the living things by families.

And Noah built an altar to the Lord and offered him burnt offerings of animals and birds. And when the Lord smelled the pleasing odor of the offerings, he said to himself, "I will never again curse the ground because of people. Nor will I ever strike down every living thing as I have done. So long as the earth lasts, there will always be seedtime and harvest, cold and heat, summer and winter, day and night."

God also said to Noah and his sons, "I make a promise to you and to your children who will come after you. . . . Never again will there be a flood that will destroy the earth." And God said, "This is the sign of the covenant between me and the earth: I will put my rainbow in the clouds. When I will bring a cloud over the earth, the rainbow will be seen in the clouds, and I will remember my promise."

8:1-13, 18-22; 9:8-16

The Tower of Babel

God blessed Noah and his sons and told them to have children and to fill the earth with people. And Noah lived for 350 years after the flood. When he died, he was 950 years old.

At first all people spoke a single language. As the population grew and people moved eastward, they settled on a plain in the country called Shinar. There they said, "Come, let us make bricks and bake them well." Then they said, "Let us build a city with a tower in it high enough to touch the sky. [In that way] let us make a name for ourselves, or else we'll be scattered and forgotten."

But the Lord came down to see the city and the tower the people were building. And the Lord said, "Now the people are all one race and speak one language. But [if they build this tower], that's only the beginning of what they will do. Nothing they might dream up will seem impossible to them. We must mix up their language, so they'll not understand one another."

[So this is what God did.] And God scattered the people from there to all parts of the earth. And they stopped building the city [and the tower]. And the name of that place was called Babel, because it was there that the Lord caused people to talk many different languages. From there he scattered them all over the earth.

9:1, 28, 29; 11:1-9

God's Promises to Abram

[In the land of Haran there lived a man called Abram. He had a wife whose name was Sarah.] One day God said to Abram, "Leave your country and your own people and go to a land that I will show you. From you I will make a great nation, and I will bless you. I will make your name great so that you will be a blessing [to others]. . . . Through you all the families of the earth will be blessed."

Well, Abram did what the Lord had told him to do. He was 75 years old when he left Haran. With him went his wife Sarah and his brother's son Lot. They took with them all their possessions and servants and went to the land of Canaan (KAY-nahn).*

[In Canaan] the Word* of God came to Abram in a dream. "Don't ever be afraid, Abram," God said to him. "I am your shield (SHEELD)* and your great reward."

But Abram said, "O Lord God, what will you give me? . . . I continue to have no children, and a slave born in my house will be my heir (AIR)."* The Lord said to

Abram, "This man will not be your heir; your own son will be your heir."

Then the Lord took Abram outside and said, "Look at the sky and count the stars, if you can. That's how many descendants (Dee-SEN-dents)* you will have." And Abram believed the Lord, and the Lord God considered Abram righteous because he believed God.

12:1-5; 15:1-6

Abram's New Name

When Abram was 99 years old, God appeared to him and said, "I am the almighty God. Walk in my ways, do what is right, and I will make a covenant with you. Your people will increase greatly."

[Hearing this], Abram knelt down and put his face to the ground. And God said to him, "My covenant with you is that you will become the father of many nations. And no longer will your name be Abram. [From now on] your name will be Abraham, because I have made you the father of many nations."

God also said, "Sarah, your wife, will have a son. You are to call him Isaac. With him and his children I will keep my everlasting promises."

17:1-5, 19

Abraham's Three Visitors

One day the Lord God appeared to Abraham as he sat in the doorway of his tent near a place called Mamre (MAHM-ray). It was the hot time of the day. As Abraham looked up, he saw three men standing a short distance in front of him. He jumped up and ran over to meet them.

Bowing himself down to the ground, Abraham said, "My lords, if I have found favor in your sight, do not pass by your servant. Let me get you a little water and wash your feet. And rest yourselves under the tree while I get you some bread to refresh you. After that you may go on. . . ."

They said, "Do as you have offered." So Abraham

hurried into his tent, where his wife Sarah was. "Quickly," he said, "bake some cakes, enough for three persons." Then he ran to his herd and got a tender calf and gave it to a younger man to prepare. When the meat was ready, he took it and the bread along with butter and milk to the three men. As they ate, he stood by them under the tree.

"Where is your wife Sarah?" they asked him. "She's in the tent," he said. One of the men, who was the Lord, said, "I will return to you in the spring, and Sarah, your wife, will have a son." Sarah was listening at the tent door behind him.

Now, Sarah and Abraham were very old and past the time for having children. Sarah therefore laughed to herself. . . . Then God asked Abraham, "Why did Sarah laugh? Does she think she's too old to have a child? Is there anything the Lord cannot do? I will return to you in the spring, and Sarah will have a son."

Because she was afraid, Sarah denied that she had laughed. But God said, "No, you did laugh."

And the Lord did as he had promised. Sarah gave Abraham a son in his old age at the time chosen by God. And Abraham called his son Isaac. And Sarah said, "God has made laughter for me."

18:1-15; 21:1-3, 6

Abraham's Greatest Test

[When Isaac had grown up and was a young man], God tested Abraham's faith once more. He said to him, "Abraham!" and Abraham answered, "Here I am." Then God said, "Take your son, your only son Isaac, whom you love, and go to the land of Moriah (Mo-RIGH-ah). There, on one of the mountains I will show you, I want you to sacrifice (SACK-ri-fighs)* your son as an offering to me."

Abraham got up early the next morning. He saddled his donkey and took with him two young men and his son Isaac. After cutting some wood to make a fire for the sacrifice, he set out for the place where God had told him to go.

On the third day Abraham looked up at the mountains and saw the place [where he was to go]. So he said to the two young men, "You stay here with the donkey while the boy and I go on ahead. We will worship there and then come back to you."

Then Abraham took the wood for the offering and loaded it on Isaac's back for him to carry. He himself carried the fire and the knife.

As they went on, the two of them together, Isaac said to Abraham, "Father?" "Yes, my son," said Abraham, "what is it?" "The fire and wood are here, but where is the lamb for a burnt offering?" asked Isaac. "God will provide for himself a lamb for a burnt offering, my son," said Abraham.

When they came to the place where God had told him to go, Abraham built an altar and laid the wood on it, stick by stick. Then he tied Isaac and laid him on the altar on top of the wood. But as Abraham reached out to take the knife, the Lord's angel called to him from heaven and said, "Abraham, Abraham! . . . Do not lay a hand on the boy or do him any harm," the voice said. "For now I know that you put God ahead of anything else. You have not kept back from me your only son."

When Abraham looked around, he saw a ram caught by its horns in some bushes. He took the ram and offered it as a sacrifice instead of his son. Then the Lord's angel called to Abraham a second time, saying, "Because you obeyed me and did not keep back your only son, I will bless you. Your children will be as many as the stars in the sky, . . . and through them all the nations of the earth will be blessed."

22:1-13, 15-18

A Wife for Isaac

[Years later] Abraham was very old, and the Lord had blessed Abraham in all things. One day Abraham said to the servant who managed everything he had,

"Swear by the Lord, the God of heaven and the God of earth, that you will . . . go to my country and there choose a wife for my son Isaac from among my own people." . . .

So the servant gave his hand to Abraham, his master, and promised to do as he had been told. Then the servant took 10 of his master's camels . . . and went to the city of Nahor (NAY-hor) in Mesopotamia (Mess-o-po-TAY-mee-ah). There he made his camels kneel down beside a well just outside the city. It was at the time of evening when the women came out to get water.

Then the servant prayed, "O Lord, God of my master Abraham, be kind to my master Abraham, and let me be successful in my errand today." . . . Before he had finished praying, a young girl appeared. She was Rebekah, whose father was the son of Nahor, Abraham's brother. . . .

Abraham's servant ran to meet her. "Let me drink a little water from your pitcher," he said. She said, "Drink, my lord." . . . The servant said to her, "Tell me whose daughter you are. And is there room in your father's house for me to spend the night?" She answered, "I am Nahor's granddaughter. Certainly we have room for you, and straw and feed for the camels as well."

Then the man bowed his head and worshiped God. "Blessed be the Lord, God of my master Abraham," he said. "He kept his love and promises to my master and led me to the house of my master's brother."

[Later] the servant took Rebekah with him to his house. Then Isaac brought her into his tent and she became his wife; and he loved her.

24:1-4, 9-18, 23-27, 61, 67

Esau and Jacob

When Isaac was 60 years old, Rebekah gave birth to twin sons. The first one born had red hair all over his body like a coat. They called him Esau. . . . His brother was called Jacob.

When the boys grew up, Esau became a good hunter, an outdoor man. But Jacob was a quiet man who lived in tents. Isaac loved Esau, because he enjoyed eating the meat Esau brought him. But Rebekah loved Jacob.

One day when Jacob was cooking his vegetables and meat, Esau came in from the field very hungry. So Esau said to Jacob, "Let me have some of that hot food; I'm starved!" . . . Jacob said, "First sell me your birthright." [Esau, being the oldest, was to be the head of the family and would have inherited most of his father's possessions.] Esau said, "I'm about to die. What good will this birthright do me?"

Jacob said, "Swear to me" [that I can have the birthright]. So Esau swore he could have it and sold his birthright to Jacob [for a dish of food]. Then Jacob gave Esau some bread and some food, and he ate it and got up and went on his way. That's how Esau threw away his birthright.

25:25-34

Isaac Blesses Jacob

When Isaac was old and his eyes became so weak he couldn't see, he had Esau, his older son, come to him. "My son," he said to him; and Esau answered, "Here I am." Then Isaac said, "Look, I am old; I don't know how soon I may die. So, take your weapons, your arrows and your bow, and go out and hunt some game for me. Then make me some tasty meat, the way I like it, and bring it for me to eat. I want to bless you before I die."

Well, Rebekah was listening when Isaac talked to his son Esau, so when Esau went out to hunt for some game to bring to Isaac, Rebekah said to her son Jacob, "I heard your father talk to your brother Esau. He asked Esau to bring him some tasty meat to eat. At the same time he wants to give him the Lord's blessing before he dies.

"Now, therefore, my son," said Rebekah, "do as I

tell you. Go to the flock and get two good young goats. From them I will prepare some tasty food, the way your father likes it. Then you must take it to your father so that he will bless you before he dies."

But Jacob said to his mother Rebekah, "Don't forget, my brother Esau is a hairy man and I am a smooth man. My father may touch me and I'll be caught deceiving (Dee-SEE-ving) him. Then I will bring a curse upon myself and not a blessing."

But his mother said, "Upon me be your curse, my son. Just do what I told you and go, get me the young goats." So Jacob went and got them and brought them to his mother. And his mother prepared the kind of tasty food his father loved.

Then Rebekah took the best robes her older son Esau had in her house and put them on her younger son Jacob. And she covered his hands and the back of his neck with the skins of the young goats. Then she handed him the tasty meat and the bread she had prepared.

So Jacob went to his father and said, "My father." And Isaac said, "Here I am, who are you, my son?" Jacob said to his father, "I am Esau, your firstborn. I have done as you told me. Now sit up and eat some of my meat and bless me." But Isaac said to his son, "How were you able to find it so quickly, my son?" He answered, "Because the Lord your God sent it to me."

But Isaac said to Jacob, "Come near, so I may feel you, my son, to know whether you really are my son Esau or not." So Jacob went near to his father Isaac, and Isaac felt him and said, "The voice is Jacob's voice, but the hands are the hands of Esau." Isaac didn't recognize Jacob because his hands felt hairy like his brother Esau's hands.

So Isaac blessed Jacob. He said, "Are you really my son Esau?" Jacob answered, "I am." Then Isaac said, "Bring the food to me, that I may eat of my son's game and bless you." Jacob brought it to him and he ate. Jacob also brought him wine and he drank.

Then his father Isaac said to him, "Come near and kiss me, my son." So Jacob came near and kissed him. When he smelled the smell of the clothes, he blessed Jacob, saying, "Ah, the smell of my son is like the smell of a field that the Lord has blessed! May God give you the dew of heaven and the fatness of the earth and plenty of grain and wine. Let [other] people serve you and nations bow down to you. Be lord over your brothers, and may your mother's sons bow down to you. May every person who curses you be cursed, and blessed be every one who blesses you!"

As soon as Isaac had finished blessing Jacob and Jacob had left his father, his brother Esau came in from his hunting. He also prepared some tasty food and brought it to his father. Esau said to his father, "May my father sit up and eat some of his son's food so that he will bless me." His father said to him, "Who are you?" He answered, "I am your son, your firstborn, Esau."

Then Isaac began to tremble badly and said, "Who was it, then, that prepared meat and brought it to me? I ate it all before you came and blessed him. Yes, and he will be blessed."

When Esau heard these words of his father, he cried out with a loud and bitter cry. "Bless me, also me, O my father!" he said. But Isaac said, "Your brother came slyly and has taken away your blessing." ... Esau said, "Haven't you saved a blessing for me?" Isaac answered, "I have made him your lord, and I have given him all his brothers for servants. I have also given him my corn and wine. What, then, can I do for you, my son?"

Esau said to his father, "Have you only one blessing [to give], my father? Bless me too, O my father." And Esau cried loudly. Then his father Isaac said to him, "See now, your home will be away from the fatness of the earth and away from the dew of heaven above. By your sword you will live, and you will serve your brother. But when you break loose, you will free yourself from his yoke (YOK) around your neck."

So Esau hated Jacob because of the blessing his father had given him. Esau said to himself, "My father will soon die; then I will kill my brother Jacob." These words of Esau were told to Rebekeh. So she sent for Jacob and said to him, "Your brother Esau is planning to kill you. Therefore, my son, do as I tell you. Hurry away to Laban (LAY-bon), my brother in Haran (HAIR-on). Stay with him for a while until your brother's anger turns away from you and he forgets what you have done to him. I will send for you from there."

27:1-45

Jacob's Dream

Jacob left home and went toward Haran. When he came to a certain place, he had to stay there all night because the sun had set. Taking a stone, he put it under his head and lay down to sleep. In a dream he saw a ladder set on the earth, with the top of it reaching to heaven. And, to his great surprise, angels of God were going up and down the ladder.

And, note this, the Lord was standing above the ladder and said, "I am the Lord, the God of Abraham and the God of Isaac. The land on which you are lying I will give to you and to your children. Your children will be like dust of the earth; they will spread to the west and to the east and to the north and to the south. Through you and your children all the families of the earth will be blessed. Behold, I am with you and will keep you wherever you go, and I will bring you back to this land. For I will not leave you until I have done all that I have promised."

When Jacob awoke from his sleep, he said, "Surely the Lord is in this place, and I didn't know it." And he was afraid and said, "How wonderful this place is! This certainly is the house of God, and this is the gate of heaven."

Early the next morning Jacob got up and took the stone he had used as a pillow, set it up like a pillar, and poured oil on the top of it. He called the name of that place Bethel.

Then Jacob made a vow saying, "If God will be with me and will guard me on my journey, and will give me bread to eat and clothing to wear, and if I will come again to my father's house in peace, then the Lord will be my God. And this stone that I have set up for a pillar will be God's house, and I will give a tenth to you, O God, of all that you will give to me."

28:10-22

Jacob's Family

Jacob went on his journey and came to the land of the people of the East. There he saw a well in a field and three flocks of sheep lying by it. It was a well from which the flocks were watered. A large stone was over the mouth of the well. When all the flocks were gathered around it, the shepherds would roll the stone from the mouth of the well and water the sheep. Then they would put the stone back on the well's mouth.

Jacob said to the shepherds, "My brothers, where are you from?" They said, "We're from Haran." He said to them, "Do you know Laban, the son of Nahor?" They said, "We know him." Jacob said to them, "Is it all well with him?" They said, "All is well with him, and see over there, his daughter Rachel is coming with his sheep."

When Jacob saw Rachel, the daughter of Laban, his mother's brother, he went and rolled the stone from the mouth of the well and watered the flock of Laban, his mother's brother. Then Jacob kissed Rachel and wept loudly. When he told Rachel he was her father's relative and that he was Rebekah's son, she ran and told her father.

When Laban heard the news about Jacob, his sister's son, he ran to meet him and brought him to his house. Jacob told Laban all the things that had happened to him, and Laban said to him, "Surely you are my bone and flesh."

When Jacob had stayed with Laban a month, Laban said to Jacob, "Just because you are my relative, should you work for me for nothing? Tell me, what shall I pay you?" Well, Laban had two daughters. The name of the older one was Leah; the name of the younger one was Rachel. Leah's eyes were weak, but Rachel was beautiful and lovely.

Jacob [of course] loved Rachel; so he said, "I will serve you seven years for your younger daughter Rachel." And Laban said, "It's better that I give her to you than to some other man. Stay with me." So Jacob served [Laban] seven years for Rachel, and they seemed to him just a few days because he loved her.

At the end of the seven years Jacob said to Laban, "Give me my wife . . . because I have completed my time. So Laban called together all the men in that place and prepared a [wedding] feast. But that evening he brought his daughter Leah to Jacob, and [Jacob married her, thinking it was Rachel].

In the morning, when Jacob saw it was Leah, he said to Laban, "What have you done to me? Didn't I serve you for Rachel? Why then did you trick me?" Laban said, "In our land the younger daughter is not given for marriage before the firstborn. Promise to serve me another seven years and I'll also give you Rachel for a wife." . . .

So Jacob married Rachel too, and he loved Rachel more than Leah. And he worked for Laban another seven years. When the Lord saw that Leah was loved less, [he gave her many sons]. But Rachel had no children. Finally God listened to her prayers for a child and gave her a son . . . and she called his name Joseph.

29:1-31; 30:22-24

Jacob Leaves Laban

[After 20 years with Laban] Jacob grew very rich and had large flocks, many servants, and many camels and donkeys. But Jacob heard that the sons of Laban were saying, "Jacob has taken all that was our father's, and from what was our father's he has gained all his wealth." Jacob also saw that Laban no longer felt the same about him as before.

Then the Lord said to Jacob, "Return to the land of your fathers and to your relatives. I will be with you." So Jacob called Rachel and Leah out to the field where he was with his flock. He said to them, "I see that your father no longer feels toward me the way he did before. But the God of my father has been with me. . . . And the angel of God said to me in a dream, 'Go from this land. . . . and return to the land of your birth.'"

Rachel and Leah answered, "Whatever God has . . . said to you, do it." So Jacob got going and set his sons and his wives on camels, and he took all his cattle [and all his goods] . . . to go to the land of Canaan (KAY-nahn)* to his father Isaac.

30:43; 31:1-6, 11-18

Jacob Meets Esau

In the country called Edom Jacob sent messengers ahead of him to his brother Esau. He told the messengers, "This is what I want you to say to my lord Esau: Your servant Jacob says, 'Until now I was staying with Laban. I have oxen, donkeys, flocks, men and women servants. I have sent someone to tell my lord so that I may find favor in your sight.'"

When the messengers returned to Jacob, they said, "We went to your brother Esau, and he is coming to meet you. He has 400 men with him." This made Jacob very afraid and upset. He divided the people who were with him into two groups, also the flocks and herds and camels. He thought, "If Esau comes to the one group and destroys it, then the other group that is left will be able to escape."

Then Jacob prayed, saying: "O God of my father Abraham and God of my father Isaac . . . save me, I pray you, from the hands of my brother, the hands of

Esau. I fear that he may come and kill us all, the mothers as well as the children. But you said to me, 'I will do you good and will make your descendants like the sands of the sea, which cannot be counted because they are so many.'"

So Jacob spent the night there and chose a present for his brother Esau from what he had with him: 200 she-goats and 20 he-goats, 200 young sheep and 20 rams, 30 milking camels and their young, 40 cows and 10 bulls, 20 donkeys and 10 colts. These he turned over to his servants in sets. Then he said to his servants, "Go on ahead of me and put a space between the groups of animals."

Then he said to the first servant, "When my brother Esau meets you and asks, 'Who do you belong to?' and 'Where are you going?' and 'Whose animals are these?' then you are to answer, 'They belong to your servant Jacob. They are a present for my lord Esau. Jacob himself is coming behind us.'"

Jacob gave the same order to a second servant, then to a third one, and to all who were walking behind the groups of animals. . . . For Jacob thought, "Perhaps I may please him with the presents I am sending ahead of me. Later, when I will see his face, he may accept me."

So the men left with the presents while Jacob spent the night in the camp.

32:3-21

[The next morning] Jacob looked up and saw Esau coming. With him were 400 men. So he divided the children between Leah and Rachel and their two maids. Then he put the maids with their children in front, then Leah with her children, and Rachel and Joseph last of all. He himself went on ahead of them and bowed himself to the ground seven times until he was near his brother.

But Esau ran to meet him and hugged him and

kissed him, and they both cried. And when Esau looked up and saw the women and children, he asked, "Who are all these with you?" Jacob answered, "Those are the children God has graciously given to your servant." . . .

"What do you mean by all these animals I met?" asked Esau. Jacob answered, "To find favor in the sight of my lord." But Esau said, "I have enough, my brother. Keep what is yours for yourself." Jacob said, "No, I beg you, if I have found favor in your sight, then accept my present, for to see your face is like seeing the face of God." . . . In that way Jacob urged Esau and he took it. . . .

Then Jacob went safely to the city of Shechem (SHE-kehm), which is in the land of Canaan. . . . And from the sons of Hamor (HAY-mor) he bought, for 100 pieces of money, the piece of land on which he had pitched his tent. There he built an altar and called it El-Elohe-Israel (EL-el-O-ay-IS-rah-ail).*

33:1-20

Jacob's Children

Jacob had twelve* sons. . . . And Jacob lived in the land of Canaan, the place where his father had lived.

When [his son] Joseph was a young man 17 years old, he used to look after his father's flocks along with his brothers. . . . And Joseph brought his father some bad reports about them.

Now, Jacob loved Joseph more than all his other sons, because Joseph was the son of his old age. So Jacob made a coat of many colors for him. When his brothers saw that their father loved Joseph more than any of his brothers, they hated Joseph and couldn't speak in a friendly way to him at all.

Well, Joseph had a dream. When he told it to his brothers, they hated him all the more. He said to them, "Listen to this dream I dreamed. We were out in a field tying up grain, and what do you know, my bundle rose and stood up straight. And your bundles stood around and bowed down to my bundle."

Joseph's brothers said to him, "So, you are going to be a king over us? Do you really think you are going to rule us?" They hated him all the more on account of his dreams and what he said about them.

Then he had another dream and told his brothers about that one too. "Listen," he said, "I've had another dream. This time the sun, the moon, and eleven stars were bowing down to me." But when he told this dream to his father and his brothers, his father became angry. He said to Joseph, "What is this dream of yours? Are your mother and I as well as your brothers to come and bow down to you?"

The brothers were very jealous of Joseph [and very angry at him], but his father kept the dream in mind.

Now, it so happened that Joseph's brothers took Jacob's flocks out to a pasture near Shechem. One day Jacob said to Joseph, "Your brothers are feeding the sheep near Shechem. . . . Go and see whether all is well with them and the flocks and bring me back a report."

Joseph went and found his brothers in Dothan (DO-thahn).* They saw him coming in the distance, so before he got to them, they began to plan how to kill him. They said, "Here comes the dreamer. Let's kill him and throw him into a hole. We can say that a wild animal ate him. Then we'll see what will become of his dreams."

But when Reuben (ROO-ben)* heard this, he saved Joseph by saying, "Let's not take his life. . . . Throw him into this hole here in the desert but don't kill him." Reuben planned to rescue Joseph later and send him back to his father.

So when Joseph came to his brothers, they pulled him out of his coat, the fine long robe his father had given him, and threw him into a hole. The hole was dry. Then they sat down to eat their meal.

Looking up, they saw a caravan of traders coming from Gilead (GIL-ee-ad). Their camels were loaded with spices and perfumes, which they were taking south to sell in Egypt. Judah said to his brothers,

"What will we gain if we kill our brother and hide his death? Come, let's sell him to the traders and let's not harm him, for he is our brother." . . . So they dragged Joseph out of the hole and sold him to the merchants for 20 pieces of silver. The merchants took Joseph to Egypt.

When Reuben returned and saw that Joseph was not in the hole, he tore his clothes. [He was upset.] He went to his brothers and said, "The boy is gone! And I, where shall I go?"

The brothers took Joseph's robe, killed a goat, and dipped the robe in the goat's blood. Then they took the coat to their father. "We found this," they said. "See whether it's your son's coat or not." Jacob recognized the coat and said, "It is my son's coat. A wild animal has eaten him. Joseph has been torn to pieces."

Then Jacob tore his clothes and put on sackcloth for many days to show his sad feelings for his son. And all his sons and daughters came and tried to comfort him, but he refused to listen to them. "I will go down to my grave weeping for my son," he said.

35:23; 37:1-35

Joseph in Egypt

Joseph was taken down to Egypt, and Potiphar (PAHT-i-far), an officer of Pharoah (FER-ah-oh)* and captain of the guard, bought him from the traders who had brought him there.

The Lord was with Joseph, and he became a successful man. He lived in the house of his master, and his master saw that the Lord was with him and that the Lord blessed all that he did. So Joseph became his favorite servant. He put Joseph in charge of his house and all that he owned.

[But when Joseph refused to make love to his master's wife, she told this lie about him]: "That Hebrew servant you brought to us came to me to insult me. As soon as I began to scream and shout, he left his clothes with me and ran out of the house."

When the master heard his wife say, "This is the way your servant treated me," he became angry and had Joseph put into prison. It was a place where the king's prisoners were kept. And there he stayed.

But the Lord God looked after Joseph and showed him kindness and made the keeper of the prison think well of him. So the prison keeper put Joseph in charge of all the other prisoners. . . . And the keeper of the prison paid no attention to anything Joseph did because the Lord was with him and whatever he did the Lord blessed.

39:1-4, 17-23

Pharaoh's Dreams

Two years passed [and then it so happened that Pharaoh had a strange dream]. Pharaoh dreamed that he was standing by the Nile River. And, to his surprise, there came up out of the river seven fine-looking fat cows, and they ate the grass near the water.

And then, note this, seven half-starved, thin cows came out of the Nile River and stood by the other cows on the bank of the river. And the thin, bony cows ate up the seven well-fed fat cows. Then Pharaoh woke up.

When he fell asleep again, he dreamed another dream. This time seven ears of corn, plump and good, were growing on one stalk. And, note this, after that seven other ears of corn, thin and dried up, came out. And the poor ears swallowed up the seven fat and full ears.

Then Pharaoh woke up again and realized it was all a dream. In the morning he was still bothered by it, so he sent for all the wise men and magicians of Egypt. He told them his dreams, but no one could tell him what the dreams meant.

But then the chief butler said to Pharaoh, "Now I remember something I should have done. When Pharaoh was angry with his servants, he put me and the chief baker into the prison of the captain of the guard. One night we both had a dream, he and I, each a different dream. And a young Hebrew was in the prison there with us. He was a servant of the captain of the guard. When we told him our dreams, he explained what each dream meant. And everything happened as he said it would." . . .

Then Pharaoh sent for Joseph, and they hurriedly brought him out of the prison. When he had shaved himself and changed his clothes, he was brought before Pharaoh.

Pharaoh said to Joseph, "I have had a dream, and no one can tell me the meaning. I have heard it said that when you hear a dream you can explain it." Joseph answered, "That power is not in me; God will give Pharaoh an answer." [So Pharaoh told Joseph both of his dreams.]

Joseph said to Pharaoh, "The two dreams of Pharaoh are one. God has shown Pharaoh what he is about to do. The seven good cows are seven years and the seven good ears are seven years. The two dreams are one. The seven thin and bony cows that came afterward are seven years and the seven empty ears withered by the east wind will be seven years of famine (FAM-in).*

"As I told Pharaoh" [Joseph continued], "God is showing Pharaoh what he is about to do. There will be seven years of great plenty throughout the land of Egypt, and then will come seven years of famine. All the plenty will be forgotten in the land of Egypt . . . because of the famine that will follow, for it will be great.

"The dream was sent to Pharaoh twice" [said Joseph], "to show that this matter has been decided by God and that God will make it happen soon. Pharaoh therefore ought to find a man who can look ahead and is wise. Make him the governor over the land of Egypt. Let him gather and store up corn during the good years so that the people will have food during the famine."

This plan seemed good to Pharaoh and to all his servants. So Pharaoh said to them, "Can we find such a man as this one in whom the Spirit of God is?" Then Pharaoh said to Joseph, "Since God has shown you all this, there is no one as wise as you are. You will be in charge of my house, and all my people will be ruled by you. Only I will be greater than you in power."

Pharaoh also said to Joseph, "Now hear this, I have put you over all the land of Egypt." Then he took off his ruler's ring from his hand and put it on Joseph's hand and dressed him in robes of fine cloth and put a gold chain around his neck. He also made Joseph ride in his second chariot* [the one that came after his own]. And Pharaoh's servants ran ahead of Joseph to tell the people, "Bow down! Bow down!" In that way Pharaoh put him in charge of all the land of Egypt. . . .

Joseph was 30 years old when he appeared before Pharaoh, the king of Egypt. After Joseph left Pharaoh, he went all over Egypt. In the seven good years plenty of food grew. So during those seven good years Joseph gathered up food and stored it in the cities. He also stored up grain from the fields that were close to the cities. . . .

Then the seven years of plenty in the land of Egypt ended, and the seven years of famine began, as Joseph had said they would. There was a great shortage of food in all the lands, but in Egypt there was [grain]. So when the people cried to Pharaoh for bread, he said to them, "Go to Joseph and do what he tells you to do."

When the famine had spread all over the country, Joseph opened up the storehouses and sold food to the Egyptians. But the famine became bad also in all other places, so people from everywhere came to Joseph in Egypt to buy grain.

41:1-57

Joseph's Brothers in Egypt

When Jacob heard that there was grain in Egypt, he said to his sons, "Why are you looking at one another [as though you don't know what to do]? I have heard that there is corn in Egypt. Go there and buy some for us, so that we won't starve to death."

So 10 of Joseph's brothers went down to Egypt to buy grain. But Jacob wouldn't let Benjamin, Joseph's brother, go with his other brothers. Jacob was afraid something might happen to Benjamin. . . .

Now Joseph was in charge of all food distribution in Egypt, so it was to him that his brothers came and bowed down to the ground. Joseph recognized them, but they didn't recognize him. In fact he treated them as though they were strangers and spoke roughly to them.

"Where do you come from?" he asked. They answered, "From the land of Canann. We have come to buy food." Joseph remembered what he had dreamed about them. He said to them, "You are spies. You have come to see where you can best attack us." They said to him, "No, my lord. We have come only to buy food. We are all sons of one man and are honest men; we are not spies."

Joseph said to them, "No, you have come to see where you can attack us." And they said, "We, your servants, are 12 brothers, the sons of one man living in the land of Canaan. The youngest is with our father and one is no more."

But Joseph said to them, "It is as I said; you are spies. . . . If you are honest men, let one of you stay here in prison while the rest of you take some grain home and bring your youngest brother to me. That will prove that you speak the truth, and then you will not die." . . .

When they came to their father Jacob in the land of Canaan, they told him all that had happened to them. . . . And when they emptied their sacks, they were surprised to find that every man's money was in his sack. This worried them. . . . Jacob said, "I'll not let my son [Benjamin] go down [to Egypt] with you, because his brother is dead and he's the only one left [of the sons of Rachel]. If anything would happen to him on the journey, my sadness would kill me."   *42:1-38*

The Brothers' Second Trip

But the famine continued to be very bad in the land [of Canaan]. When Jacob's family had eaten up the grain the brothers had brought from Egypt, their father said to them, "Go again and buy us a little food." But Judah told him, "The man seriously warned us that we would not see his face again unless our brother was with us. If you will send our brother [Benjamin] with us, we will go down and buy you food, but if you will not send him, we will not go."

"Why were you so unkind to me as to tell the man you had another brother?" asked Jacob. They said, "The man asked many questions about us and our family. . . . How could we know he would say, 'Bring your brother down'?"

Then Judah said to his father, "Send the lad with me, and we will get started and go so that we may live and not die, me and you and all our little ones. I will be responsible for him. . . . If I do not bring him back to you, then I'll take the blame forever. If we hadn't waited so long, we could have been back a second time already."

Then their father said to them, "If it must be so, then do this: Take some of the best fruits of our land in your bags and carry some presents down to the man—a little honey, spices and perfumes, and nuts. Take double the money with you and carry back with you the money that was returned in your sacks. Perhaps it was a mistake. Take also your brother and go again to the man. May God Almighty make the man merciful so that he will send back your other brother and Benjamin." . . .

So they went down to Egypt and stood again before Joseph. When Joseph saw Benjamin with them, he said to the ruler of his house. "Take these men to my house and prepare some meat; these men are to dine with me at noon." So the servant did as Joseph told him and took the brothers to Joseph's house. The brothers were afraid when they were brought to Joseph's house. They said, "It's because of the money that was returned in our sacks the first time." . . .

When Joseph came home, they presented to him the presents they had brought to the house, and they bowed themselves down to the ground in front of him. He asked them how they all were and said, "Is your father well, the old man about whom you spoke? Is he still alive?" They answered, "Your servant, our father, is in good health. He is still alive." And they bowed their heads respectfully.

Then, looking around, Joseph saw his brother Benjamin, his own mother's son. "Is this the youngest brother about whom you told me?" asked Joseph. Then he said, "God be good to you, my son" and hurried away, looking for a place to cry. He still loved his brother very much. He went to his room and cried there.

After he washed his face and controlled himself, he came out and said, "Let the food be served!" Then the servants served him separately and the brothers by themselves and the Egyptians by themselves. . . . Joseph sent servings to the brothers from his table, and Benjamin's serving was five times as much as any of the others. They drank and were merry with him.

Then Joseph gave these orders to his steward (STOO-werd),* "Fill the men's sacks with food, as much as they can carry; and put each man's money in the mouth of his sack." He also said, "Put my cup, the silver cup, into the sack of the youngest brother, along with his money for the grain." The steward did everything Joseph told him to do.

At daybreak the men were sent on their way, they and their loaded donkeys. When they had left the city but had not yet gone very far, Joseph said to his steward, "Go after them. When you have caught up with them, say to them, 'Why have you repaid good with evil? Why have you stolen my silver cup? Isn't this cup the one from which my lord drinks and the one by which he discovers secrets?"

When the steward caught up with the brothers, he accused them as Joseph had said he should. But they said to him, "Why does my lord say these things. God forbid that your servants should do anything like this. . . . Let whoever has this object die and the rest of us will be your lord's slaves." The steward said, "Let it be as you say. Whoever is found to have it will be my slave, but the rest of you will not be blamed."

Then each man hurriedly put down his sack on the ground, and each man opened his sack. The steward searched the sacks, beginning with the oldest and ending with the youngest brother. And the cup was found in Benjamin's sack. Then the brothers tore their clothes [to show how upset they were], and everyone of them loaded his donkey and returned [with Benjamin] to the city.

When Judah and his brothers came back to Joseph's house, he was still there. They lay down in front of him on the ground. Joseph said to them, "What is this you have done? Don't you know that a man like me can discover secrets?" Judah said to him, "What can we say to you, my lord? How can we clear ourselves? God knows your servants are all guilty of doing wrong, and so we are all your slaves, the one in whose sack the cup was found and the rest of us too."

Joseph said, "Far be it from me that I should do that. Only the one in whose sack the cup was found will be my slave. The rest of you may go in peace to your father." Then Judah went up to Joseph and said, "My lord, let your servant, I beg you, say a word to you in private and do not be angry with me. . . . Your servant promised to bring the lad back to my father. I said, 'If I do not bring him back to you, then I'll bear the blame all my life.' Therefore, I beg you, let your servant remain as a slave to my lord instead of the lad, and let the lad go back with his brothers. For how can I go back to my father if the lad is not with me? I couldn't bear to see such trouble come to my father."

43:1-18, 26—44:34

Jacob Moves to Egypt

When Joseph could keep his secret no longer, he shouted, "Get out, everyone, except these men." And when there was no one else with them, he made himself known to his brothers. He cried so loud that the Egyptians heard it.

And Joseph said to his brothers, "Come near to me, please." So they came nearer. And he said, "I am your brother Joseph, whom you sold into Egypt. Do not be upset or angry with yourselves because you sold me to be a slave in this place. God sent me here ahead of you to save lives. For there has been a famine in the land for two years and another five years are coming in which there will be neither plowing nor harvest.

"God sent me here ahead of you," Joseph continued, "to keep alive a part of our people and to save you. So it was not you who sent me here. It was God. He made me Pharaoh's counselor and ruler over the whole land of Egypt. So now go home as quickly as you can and tell my father that his son Joseph sends him this message: 'God has made me lord over all of Egypt. Come here to me without delay. You shall live here with me in Goshen (GO-shen), a part of Egypt, you and your children and grandchildren. . . .'"

Then the brothers went to their father Jacob in the land of Canaan and told him their news. "Joseph is still alive," they said, "and he is in charge of the whole land of Egypt." At first Jacob couldn't believe them; he was so shocked he felt faint. But when they told him all that Joseph had said to them and he saw the wagons Joseph had sent, he recovered. "I'm convinced," he said. "My son Joseph is alive. I will go and see him before I die."

45:1-28

Then Jacob left with all that he owned and came to

Beer-sheba (Beer-SHEE-bah) [on the way to Egypt].
There he offered sacrifices to the God of his father
Isaac. And God spoke in a dream vision to Jacob in the
night and said, "Jacob, Jacob." Jacob answered, "Here I
am." And God said, "I am the God of your father. Do not
be afraid to go down to Egypt, for there I will make you
a great nation. I will go down with you into Egypt, and
I will surely bring you back again. Joseph's hand will
close your eyes" [after you die].

So Jacob left Beer-sheba, and his sons carried their
father Jacob and their little ones and their wives in the
wagons Pharaoh had provided for them. And they took
their cattle and all their possessions. And so Jacob
came to Egypt, and all his family with him: his sons
and his sons' sons, his daughters and his sons'
daughters. All of them he brought with him to Egypt.

Then Joseph went to meet his father in Goshen
(GO-shen) and presented himself to him. And he
hugged him and cried on his neck a long time. And
Jacob said to Joseph, "Now I'm willing to die, since I've
seen your face and know you are still alive."

46:1-7, 29, 30

Jacob Buried in Canaan

[Jacob lived in the land of Egypt for 17 years and
became a very old man. Before he died, he asked Joseph
to bury him in the land of Canaan, where Abraham and
Sarah and Isaac and Rebekah were buried. So Joseph
did this.]

After their father was buried, Joseph's brothers
said, "If Joseph ever hated us, he will surely pay us
back now for all the harm we did to him." So they sent a
message to Joseph, saying, "Before he died, your father
told us to say to you: 'Forgive the sins of your brothers,
the evil which they did to you.'"

When Joseph heard them speak this way to him he
cried. And his brothers came to him and knelt down
before him and said, "See, we are your servants!" But
Joseph said, "Don't be afraid. Am I here in place of

God? You meant to hurt me, but God meant it to turn out good and to keep many people alive, as they are today. So don't be afraid. I will provide for you and your little ones." In that way Joseph spoke kindly to them and made them feel better.

And Joseph lived 110 years and died. . . . And he was buried in Egypt.

50:14-21, 26

THE BOOK OF
Exodus*

Joseph died, and all his brothers and all their families died. But the Israelites, the descendants of Jacob, increased greatly. Soon the land [of Egypt] was filled with them.

Then a new king began to rule Egypt. He didn't know Joseph and what he had done. This new pharaoh said to his people, "Look here, the people of Israel are stronger than we are, and there are more of them. Let us deal wisely with them. Otherwise, if they keep on increasing, they may join our enemies and will fight against us in a war. In that way they will set themselves free."

So the Egyptians put taskmasters over the people of Israel and forced them to work hard and long for them. They were forced to build Pithom (PIT-hum) and Raamses (Rah-AM-zees) for Pharaoh [the king], cities where weapons and treasures were stored. But the more the Egyptians mistreated the Israelites, the more they increased. The Egyptians became afraid of the people of Israel.

Then the king of Egypt gave these orders to his people: He said, "Every Israelite son that is born you are to throw into the river, but every daughter you will let live."

1:6-12, 22

The Birth of Moses

Now, there was a man in the tribe of Levi (LEE-vigh)* who married a daughter of [the tribe of] Levi. The woman had a son. When she saw that he was a fine child, she hid him for three months.

When the woman couldn't hide the baby any longer, she took a basket made of papyrus (pah-PIGH-ruhs)* reeds and made it watertight by covering it with tar. Then she put the baby into the basket and hid it among the tall reeds at the edge of the river. His sister stood nearby to watch what would happen to him.

One day the daughter of Pharaoh came down to the river to wash herself. Her maids walked with her along the bank of the river. When she saw the basket among the tall reeds, she sent one of her maids to get it.

Pharaoh's daughter opened the basket and saw the baby. He was crying. She felt sorry for him. "This is one of the Hebrew's (HEE-broos)* children," she said.

Then the baby's sister said to Pharaoh's daughter, "Should I go and get you a nurse, a Hebrew woman, to take care of the child for you?" Pharaoh's daughter said, "Yes, do so." So the girl went and got the baby's mother.

Pharaoh's daughter said to the mother, "Take the baby and nurse him for me and I will give you your wages." So the woman took her child and nursed him. When he grew old enough, she took him to Pharaoh's daughter, and he became her son. She named him Moses (MO-zehs),* because, she said, "I drew him out of the water."

2:1-10

Young Moses

When Moses had grown up [and was a young prince], he went out among his people and saw how badly they were being treated. One day he saw an Egyptian beating a Hebrew man, one of his own kind of people. He looked this way and that. Seeing no one,

Moses killed the Egyptian and hid his body in the sand.

The next day when Moses went out, it so happened that he saw two Hebrews fighting. He said to the one who was doing the wrong, "Why are you hitting your own countryman?" The man said, "Who made you a prince and a judge over us? Do you mean to kill me the way you killed the Egyptian?"

Then Moses became afraid. He said to himself, "What I did must be known." And when Pharaoh heard about it, he tried to have Moses killed. But Moses escaped from Pharaoh and lived in the land called Midian (MID-ee-an).

In Midian Moses sat down beside a well one day. And the seven daughters of the priest of Midian came to get water from the well. They wanted to water their father's flock. But some shepherds came and chased them away. Moses stood up and helped them and watered their flock.

When they went home, their father said, "How did you get back so early today?" They said, "An Egyptian saved us from the shepherds and even drew water for us and watered the flock." He said to his daughters, "Where is he? Why did you leave the man behind? Invite him to eat with us."

Moses was happy to live with this man, and the man gave Moses his daughter Zipporah (Zip-PO-rah) for a wife. . . .

After some time the king of Egypt died. But the people of Israel (IS-rah-ail)* continued to suffer slavery and cried for help. Their cries went to God and he heard them. God also remembered his promise to Abraham, to Isaac, and to Jacob. When he saw how the people of Israel were suffering, he pitied them.

2:11-25

The Burning Bush

Moses helped take care of the flock of his father-in-law, Jethro (JETH-ro), the priest of Midian. One day he led his sheep to the west side of the desert and came to the mountain of God called Horeb (HOR-eb). There the angel of the Lord [God] appeared to him in a flame of fire out of the middle of a bush.

Moses looked and saw that the bush was burning but was not burning away. So he said [to himself], "This is a wonderful sight. I must go and see why the bush is not burning up."

When God saw that Moses had stopped to look, he called to him from out of the bush, "Moses, Moses!" Moses answered, "Here I am!" God said to him, "Do not come near. Take your shoes off your feet, because the place on which you are standing is holy ground." Then he said, "I am the God of your father, the God of Abraham, the God of Isaac, and the God of Jacob."

Moses covered his face, because he was afraid to look at God. Then God said, "I have seen the suffering of my people in Egypt. I have heard them cry out under their taskmasters. I know their troubles, and I have come to save them from the Egyptians. I will bring them out of that land to a good and large place, a land where milk and honey flow. . . .

"Come, I will send you to Pharaoh" [the voice of God continued], "so that you may lead my people, the children of Israel, out of Egypt." But Moses said to the Lord, "Who am I, to go to Pharaoh and to lead the people of Israel out of Egypt?" God said, "I will certainly be with you; and this will be a proof that I have sent you: When you have brought the people out of Egypt, you will worship me on this mountain."

"But," said Moses, "if I go to the people of Israel and say that the God of their fathers has sent me to them, they will ask, 'What is his name?' What am I to say to them?" God answered, "I AM WHO I AM. So say this to the people of Israel, 'I AM has sent me to you.'"

God also said, "I know that the king of Egypt will not let you go unless he is forced. So I will stretch out my hand and will deal a blow to the Egyptians through all the wonders I will do. After that Pharaoh will let you go."

Then said Moses, "O my Lord, I'm not a good speaker. I haven't been, and I'm not now, since you've spoken to me. I am slow in speaking." The Lord said to Moses, "Who made man's mouth? Who makes the dumb or the deaf or the seeing or the blind? Is it not I, the Lord? Go then, and I will be with you as you speak, and I will teach you what to say."

But Moses said, "O my Lord, please send some other person." Then the Lord became angry with Moses. He said, "Isn't Aaron (AIR-on),* the Levite (LEE-vight), your brother? I know he can speak well. He is coming out to meet you, and when he sees you, he'll be glad. You will speak to him and tell him what to say. And I will help both of you to speak, and I will teach you what to say. . . ."

So Moses went to Jethro, his father-in-law, and said, "Please let me go back to my people in Egypt and see whether they still are alive." And Jethro said, "Go in peace." And the Lord said to Moses, "Go back to Egypt; all those who wanted to kill you are dead." So Moses set his wife and sons on a donkey and went back to Egypt.

3:1-15, 19, 20; 4:10-20

Moses Before Pharaoh

Moses and Aaron went to Pharaoh and said, "This is what the Lord, the God of Israel, says: 'Let my people go, so that they may hold a [religious] feast in the desert and worship me there.'" But Pharaoh said, "Who is the Lord that I should obey him and let the Israelites go? I don't know the Lord, and I won't let Israel go!"

Then Moses and Aaron said, "The God of the Hebrews has met with us. We beg you, let us go on a three-day journey into the desert. We want to sacrifice to the Lord our God so that he won't send sickness or a battle to us." But the king of Egypt said to them, "Moses and Aaron, why do you take the people away from their work?" . . .

That same day Pharaoh ordered the taskmasters

and their helpers not to give the people straw to make bricks, as they had been doing. "Let them go and gather straw for themselves," he said. "But you are still to demand from them the same number of bricks they have been making. They haven't enough work to do. That's why they say, 'Let us go and sacrifice to our God.'"

Then the leaders of the people of Israel met Moses and Aaron. . . . They said to them, "May the Lord look at you and judge you, because you have made us hated in the sight of Pharaoh and his servants. Now they want to kill us."

Then Moses went to the Lord and said to him, "Lord, why have you treated these people so badly? Why did you ever send me here? Even since I came to Pharaoh to speak for you, he has harmed them more, and you have not saved them at all."

Then the Lord said to Moses, "You will see what I will do to Pharaoh. By my power he will be made to let the people go, and by my power he will drive them out of his land." And God said to Moses, "I am the Lord. I appeared to Abraham, to Isaac, and to Jacob as God Almighty. . . . I also made a promise to them, to give them the land of Canaan. . . . Say to the people of Israel, 'I am the Lord, and I will bring you out from slavery under the Egyptians, . . . and I will make you my people, and I will be your God. . . .'"

Moses told the people of Israel all that the Lord had said, but in their suffering and misery they didn't listen to him.

5:1-8; 20-23; 6:1-9

The Ten Plagues

Moses and Aaron went before Pharaoh and did what the Lord told them to do. Aaron threw down his walking stick in front of Pharaoh and his servants, and the walking stick became a snake. Then Pharaoh called together the wise men and magicians of Egypt, and they did the same by their secret art. But Aaron's walking stick swallowed up their walking sticks. Still, Pharaoh's heart was hard, and he wouldn't listen to them.

Then Aaron took his walking stick and struck the water in the Nile River. At once all the water in the river turned to blood. [And the fish in the river died.] The river smelled so bad the Egyptians couldn't drink the water. But the magicians also were able to do this, so Pharaoh's heart became harder, and he wouldn't listen to Moses and Aaron.

Then Aaron stretched his hand over the waters of Egypt, and frogs came out and covered the land. . . . [The frogs went into the houses and bedrooms and beds and kitchens and ovens.] Then Pharaoh called for Moses and Aaron and said, "Ask the Lord to take the frogs away from me and my people, and I will let the people go to make sacrifices to the Lord." . . .

So Moses prayed to the Lord and the frogs died. The people gathered them up in big piles and the whole country smelled bad. But when Pharaoh saw that they were gone, he made his heart harder and would not listen to Moses and Aaron, just the way the Lord had said.

Then Aaron took his walking stick and struck the ground. And the dust became lice (LIGHS)* on the people and animals all over Egypt. The magicians tried to do the same but couldn't. So they said to Pharaoh, "This is the work of God." But Pharaoh's heart was hard, and he wouldn't listen to them, as the Lord had said [would be the case].

[Then the Lord sent other plagues (PLAYGS):* swarms of flies, a disease that caused all the cattle to die, painful sores that covered the bodies of the people and the animals, hail that struck down everything in the fields, grasshoppers that ate up all that was left after the hail, and thick darkness over all of Egypt for three days. None of these plagues came to where the Israelites lived in the land of Goshen (GO-shen). Still,

71

Pharaoh's heart was hard, and he wouldn't let the people of Israel leave his country.]

7:10-13, 20-22; 8:6-15, 17-19

The Passover

Then the Lord said to Moses, "I will bring one more plague upon Pharaoh and upon Egypt. After that he will let you go. In fact, he will drive you out for good."

Then Moses called the leaders of the Israelites together and said to them, "Take a lamb from your flocks according to the size of your families and kill it. Also take a bunch of plants and dip it in the blood [of the lamb]. Then paint with the blood the top and two side posts of the doorways of your houses. And none of you are to go out of your houses until morning."

[Moses also told the people to roast the lamb and eat the meat with flat bread and with bitter herbs (ERBS).* While eating the meal, they were to be dressed and ready to leave.] "For the Lord will pass through and strike down the Egyptians," said Moses. "And when he sees the blood on the door top and side posts, he will pass over that house and will not allow death to go in.

"And you are to observe this [passover meal] as a covenant (KUHV-eh-nuhnt),* for you and your children forever," said Moses. "And when you come to the land that the Lord will give you, as he has promised, you are to keep this service. When your children ask, 'What do you mean by this service?' you will say, 'It is the service of the Lord's passover. He passed over the houses of the children of Israel in Egypt when he struck down the Egyptians. He saved all our families.'"

[When the people heard this], they bowed their heads and worshiped God. Then they went and did as the Lord had commanded Moses and Aaron.

11:1; 12:21-28

The Firstborn Die

When midnight came, the Lord God struck down all the firstborn sons of the Egyptians, from the oldest son of Pharaoh, the king, to the oldest son of a prisoner in a jail, and even the first calves of the cattle. Pharaoh got up in the night and so did all the people of Egypt. And there was a great cry throughout the whole land, because there wasn't a single house where someone wasn't dead.

That night Pharaoh sent for Moses and Aaron. "Get out!" he said, "Go away from my people, you and all the Israelites. Go and worship your God, as you said, and take your flocks and your herds with you. Be gone." And all the Egyptians urged the Israelites to leave their country as quickly as they could. "Otherwise," they said, "we're as good as dead."

So the people of Israel took their bread dough as it was [before it had raised] and tied their bread boards in their clothes bundles on their shoulders. Then they left and traveled from Rameses (RAM-zees)* to Succoth (SUCK-oth).* There were about 600,000 of them, counting only the men. And with them also went a crowd of other people and flocks and herds in great numbers.

From Succoth they went on to Etham (EE-tham), on the edge of the desert, and camped there. And the Lord went with them. In the daytime he led them along the way by a cloud in the shape of a pillar. At night he led them with a pillar of fire.

12:29-34, 37, 38; 13:20-22

Crossing the Red Sea

When the king of Egypt was told that the Israelites had left [his country], he and his servants changed their minds. "Why did we let them go, these slaves of ours?" they said. So the king got his chariot (CHAIR-ee-ot)* ready and went after them with his army. . . .

When the people of Israel saw the Egyptians coming, they became very frightened. They cried out to the Lord and said to Moses, "Why have you brought us out here to die in the desert? Were there no graves in Egypt? Didn't we tell you in Egypt, 'Let us alone; let us go on serving the Egyptians'? Slavery would have been better than to die here."

But Moses said to the people, "Don't be afraid. Wait and you'll see how God will save you, for you'll never see these Egyptians again. The Lord will fight for you and you just have to be calm."

Then the cloud moved from in front of the Israelites and went behind them, coming between them and the Egyptians. That night it caused darkness and kept the two camps apart. Then Moses held out his hand over the sea [as God had ordered him]. And all during the night the Lord drove the water back with a strong wind.

Now the people of Israel walked through the middle of the sea on dry ground. The waters were like a wall on both their right and left sides. Then the Egyptians went into the sea after them, all of Pharaoh's horses and chariots and horsemen.

When morning came, the Lord . . . clogged the chariot wheels so that they wouldn't turn. The Egyptians said, "Let's turn back to escape from the Israelites, because the Lord is fighting for them against us."

Then the Lord said to Moses, "Stretch out your hand over the sea so that the water will flow back over the Egyptians." So Moses stretched out his hand over the sea, and the water returned and covered the chariots and the horsemen and all the army of Pharaoh. Of all the army of Pharaoh not a man remained. But the Israelites were safe, having walked on dry ground through the sea. . . . In this way the Lord saved the Israelites from the Egyptians.

When the people of Israel looked back, they saw the Egyptians lying dead on the seashore. Seeing what the Lord had done against the Egyptians, the people of

Israel were full of holy fear. Now they believed in the Lord and in his servant Moses.

14:5-14, 19-31

In the Wilderness (WIL-der-ness)*

Moses led the people of Israel from the Red Sea into the wilderness called Shur (SHOOR). For three days they traveled and found no water. When they came to a place called Marah (MAH-rah), they couldn't drink the water they found there. It was bitter. For this reason it was given the name Marah [which means "bitterness"].

The people grumbled and blamed Moses, saying, "What are we to drink?" Moses talked to the Lord, and the Lord showed him a tree [to sweeten the water]. When he threw the tree into the water, the water became sweet. . . .

Then they came to Elim, where there were 12 wells of water and 70 palm trees, and they camped there by the water. When they left Elim, they came to the wilderness called Sin, which is between Elim and Mt. Sinai. This was on the 15th day of the second month after they had left Egypt.

And the people of Israel grumbled against Moses and Aaron. They said, "It would have been better for us if we had died by the hand of the Lord in the land of Egypt. There we sat down and had bowls of meat and ate our fill of bread. You have brought us into this wilderness to kill all of us with hunger."

Then the Lord said to Moses, "You will see. I will rain bread from heaven for you. The people are to go out and collect a day's supply every day. This will test them on whether they will obey my laws or not. Then on the sixth day they are to bring in twice as much as they collect on other days."

So Moses and Aaron said to all the people of Israel, "When evening comes, you will know that it is the Lord who brought you out of the land of Egypt. And in the morning you will see the glory of the Lord, because he has heard your grumblings against him. Your complaints are not against us—for what are we?—but against the Lord." . . .

And it so happened that in the evening quails (KWAYLS)* flew all over the camp, and in the morning dew lay all around the camp. And when the dew had disappeared, the people saw small, round things lying on the ground. . . . And Moses said to them, "This is the bread the Lord has given you to eat. And this is what the Lord has commanded: Every person is to gather only as much as he can eat. You are to take an omer [about one tenth of a bushel] for each person in your tent."

Well, the people of Israel did so. Some gathered more, some less. But when they measured it out with an omer, those who had gathered a lot had nothing left over and those who had gathered just a little had enough. Everyone had enough to eat.

"Don't leave any of it until morning," said Moses. But some people didn't listen to him. They saved some of the bread wafers until morning, and it got wormy and smelled bad. Moses was angry with them.

But from then on they gathered the bread every morning, each gathering the amount needed for the day. When the sun grew hot, the wafers melted. On the sixth day they gathered twice as much, two omers for each.

And the children of Israel ate manna (MAN-nah)* for 40 years, until they came to the borders of the land of Canaan.

15:22-27; 16:1-21, 35

The Ten Commandments

In the third month after the Israelites had left Egypt, they came to the desert area called Sinai (SIGH-nah-igh). There, at the foot of Mount Sinai, they pitched their tents.

And Moses went up the mountain to talk to God, and the Lord spoke to him, saying, "This is what you are to say to the people of Israel: You have seen what I did to the Egyptians, and how I carried you on eagles' wings and brought you to myself. Now, if you will obey my voice and keep my covenant, then you will be my special possession, more' so than any other people. . . . These are the words you are to speak to the people of Israel."

Moses called all the leaders of the people to him and told them what the Lord had said. All the people answered, "We will do everything that the Lord has told us to do." . . .

Then Moses told the Lord what the people had said, and God said to Moses, "Go and get the people ready. These next two days they are to wash themselves and their clothes. On the third day from now, I, the Lord their God, will come down to Mount Sinai in the sight of all."

In the morning of the third day there was thunder and lightning, and a thick cloud hung around the mountain. A very loud trumpet sound was heard; it made everyone in the camp tremble.

Then Moses led all the people out of the camp to meet God, and they stood at the foot of the mountain. And Mount Sinai was wrapped in smoke, because the Lord came down to it in fire. And the whole mountain shook and trembled. . . .

Then the Lord called Moses to the top of the mountain, and Moses went up. And God spoke these words: "I am the Lord your God, who brought you out of the land of Egypt, out of slavery. You must have no other gods besides me. . . ."

God also said, "You must not use the name of the Lord, your God, carelessly. Whoever does so will be considered guilty by God himself. Remember to keep the sabbath (SAB-bahth)* day holy. . . . Honor your father and your mother. . . . You must not murder. You must not commit adultery. You must not steal. You must not tell lies about your neighbor. You must not long for your neighbor's house, or his wife, his servants, his property, or anything else belonging to him."

When all the people saw the lightning and smoke coming from the mountain, and when they heard the thunder and the sound of a trumpet, they were afraid and went and stood farther away. They said to Moses, "You speak to us and we will listen, but don't let God speak to us, for we may die."

Moses said to the people, "Don't be afraid. God has come to test you. This fear that you have of him is to keep you from doing what is wrong." But the people drew back from the mountain and waited while Moses went into the thick smoke where God was.

And the Lord spoke to Moses, and Moses told the people all the words of the Lord and all his laws. And the people answered, "Everything the Lord has said we will do."

Then the Lord said to Moses, "Come up to me on the mountain and wait there. I will give you [two] tablets of stone with the laws and commandments that I have written, so you can teach the people." . . . So Moses went up on the mountain. . . . And Moses was on the mountain 40 days and 40 nights.

19:1-11, 16-20; 20:1-21; 24:12-15

The Golden Calf

When the people saw that Moses wasn't coming down from the mountain right away, they said to Aaron (AIR-on),* "Make us some gods who will lead us, for we don't know what has happened to Moses, who brought us out of the land of Egypt."

Aaron said to them, "Break off the gold earrings that your wives, sons, and daughters are wearing and bring them to me." So all the people broke off their gold earrings and brought them to Aaron. He took them and melted the gold and made it into the shape of a calf.

Then the people said, "Let this be your god, O

Israel, that brought you out of the land of Egypt." And Aaron built an altar in front of the golden calf. Then he made a proclamation, saying, "Tomorrow is a feast day to the Lord." So the people got up early the next morning and offered burnt offerings and peace offerings, and then they ate and drank and played.

Then God said to Moses, "Go down, for your people . . . have quickly gone out of the way I told them to go. They had made for themselves a golden calf and are worshiping it. So Moses went down from the mountain carrying two [stone] tablets of laws. The tablets were covered with writing on both sides and were the work of God. . . .

As Moses came close to the camp, he saw the calf and the dancing and he became very angry. He threw down the stone tablets and they broke. Then he took the calf the people had made and burned it in a fire. He ground what was left into powder, sprinkled it on the water, and made the people drink it.

On the following day Moses said to the people, "You have done a great sin. Now I will again go up to the Lord. Perhaps I can get forgiveness from him for the sin you have done."

And the Lord said to Moses, "Cut two tablets of stone like the first ones, and I will write upon these the words that were on the tablets you broke." . . . So Moses cut two tablets of stone like the first ones and climbed Mount Sinai with the two tablets, as the Lord had commanded.

And God came to Moses in a cloud and said, "I am the Lord, the Lord God. I am merciful and gracious, patient, and full of goodness and truth. I show mercy to thousands and forgive evil, wrongdoing, and sin. But I punish the guilty even in their children and their children's children."

Moses bowed his head and worshiped God and said, "O Lord, . . . forgive our wrongdoing and our sin and let us be your people." Then the Lord said, "I will make a promise: I will do wonders for all your people [but you must keep all my commandments and worship me according to my laws]. . . .

Moses stayed there with the Lord [on the mountain] 40 days and 40 nights. During this time he didn't eat or drink. And he wrote upon the tablets the words of God's promise and the 10 Commandments.

32:1-8, 15-20, 30; 34:1-28

The Making of a Tabernacle

When Moses came down from Mount Sinai with the two tablets in his hands, he didn't know that the skin of his face shone from his visit with God. When Aaron and the people of Israel saw Moses, they were afraid to come near him because of the way his face shone. But Moses called to them, and Aaron and the rulers of the people came to him, and he talked with them.

Afterwards all the children of Israel came, and Moses told them all that the Lord had said to him on Mount Sinai. Moses put a veil over his face until he had finished speaking to them.

Then Moses said to all the people of Israel, "This is a thing the Lord has commanded: Take an offering to the Lord. Whoever has a generous heart, let him bring the Lord's offering. . . . And let every able man among you come and . . . make the tabernacle (TAB-er-nack-l)* that the Lord wants. . . . "

Then all the people of Israel came, everyone whose heart stirred him and whose spirit moved him. They all brought an offering to the Lord—to be used for a meeting tent and for its services and for the holy garments [what the priests were to wear]. . . .

And Moses [chose certain architects and artists to plan the tent church and] asked every one whose heart stirred him up to come and do the work. They received from Moses all the freewill offerings that the people of Israel had brought for doing the work of the tent church.

But the people kept bringing offerings every morning. Finally the men doing the tasks went to

Moses and said, "The people are bringing much more than enough for doing the work the Lord has asked us to do." So Moses sent out this order throughout the camp: "No one is to do anything more for the offering for the tabernacle."

So Moses finished the work and a cloud covered the meeting tent. . . . Whenever God raised the cloud from over the tabernacle, the people of Israel continued their journey. But when the cloud covered the tabernacle, they would not travel until it was raised.

34:29-33; 35:4-35; 36:2-6;
and 40:33-37

THE BOOK OF
Leviticus*

The Lord said to Moses, "Say to the whole congregation of the people of Israel, 'You are to be holy, for I, the Lord your God, am holy. Every one of you is to honor his mother and his father, and you are to observe my sabbaths. I am the Lord, your God. Do not turn to idols or make for yourselves metal gods. I am the Lord, your God. . . .'"

Holy Behavior

When you harvest the grain of your land, you are not to cut it to the very border. Neither are you to gather what's left after your harvest. And you are not to strip your vineyard bare; nor are you to gather the fallen grapes in your vineyard. You are to leave them for the poor people and the traveler. I am the Lord, your God.

You must not steal or deal falsely [with others] or lie to one another. And you are not to lie or swear falsely when using my name, thereby misusing the name of your God. I am the Lord.

You must not make life hard or miserable for your

neighbor or rob him. The wages of a hired man ought not be kept by you overnight. [You are to pay him as soon as he has finished his work.] You must not curse the deaf or trip a blind man. You are to fear your God. I am the Lord.

You must always be fair in what you decide. The poorness or richness of people doesn't really matter, so always treat them with fairness. Don't go around talking bad about people, and don't try to get your neighbor into trouble. I am the Lord.

Don't ever hate your brother. Reason with him so that you won't have to carry the blame for the sins he does. Don't seek revenge and don't bear a grudge. Love your neighbor as yourself, for I am the Lord.

19:1-4, 9-18

Blessings and Punishments

The Lord said to Moses, . . . "If you will live according to my directions and do my commandments, I will give you regular rains. Then the lands will produce bumper crops, and the trees will be loaded with fruit.

"Your grain harvest will last until your grape harvest, and your grape harvest will last until the time for sowing. And you will be able to eat all you want and live safely in your land.

"I will give you peace" [the Lord said to Moses], "and you will be able to go to sleep without being afraid of anyone. And I will remove the dangerous animals from your land, and war will not go through your land. . . . [You will defeat all your enemies.]

"And I will look after you and will multiply you and will keep my covenant with you. You will still be eating the old crops when you will have to clear them out to make way for the new.

"I will live among you" [said the Lord], "and will be your God, and you are to be my people. . . .

"But if you will not listen to me and will not do my commandments, this is what I will do to you" [said the

Lord]: "I will punish you with sudden panic and fever that weakens the eyes and causes life to drift away. And you will plant your seeds for nothing, because your enemies will eat your crops.

"I will show my anger against you" [said the Lord], "and those who hate you will rule you. You will even run when no one is chasing you!" . . .

These are the laws and instructions the Lord God gave to the people of Israel on Mount Sinai through Moses.

26:3-12, 14-17, 46

THE BOOK OF
Numbers*

The Lord said to Moses, "Say to Aaron and his sons: This is the way you are to bless the people of Israel: You shall say to them,

The Lord bless you and keep you;
The Lord make his face shine on you
and be gracious to you;
The Lord lift up his countenance
(KOWN-teh-nehns)* on you
and give you peace."

6:22-26

Spies Sent to Canaan

And the Lord said to Moses, "Send some men to spy out the land of Canaan, which I have promised to give to the people of Israel. Send a man from every tribe, every one a leader among his people."

So Moses chose 12 men [one from each of the tribes of Israel], as the Lord had commanded. . . . And Moses sent them to spy out the land of Canaan.

Moses said to them, "Go up into . . . the hill country and see what the land is like. See whether the people who live there are strong or weak, few or many. See

whether the land itself is good or bad, and whether the
people live in tents or in strong buildings. See also
whether there is wood in the land, and bring back some
of the fruit of the land."

Now, it was the time of the first ripe grapes. So the
men went and spied out the land.... When they came to
the Valley of Eshcol (ESH-kohl), they cut down a
branch with a single bunch of grapes on it. [It was so
large and heavy] they carried it on a pole between two
men....

13:1-24

The Spies Return

At the end of 40 days the spies returned from
spying on the land. They showed Moses and Aaron and
all the people of Israel the fruit and told them, "The
land to which you sent us is flowing with milk and
honey, and this is some of its fruit. But the people who
live in the land are strong, and the cities are well
protected and very large...."

Caleb (KAY-leb), one of the men sent to spy out the
land, said, "Let's go at once and occupy the land, for we
are able to overcome it." But the others who had gone
with him said, "We aren't able to fight those people;
they are stronger than we."

So the other spies gave a bad report to the people of
Israel. They said, "The land we went to look over is a
land that eats up the people who live there. All the
people we saw in it were very tall. We saw giants there.
We felt like grasshoppers beside them."

13:25-33

The People Grumble

Then all the people cried that night and complained to Moses and Aaron. They said, "If only we had died
in the land of Egypt or in this wilderness! Why has the
Lord brought us to this land to be killed in battle? Our
wives and our little ones will be captured. Wouldn't it
be better for us to go back to Egypt?"

And the people said to one another, "Let's choose a captain and go back to Egypt." Then . . . Joshua (JAH-shoo-ah) and Caleb, who had been with those who had spied out the land, . . . said to all the people of Israel, "The land that we passed through to look over is a very good land. If the Lord is pleased with us, he will . . . give it to us. . . ." But the people said to stone them with stones.

Then the glory of the Lord appeared at the meeting tent, and God said to Moses, "How long will these people try me? How long will they not believe in me in spite of all the proof [of my power] I have given them. I will destroy them with a plague (PLAYG)* and will make you into a greater and mightier nation than they are."

But Moses said to the Lord, "The Egyptians will hear about this and . . . will say, 'Because the Lord was not able to bring these people into the land he promised to give them, he destroyed them in the wilderness.' So I beg you, . . . pardon the sin of these people by the greatness of your mercy, as you have forgiven them since Egypt even until now."

Then the Lord said to Moses, "I have pardoned, as you ask. But as surely as I live, . . . none of the people who saw my glory . . . but did not listen to my voice will see the land that I promised to give to their fathers. . . . Of all who are 20 years old and up . . . not one will get to enter the land . . . except Caleb and Joshua. . . ."

When Moses told these words to all the people of Israel, they were very sad. So early the next morning they went to the top of the hill country and said, "See, we are here. We will go to the place the Lord has promised. We have sinned" [in being afraid to go].

But Moses said to them, "Why are you now disobeying God [in going up the mountain]? That will not succeed. . . . Because you have stopped following the Lord, the Lord will not be with you."

14:1-16, 20-22, 26-30, 39-43

The Wandering in the Desert

The people of Israel continued their wandering and came to the desert called Zin. They stayed [for a while] at Kadesh (KAY-desh). Miriam (MEER-ee-am)* died and was buried there.

Once again there was no water for the people, so they came together to complain to Moses and Aaron. They said, "We wish we had died when our brothers [and sisters] died. Why did you bring the people of the Lord into this desert? That we should die here, we and our cattle? . . . There is no water to drink. . . ."

Then the Lord said to Moses, "Take your rod and call the people together, you and your brother Aaron, and tell the rock in front of them to give them water...." So Moses and Aaron called the people together in front of a huge rock and said to them, "Listen now, you rebels. Must we bring water for you out of this rock?" Then Moses raised his hand and struck the rock with his rod two times. At once lots of water came running out, and the people drank and so did the cattle.

Then the Lord said to Moses and Aaron, "Because you did not believe in me, . . . you will not bring these people to the land I have given them."

20:1-12

The Brass Serpent

From Mount Hor the Israelites traveled by way of the Red Sea in order to go around the land of Edom. And the people became very discouraged along the way. They spoke against God and against Moses, saying, "Why have you brought us out of Egypt to die in the desert? For there is no food and no water, and we hate this awful manna."

So the Lord sent poisonous snakes among the people to punish them, and many were bitten and died. Then the people came to Moses and said, "We have sinned, because we spoke against the Lord and against you. Pray to the Lord to take away the snakes." And Moses prayed for the people.

Then the Lord said to Moses, "Make a brass snake and put it on a pole. Anyone who is bitten will live simply by looking at it." So Moses made a metal snake, and when anyone who was bitten looked at the brass snake, he recovered.

21:4-9

THE BOOK OF
Deuteronomy*

Moses called all the people of Israel together and said to them, "Listen carefully to all the laws I will now tell you. Learn them and be sure to do them. The Lord, our God, made a covenant with us at Mount Horeb (HOR-eb). . . . He said:

"I am the Lord, your God, who brought you out of slavery in Egypt. You must not have any other gods but me. You are not to make for yourselves and worship any carved statues of birds, animals, or fish. You must not bow down to them or worship them in any way, for I, the Lord your God, am a jealous God. . . .

"You must never use the name of the Lord, your God, without a good reason. The Lord will never overlook any misuse of his name.

"Keep the sabbath day holy, as the Lord, your God, has commanded. Do all your work on the other six days, but the seventh day is a sabbath day to the Lord, your God. On it you are not to do any work. . . .

"Honor your father and mother, as the Lord has commanded, so that you will have a long and good life in the land the Lord, your God, will give to you.

"You are not to murder. Neither are you to commit adultery. Nor are you ever to steal. Neither are you to tell lies against your neighbor. And you must not ever covet another man's wife and desire his house or his land or his servants or his animals or anything that he owns.

"These words," said Moses, "the Lord spoke to all the people at the mountain. He spoke with a loud voice out of the fire and the cloud and the thick darkness. Those were the only commandments he gave at that time. And he wrote them on two stone tablets and gave them to me.

"Now, these are the commandments, the laws, which the Lord your God told me to teach you," said Moses, "so that you will do them in the land to which you are going. . . . Listen closely, therefore, O people of Israel, and be careful to do them, so that all will go well with you. . . .

"Listen, O Israel: The Lord is our God, the Lord alone. And you are to love the Lord your God with all your heart and with all your soul and with all your might. And these words that I command you this day are to be in your heart, and you must try hard to teach them to your children. Talk about them when you are at home or out walking and at bedtime and the first thing in the morning. . . ."

5:1-22; 6:1-9

Moses' Farewell and Death

Moses continued to speak such words to all the people of Israel. Then he said to them, "I am 120 years old this day. I can no longer go here and there. And the Lord has said to me, 'You will not get to go over this Jordan River.' But the Lord your God will go over with you; . . . and Joshua (JAHSH-oo-ah) will be your leader, as the Lord has decided." . . .

Then Moses called for Joshua and said to him in front of all the people of Israel, "Be strong and brave, for you will go with these people into the land the Lord has promised he would give to them. You must help them take possession of it. Don't be afraid or worried. The Lord will go ahead of you. He will not let you down or leave you." . . .

Then Moses went from the plains of Moab (MO-ab), up the mountain of Nebo (NEE-bo) to the peak of Pisgah (PIZ-gah) near Jericho (JAIR-ee-ko). There the Lord showed him all the land [he was giving to each of the tribes of Israel]. And the Lord said to Moses, "This is the land I promised Abraham, Isaac, and Jacob I would give to their descendants. I have let you see it, but you will not get to go over there."

So Moses, the servant of the Lord, died in the land of Moab, as the Lord had said he would. And he was buried in a valley in the land of Moab, but to this day no one knows where his grave is.

Moses was 120 years old when he died, but his eyesight was still good and he was still physically strong. The people of Israel wept for Moses on the plains of Moab for 30 days. Then the days of weeping for Moses were over.

And Joshua, the son of Nun, was full of wisdom, for Moses had laid his hands on him and had blessed him. So the people of Israel listened to Joshua and did what the Lord had told Moses.

Never since then has there been in Israel a prophet like Moses. [He was a man] the Lord knew face to face. No one has ever done wonders like the wonders the Lord sent him to do in the land of Egypt. . . . And no one ever had power like his or did the great deeds Moses did among the people of Israel.

34:1-12

THE BOOK OF
Joshua

After the death of Moses, the servant of God, the Lord spoke to Joshua, the son of Nun, who had served Moses. God said, "My servant Moses is dead. Therefore get ready and cross the River Jordan, you and all the people, into the land I am giving them. . . . As I was with Moses I will be with you. I will not let you down or leave you. . . . Be strong and brave and don't be afraid or worried. The Lord, your God, is with you wherever you go."

1:1-2, 5, 9

Joshua Sends Spies

So Joshua sent two men to spy secretly. "Go, see what the land is like, especially Jericho (JAIR-ee-ko)," he told them. They went there and came to the house of a woman named Rahab (RAY-hab). There they rented a room.

But someone told the king of Jericho, "Some Israelite men have come here tonight to spy out the land." So the king sent a message to Rahab. "Bring out the men who came to you and are now in your house. They have come to spy against our country." But the woman had hidden the two men.

[When she was questioned, she said], "It's true that two men came here, but I didn't know where they came from. And the men left about the time it was getting dark and the gate was to be closed. Where they went I don't know. If you will go after them quickly, you'll catch them."

So the king's men chased after the spies all the way to the Jordan River. As soon as they had left the city, the gate was shut.

But the woman had hidden the two spies under some stalks of grain on her roof. Before they lay down for the night, Rahab came up to them and said, "I know that the God Jahweh (YAH-way)* has given you this land and that all the people in it are afraid of you. For we have heard how Jahweh dried up the water of the Red Sea for you when you came out of Egypt. . . . Now then, promise by God that as I showed kindness to you, you also will show kindness and will save the lives of my father and mother and brothers and sisters and all who belong to them. Keep us from being killed."

The men said to her, "We will save your lives if you

will save ours. If you will not give us away, we will deal kindly with you when the Lord gives us the land."

Then she let the men down by a rope through a window. Her house was built on top of the city wall. And she said to the spies, "Go and hide in the hills for three days, until the men looking for you have come back here. After that you can safely go on your way."

The men said to her, "We'll try to keep this promise you made us give you. But when the people of Israel invade your country, you must tie a piece of purple cord in the window through which you let us down. And you must bring your father and mother and your brothers and your father's whole family into your house. . . . We will see that no one harms whoever is with you in your house. But if you tell anybody what we were doing here, we'll not keep our promise."

The woman said, "It will be just as you say it should be." Then she sent them away. As soon as they had left, she tied a purple cord in her window.

2:1-21

Crossing the Jordan River

When the spies returned, they said to Joshua, "The Lord most certainly has handed the whole country over to us. All the people of Jericho feel faint when they hear of us." . . .

Early the next morning Joshua and all the people of Israel moved on toward Canaan (KAY-nahn).* When they came to the Jordan River, they camped there before crossing over. After three days . . . the priests went ahead of the people, carrying the ark* of the covenant. And when the feet of the priests carrying the ark touched the edge of the water, the waters coming down from upstream backed up and those that went downstream toward the salt sea ran off.

So the people crossed over the Jordan River opposite the city of Jericho. And the priests who carried the ark of the covenant of the Lord stood on dry ground in the middle of the Jordan until all the people had finished crossing over the Jordan. . . . When the priests carrying the ark of the covenant of the Lord came out of the river and their feet touched dry ground, the waters of the Jordan began to flow again and overflowed its banks as before.

2:23-24; 3:1, 14-17; 4:18

The Fall of Jericho

Now Jericho was tightly shut up because of the people of Israel [who were camping nearby]. No one went out of the city and no one came in.

Then the Lord said to Joshua, "You'll see, I have given Jericho into your power, along with its king and all its brave men. You are to march around the city with all your fighting men every day for six days. And seven priests are to carry rams-horn trumpets in front of the ark. On the seventh day you are to march around the city seven times, and the priests are to blow the trumpets. . . ."

So Joshua had the ark of the Lord circle the city once [each day for six days]. On the seventh day the people of Israel got up early at the dawn of the day and marched around the city in the same way seven times. It was only on that day that they marched around the city seven times.

At the seventh time, when the priests had blown their trumpets, Joshua yelled to the people, "Shout! The Lord has given you the city! . . ." So the people shouted and the trumpets were blown. As soon as the people heard the sound of the trumpets, they all shouted still more and down fell the walls of Jericho.

Now the people of Israel went into the city . . . and took it. They completely destroyed everything in the city. . . . But Joshua said to the two men who had spied out the land, "Go to that woman's house and bring her and all who are with her safely out of it, as you promised." So the young men who had been spies went and brought Rahab and her family out and put them in the camp of the Israelites. . . .

And Joshua saved Rahab's life and her father's family and all that she had, and she lived with the people of Israel. Joshua did this because Rahab had hidden the men Joshua had sent to spy on the city of Jericho.

6:1-4, 11, 15-25

Joshua's Last Days

[Joshua conquered all the kings of Canaan and divided their land among the tribes of Israel. But to the tribe of Levi (LEE-vigh)* he gave no land, because they received the offerings of the people for the Lord, the God of Israel. And they set up the tabernacle in a place called Shiloh (SHIGH-lo).]

A long time after this, when the Lord had helped the Israelites conquer all their enemies, Joshua called all the leaders and officers of the people together. "I am now old," he said to them, "and you have seen what the Lord, your God, has done for you . . . , for the Lord, your God, fought for you.

"And now" [said Joshua], "I am about to go* the way of all things on earth. And you know in your hearts, all of you, that everything the Lord, your God, promised has come true; not one has failed."

Then Joshua gathered together all the tribes of Israel at Shechem (SHEE-kehm). And Joshua said to the people, " . . . Now, then, fear the Lord, and serve him sincerely and faithfully. . . . And if you are unwilling to serve the Lord, choose this day whom you will serve, . . . but as for me and my house we will serve the Lord."

Then the people answered, "Far be it from us that we should leave the Lord to serve other gods. It is the Lord, our God, who brought us and our parents out of Egypt and out of slavery. He did great things for us . . . and drove out all the people who lived in this land. Therefore we too will serve the Lord, for he is our God."

So Joshua made a covenant with the people that day . . . and then sent the people away. After these things Joshua, the son of Nun, the servant of the Lord, died. He was 110 years old.

23:1-3, 14; 24:1, 14-18,
25, 28-29

THE BOOK OF
Judges *

The people [of Israel] served the Lord as long as Joshua was alive and as long afterward as the old people were still living—those who had seen what the Lord had done for Israel. . . . But all those people died, and another generation grew up after them. They didn't know the Lord and what he had done for the people of Israel.

And the people did many things that the Lord considered very wrong. . . . They stopped worshiping the Lord, the God of their ancestors, who had brought them out of the land of Egypt. Instead, they began to bow to other gods from among the gods of the people around them. This made the Lord [the God Jahweh] angry. So the Lord let them fall into the power of their enemies.

Then the Lord gave the people of Israel judges. These leaders saved them from the power of their enemies around them. Whenever the Lord gave them judges, the Lord helped the judge and saved the Israelites from the power of their enemies. [Some of these judges were Deborah (DEH-ba-rah), Gideon (GID-ee-on), Jephthah (JEFF-thah), Samson, Eli (EE-ligh), and Samuel (SAM-yoo-el).*]

2:7, 10-12, 14, 16, 18

Gideon Chosen by God

The people of Israel did things that were wrong in the eyes of God, worshiping, for example, the gods called Baal (BAY-al)* and Asheroth (ASH-er-oth). So God allowed the people of Midian (MID-ee-ahn) to conquer and rule them for seven years. Because of the Midianites the people of Israel took to living in caves in the mountains, but still the people from Midian would come like a swarm of grasshoppers to destroy their crops and steal their cattle.

In their misery the people of Israel cried to the Lord, so he sent a prophet to them. [The prophet reminded the Israelites that their God had given them their land and warned them not to worship the gods of the people around them.] Also, the angel of the Lord came [with a message] to a man named Gideon.

When the angel of God appeared to Gideon, the son of Joash, he was beating out some wheat in a pit used for pressing out grapes. He didn't want the Midianites to see what he had. "Gideon," said the angel, "the Lord is with you, and you are a strong and brave man."

Gideon said to the angel, "If the Lord is with us, why has all this trouble come to us? And where are all those wonderful deeds our fathers told us he did for them? . . ." The Lord said to him, "You are to go with this power and save Israel from the Midianites. Am I not sending you?"

That night God told Gideon what to do. He said, "Take a bull from your father's herd and pull down the altar that your father has set up for sacrifices to Baal. Also cut down the totem pole beside it. Then take the bull and offer it [to the true God]. Make a fire with the wood from the sacred pole you will cut down."

So Gideon took 10 of his father's servants and did what God had told him to do. Because he was too afraid of his family and the people of the town to do it in the daytime, he did it at night.

When the people of the town got up in the morning and saw that the altar of Baal was pulled down and that the pole beside it had been cut down, . . . they said to one another, "Who did this?" When they discovered that Gideon, the son of Joash, had done this thing, they went

95

to Joash. "Bring out your son," they said. "He must die, because he has pulled down the altar of Baal. . . ."

But Joash said to all who were against him, "Do you have to fight for Baal or defend him?. . . If he is a god, let him fight for himself. Let him fight the one who pulled down the altar. Whoever fights for Baal will be dead by morning." [So the people were afraid to harm Gideon.]

6:1-14, 25-32

Gideon Defeats the Midianites

When the Midianites and their friends crossed the Jordan River and camped again in the land of Israel, the Spirit of the Lord caused Gideon to send out a call for men to come and help him fight the invaders. Men from everywhere came to join his army.

Gideon and his men gathered and camped by the spring of Harod (HAIR-ahd). The camp of Midian was north of them. The Lord said to Gideon, "There are too many of you for me to give you a victory over the Midianites. The men of Israel will proudly say, 'We saved ourselves.' Go, therefore, and tell those who are afraid, to go back home." So 22,000 left and 10,000 stayed.

Then the Lord said to Gideon, "There are still too many. Take them down to the water, and I will test them for you there. . . ." So Gideon brought the men down to the water. And the Lord said to Gideon, "Separate those who lap the water with their tongues, as a dog laps, and those who kneel down to drink."

The number of those who lapped [the water], putting their hands to their mouths, was 300 men. All the rest knelt down to drink.

The Lord said to Gideon, "With the 300 men who lapped I will save you and will put the Midianites into your hands. Let all the others go back to their homes." So after collecting all the clay jars and trumpets they had among them, Gideon kept the 300 men and sent the rest to their tents. The camp of Midian was below him in the valley.

That night the Lord said to Gideon, "Go down to the camp, for I have given it to you. But if you're afraid, first go down with your servant Purah (POO-rah) and listen to what they're saying down there. Then you'll be ready to attack."

So Gideon went down with his servant Purah to the outposts of the enemy camp. There he saw the Midianites and their allies camped in the valley like grasshoppers. . . . When Gideon came nearer, a man was telling a dream to his comrade.

The man said, "I dreamed a dream. In it a piece of barley bread tumbled into the Midian camp. When it struck a tent, the tent fell and turned upside down." His partner said, "This means nothing other than the sword of Gideon, the son of Joash, a man of Israel. God is giving him a victory over the whole army of Midian."

When Gideon heard the telling of the dream and its meaning, he worshiped God. Then he returned to his men and said, "Get up! The Lord has given the Midian army to you."

Then he divided the 300 men into three groups. To each man he gave a trumpet and an empty jar with a torch in it. "Watch me," he said, "and when I come to the edge of the camp, do what I will do. When I and those with me blow our trumpets, then blow your trumpets too on all sides of the camp. And shout, 'For the Lord and for Gideon.'"

So Gideon and the 100 men who were with him came to the edge of the camp at the beginning of the middle watch just after a new watch had been posted. And they blew on their trumpets and smashed the jars they held in their hands. And all three companies blew the trumpets and broke the jars, holding the lights in their left hands and the trumpets in their right hands. And they all shouted, "The sword of the Lord and of Gideon."

Every soldier stayed in his place around the camp, and all the men of Midian awoke with fear and began to run. When the 300 men of Israel blew on their trumpets, the Lord caused the Midianite men to use their swords against each other and then to run away. [The men of Israel chased them beyond the Jordan, killing their leaders. After that the country lived in peace for 40 years.]

6:33-35; 7:1-25

The Mighty Samson

[In time] the people of Israel again did much evil in the eyes of the Lord, and so the Lord let them be ruled by the Philistines (Fil-ISS-tins) for 40 years.

And there was a certain man in the tribe of Dan whose name was Manoah (Man-OH-ah). At first his wife had no children. Then the angel of the Lord appeared to her and said, "You have no children, but now you will have a son. Therefore take care, drink no wine or any strong drink and do not eat anything unclean. No razor is even to touch his head, because the boy is to be a special servant of God, dedicated to him from the day of his birth. And he will begin to save Israel from the Philistines."

After that the woman had a son and named him Samson. The boy grew up and the Lord blessed him. [When he was a young man], Samson asked his parents to get him a Philistine girl for a wife. At first his parents wanted him to marry one of his own people. They didn't know that this marriage was part of God's plan to free the people of Israel from the Philistines. Samson insisted.

As he and his parents were on their way [to where the young woman lived], a young lion tried to attack Samson. The Spirit of God came over him and he tore the lion apart with his bare hands. . . . Then he met the Philistine girl and talked to her. She pleased him very much.

When he returned after a while to get the girl, he

looked for the body of the lion he had killed. In the body of the lion was a swarm of bees and honey. Samson scooped a handful of the honey and ate it. He also gave some to his parents, but he didn't tell them he had taken the honey from the body of a lion.

[Later the marriage was arranged and Samson prepared a wedding feast. . . . 30 young Philistine men were present.] Samson said to them, "Let me give you a riddle. If, in the seven days of the feast, you can tell me what it is, I will give you 30 suits of clothes. But if you cannot tell me what it is, then you must give me 30 changes of clothes."

So they said, "Tell us your riddle." He said to them, "Out of the eater came something to eat; out of the strong came something sweet." Three days passed and the Philistines had found no answer to the riddle.

On the fourth day they said to Samson's wife, "Coax your husband to tell you what the riddle is. Otherwise we'll set fire to your father's house and burn you alive. . . ." So Samson's wife cried and said to him, "You hate me; you don't love me. You have given my people a riddle to solve, and you haven't told me the answer."

Samson said, "I haven't even told my father or my mother. Why should I tell you?" So she went on crying all during the seven days that the wedding feast was going on. On the seventh day he told her because he couldn't stand her any longer. She told the riddle immediately to her countrymen.

So before the seventh day was over, the men of the city said to Samson, "What is sweeter than honey? And what is stronger than a lion?" Samson [seeing what had happened] said, "You would never have found the answer to my riddle if you hadn't used my wife."

So Samson went . . . and killed 30 men and took their clothes and gave these to the men who had answered the riddle. Then he went back to his father's house. He was very angry [at the Philistines and with the woman he had married].   *13:1-7, 24-25; 14:1-19*

99

Samson and Delilah (Dee-LIGH-lah)

Samson became a judge in the land of Israel, and for 20 years he judged his people living under the Philistines (Fil-ISS-tins).

After some time he fell in love with a woman whose name was Delilah.

One day the leaders of the Philistines came to her and said, "Coax him and find out what gives him his great strength. We want to know how we can over-power him so we can tie him up and control him. For this each one of us will give you 1,100 pieces of silver."

So Delilah said to Samson, "Tell me, Samson, please, what makes you so strong? And how could anyone tie you down?" Samson said to her, "If someone tied me with seven bowstrings, I would be as weak as any other man."

Not long after this the leaders of the Philistines brought Delilah seven fresh bowstrings. She tied Samson with them and had men hiding in a nearby room.

As soon as she had tied Samson, she said to him, "Samson, the Philistines are here." But he broke the strings off his arms like a rope snaps when fire touches it. So the secret of his strength wasn't known.

Delilah then said to Samson, "You played with me and told me lies. Please tell me how you could be tied down." He said to her, "If I would be tied with new ropes that have never been used, then I would be as weak as any other man." So Delilah took some new ropes and tied him with them. Then she said to him, "Samson, the Philistines have come to get you."

Again there were men waiting in a nearby room, but Samson snapped the ropes off his arms like a thread. Again Delilah said to Samson, "Until now you've had fun with me and told me lies. Tell me now how you really could be tied." He said to her, "If you would weave my hair with cloth and make it tight with a pin, then I would become weak and be like any other man."

So while Samson slept, Delilah wove his hair into a web and made it tight with a pin. Then she said to him, "Samson, the Philistines are here to get you." But when he woke up out of his sleep, he pulled out the pin and the web.

Then she said to him, "How can you say 'I love you' when you don't trust me? Three times you have made fun of me and have not told me what the secret of your great strength is." Day after day she kept after him until he couldn't stand it any longer.

Finally he told her, "A razor has never touched my head because I have been dedicated to God since before I was born. If I would be shaved, my strength would leave me, and I would become weak and like any other man."

When Delilah saw that he had told her his secret, she sent for the Philistine leaders, saying, "Come up once more, because he has told me his secret." So the leaders of the Philistines came and brought along their money.

That evening Delilah made Samson go to sleep with his head on her knees. Then she called for a man and had him shave off Samson's hair. When she began to poke him, she saw that his strength was leaving him.

Then she said, "Samson, the Philistines are here to capture you!" As he awoke, he thought, "I'll do as before and just shake myself free." He didn't realize that the power of God had gone out of him.

So the Philistines quickly grabbed him and put out his eyes and took him to Gaza (GAY-zah).* There they tied him up with chains and made him grind the mill in their prison. But the hair of Samson's head began to grow again after it had been shaved.

Then the leaders of the Philistines planned a great celebration to offer a sacrifice to their god Dagon (DAY-gon). "Our god gave our enemy Samson to us," they said. And when the people saw him they praised their god. . . .

Later, when the people were merry, they said, "Bring Samson out, so he can entertain us." So they brought Samson out of the prison and made fun of him. When they stood him up between two pillars, Samson said to the boy who held him by the hand, "Let me feel the pillars that hold up the house, so I may lean on them."

Now, the house was full of men and women, and all the leaders of the Philistines were there. And on the roof there were about 3,000 men and women watching Samson and laughing at him. Then Samson said to the Lord, "O Lord God, remember me, I beg you, and make me strong again just this once, O God."

Then Samson took hold of the two middle pillars on which the building rested and leaned his weight on them, his right hand on the one and his left hand on the other. And Samson said, "Lord, let me die with the Philistines." Then he bent himself with all his might, and the building fell upon all the people that were in it.

15:20; 16:4-30

THE STORY OF
Ruth

In the days [long ago] when judges ruled the people of Israel, there was a famine in the land. And a certain man from the town of Bethlehem, in the country of Judah, moved to the country called Moab (MO-ab), he and his wife and two sons. The man's name was Elimelech (Ee-LIM-eh-lech). His wife's name was Naomi (Nay-O-mee). The names of the two sons were Mahlon (MAH-lahn) and Chilion (KIL-lee-ahn).

Elimelech, the husband of Naomi, died in Moab, and she was left with her two sons. The two sons married women of that country. Their names were Orpah (OR-pah) and Ruth (ROOTH).

After Naomi had lived in Moab for 10 years, both of her sons died too. Then she decided to go back to her home country. She had heard that the Lord had again given his people plenty of food there.

Naomi started out for Bethlehem with her two daughters-in-law, but on the way she told them to go back to their own people. "May the Lord treat you kindly," she said, "as you treated your husbands and me. . . ." Then she kissed them and they all began to cry. "No, we will go with you to your people," they said.

[But Naomi again told them to return and again they cried.] Then Orpah kissed Naomi good-bye, but Ruth hung on to her. Naomi said to Ruth, "See, your sister-in-law is going back to her people and to her gods. Go back with her."

But Ruth said, "Don't ask me to leave you or to stop following you. Where you will go I will go, and where you will stay I will stay. Your people will be my people and your God will be my God." . . .

When Naomi saw that Ruth was determined to go with her, she said no more. So the two of them went on together. They arrived in Bethlehem at the beginning of the barley (BAHR-lee)* harvest.

1:1-22

Ruth in Bethlehem

Now in Bethlehem there lived a relative of Naomi's dead husband. He was a very rich and powerful man. His name was Boaz (BO-az). Ruth said to Naomi, "Let me go to the fields and pick up grain that the workers have left behind if they give me permission." Naomi said to her, "Go, my daughter." So Ruth went and picked up grain the workers left behind. And she happened to go to a field that belonged to Boaz.

One day Boaz came from Bethlehem [and saw Ruth picking up grain in his field]. He said to the man who was in charge of the workers, "Whose girl is that?" The servant answered, "It's the Moabite girl who came back with Naomi from the country of Moab. She asked permission to pick up leftover grain and has worked since early morning until now without resting."

Then Boaz went over to Ruth and said, "Listen, my daughter, don't go to another field, but follow my servants. I have ordered them not to touch you. And when you are thirsty, go and drink from the water they have brought."

Ruth bowed herself to the ground and said to Boaz, "Why have I found favor in your eyes, since I am a stranger?" Boaz answered, "I have heard all that you have done for your mother-in-law since the death of your husband and how you have left your father and mother and the country where you were born and have come to a people you never knew before. May the Lord God of Israel reward you for what you have done. . . . "

At mealtime Boaz invited Ruth to eat with him and his workers. When she went back to picking up grain, he said to his young men, "Let her pick up grain also among the sheaves, and let some handfuls fall on purpose for her. . . .

So Ruth gathered it up and went and showed her mother-in-law what she had collected. Naomi said to her, "Where did you work today? Blessed be the man who took notice of you." When Ruth told her mother-in-law where she had worked, Naomi said, "The Lord has not stopped showing kindness to the living or the dead." . . .

Not long after this Boaz married Ruth and the Lord gave them a son. Then the women of Bethlehem said to Naomi, "Thanks be to God who has not left you without a descendant. May his name become famous in Israel! He will make you happy again and be a comfort to you in your old age. He is the child of your daughter-in-law, who loves you and is better to you than seven sons."

Then Naomi took the child and became his nurse. And the women who were her neighbors said, "It is as though a son has been born to Naomi." So they called him Obed (O-behd). He later became the father of Jesse, who was the father of David.   *2:1-20; 4:13-17*

THE FIRST BOOK OF
Samuel*

Once there was a man whose name was Elkanah....He had two wives. The name of one of them was Hannah (HAN-nah). The name of the other one was Peninah (Peh-NIN-ah). Peninah had children, but Hannah had none.

Now, every year this man used to go to Shiloh (SHIGH-lo) [where the tent church was]. He went there [with his wives] to worship the Lord God Jahweh....[While there] Hannah prayed to the Lord and cried sadly [over not having any children]. She also made a promise, saying, "O Lord, if you will...give me a son, then I will give him back to you all the days of his life."....

As Hannah continued praying to God, Eli [the priest] noticed how her mouth was moving. . . . He thought she was drunk. So he said to her, "Woman, how long are you going to stay drunk?" But she answered, "I haven't drunk any wine or strong drink. I've been pouring out my soul to the Lord...." Then Eli said, "Go in peace. And may the God of Israel give you what you asked him to give you."

Not long after that, Hannah had a son. She gave him the name Samuel because, she said, "I asked the Lord for him."...When she stopped nursing Samuel,... she brought him to the house of God at Shiloh and said to Eli, "I am the woman who stood here and prayed for this child, and the Lord gave me what I requested. Therefore as long as he lives I shall lend him to the Lord."

So when Elkanah [and Hannah] returned to their home, the boy was left with Eli the priest. There he [grew up and was taught by Eli] and served the Lord with Eli. . . . And the boy Samuel grew not only in body but also in favor with the Lord and with people.

1:1-3, 10-17, 20, 24-28;
2:11, 26

God Calls Samuel

One evening, when the lamp over the altar was still burning, Eli lay down to rest in his place [in the tent church]. Samuel was lying down in that part of the temple where the ark* of the covenant was kept. There the Lord called Samuel. He said, "Here I am." Then he ran to Eli and said, "Here I am, Eli; you called me." But Eli said, "I didn't call you. Go lie down and sleep." So Samuel went and lay down.

Pretty soon God called again. "Samuel," he said. So Samuel got up and went to Eli. "Here I am," he said, "because you called me." But Eli said, "I didn't call you, my son. Go lie down again." . . . Then God called Samuel a third time, so he got up and went to Eli and said, "Here I am; you called me."

Now Eli understood that God was calling the boy. So he said to Samuel, "Go and lie down, and if the Lord calls you, say: 'Speak, Lord, for your servant is listening.'" So Samuel went and lay down in his place.

Then God came and called as he had the other times, "Samuel, Samuel." And Samuel answered, "Speak, for your servant is listening." Then God said to Samuel, "I am about to do something over which the ears of everyone in Israel will tingle. On a certain day I will do all the things I said I would do against Eli. I am about to punish his family forever . . . because his sons make fun of God and he didn't stop them."

Well, Samuel just lay on his bed until morning. He was afraid to tell Eli what he had heard God say to him. But when Samuel opened the doors of the house of the Lord, Eli called to him and said, "Samuel, my son." Samuel said, "Here I am." And Eli said, "What did the Lord say to you? Don't try to hide it from me. May God do the same to you, and more so, if you will hide from me any of the things he said to you."

So Samuel told him everything and kept nothing from him. And Eli said, "It is the Lord [talking]; let him do whatever seems good to him." After that Samuel kept on growing, and the Lord was with him. And all the people of Israel . . . knew that Samuel would someday be a prophet of the Lord.

When the people of Israel went to war against the Philistines (Fil-ISS-tins), the Philistines defeated the Israelites. . . . And the ark of God [which had been taken into battle] was captured. Also, the two sons of Eli . . . were killed. A man from the battle ran to Shiloh [to tell what had happened]. . . .

When the man came to the city and told the news,... Eli fell over backward from his seat by the side of the city gate and broke his neck and died. . . . He had been a leader of Israel for 40 years. [After that, Samuel became the leader of the people.]

3:2-20; 4:1, 10-18

The Israelites Want a King

When Samuel became old, he made his sons the judges over the people of Israel. . . . But his sons didn't follow the ways of their father because they looked for selfish advantages. They accepted bribes and were very unfair in handing out justice.

So all the leaders of Israel came together. Then they went to Samuel and said to him, "See here, you are old and your sons aren't like you. Let a king rule us like kings rule all the other nations."

Samuel wasn't pleased by their saying, "Give us a king to rule us." He prayed to the Lord about it. God said to Samuel, "Listen to what the people say to you. It's not you they're against. They just don't want me to rule them. . . . So give them what they want. But first warn them and show them the ways of a king who will rule them."

Then Samuel told the people what the Lord had said to him and showed them how a king would treat them. He said, "A king will take your sons to be his men. . . . He will take your daughters, too, to bake and cook and do other services in his house. He will take your lands, too, . . . to give to his officers, and a tenth of all you produce—your fruit, your seed, your flocks. When that day comes, you will complain loudly because of the king you wanted to have, and then the Lord won't answer you."

But the people wouldn't listen to Samuel's advice. "No, no," they said, "we want a king. We want to be like all the other countries. We want a king who will rule us and lead us in our battles." So Samuel told all this to the Lord, and the Lord said, "Listen to their request. Give them a king."

8:1-22

Saul Is Anointed King

There was a man in the tribe of Benjamin whose name was Kish. He had a son whose name was Saul (SAWL). Saul was a handsome young man. There was not a man among the people of Israel more handsome than he. He stood head and shoulders above everyone else.

Now, Kish, Saul's father, had lost some of his donkeys. So he said to his son Saul, "Take one of the servants with you and go and look for my donkeys." So Saul traveled around . . . but didn't find the animals.

When they came to the land of Zuph (ZUFF), Saul said to the servant who was with him, "Come on, let's go back or my father will stop worrying about the donkeys and will start to worry about us." But the servant said, "There's a man of God in this city. He's a man held in high honor. . . . Let's go see him. Perhaps he can tell us which way to go" [to find the animals].

Saul said to his servant, "But if we go [to get some advice from the man], what can we bring him? . . . What have we?" Saul's servant said, "Here, I have a fourth part of a piece of silver. We can give that to the man of God to have him tell us the way. . . ." Saul said to the servant, "Well said. Let's go." So they went to the city where the man of God was.

As they were entering the city, they saw Samuel coming toward them on his way to the place for worship. Now, on the day before, the Lord had told Samuel, "Tomorrow about this time I will send you a man . . . and you are to anoint (ah-NOYNT)* him to be the ruler over my people Israel. . . ." When Samuel saw Saul, the Lord told him, "Here is the man I spoke to you about. He is the one who is to rule over my people."

When Saul went up to Samuel and asked where the prophet of God lived, Samuel answered, "I am the prophet." Then he asked Saul to go with him to the place for worship and told him not to worry about his lost animals. They had been found. "Anyway," he said, "all the wealth of Israel is yours now."

Saul said, "I'm a Benjamite (BEN-jah-might), a member of the smallest tribe of Israel. My family is the least important family in the tribe. Why do you say what you've said?" Then Samuel took Saul and his servant into his house and had them sit ahead of all the other guests, of which there were about 30. And Samuel told the cook to serve Saul a special piece of meat that had been saved for the guest of honor. . . .

The next morning Samuel took a small bottle of oil and poured it on Saul's head and kissed him. He also said, "The Lord has anointed you to be the ruler over his people Israel. You will rule over the people of the Lord and will save them from their enemies around them."

When Saul left Samuel [to go back home], God gave Saul a different heart. . . . The Spirit of God came to Saul. . . . When the people who knew him saw how he spoke the Word of God, they said to one another. "What has come over the son of Kish? Is Saul also a prophet?"

When Saul's uncle asked him where he had been, Saul said, "To find the donkeys. When we couldn't find them, we went to Samuel." Saul's uncle said, "Tell me what Samuel said to you." Saul said to his uncle, "He told us that the donkeys had been found." But about him becoming the king Saul said nothing.

9:1-10, 14-24; 10:1, 9-16

The First King of Israel

Soon after this Samuel called the people of Israel together at a place called Mizpeh (MIZ-peh). There he said to them, "This is what the Lord, the God of Israel, says: 'I brought Israel out of Egypt.' . . . But this day you have rejected your God, who saves you from all your troubles. You have said to him, 'No, put a king over us.' Now therefore present yourselves before the Lord by tribes."

When Samuel had all the tribes of Israel before him, Saul, the son of Kish, was chosen [to be the king]. When they looked for him, he couldn't be found. [He was hiding among the baggage.] When they found him and brought him among the people, he stood head and shoulders higher than anyone else.

And Samuel said, "Look, here is the man the Lord has chosen. There is nobody like him among all the people." And all the people shouted, "Long live the king!"

10:17-24

Saul Disobeys God

[Saul took over the ruling of Israel and led the fighting against Israel's enemies who were all around them.] One day Samuel said to Saul, "The Lord says, 'I remember what the people of Amalek (AM-ah-lek) did to the people of Israel. . . .' Go and attack Amalek and completely destroy them and all that they have. . . ."

So Saul defeated the Amalekites. . . . But Saul and his men spared Agag (AY-gag) [the king] and the best of the sheep and the lambs and the oxen. . . . Then the Lord said to Samuel, "I'm sorry I made Saul the king, because he has stopped following me and has not done my commands." This made Samuel angry, and he cried to the Lord all that night.

The next morning Samuel went to Saul, and Saul said to him, " . . . I have done the commandment of the Lord." But Samuel said, "What then is this bleating of sheep I hear and the sound of oxen?" Saul said, "The people spared the best of the sheep and oxen to sacrifice to the Lord, your God. The rest we completely destroyed."

Samuel said to Saul, "Stop! I will tell you what the Lord said to me last night. . . . 'Obedience is much better than sacrifice.' . . . Because you have rejected the Word of the Lord, he has rejected you from being king."

As Samuel turned to go away, Saul grabbed the bottom of his robe and it tore. Samuel said to Saul, "This day the Lord has torn away the kingdom of Israel from you and has given it to a neighbor of yours who is a better man than you." . . . Then Samuel went to a place called Ramah (RAY-mah) and never saw Saul again until the day of his death.

15:2-3, 10-11, 12-16, 22-23, 27-28, 34-35

Samuel Anoints David

One day the Lord said to Samuel, "Fill your horn with oil and go . . . to Jesse (JES-see),* who lives near Bethlehem, for I have chosen a king from among his sons." . . . Samuel did what the Lord told him to do. When he came to Bethlehem, the rulers of the city came out to meet him. "Do you come peacefully?" they asked, shaking with worry. He said, "Peacefully. I have come to sacrifice to the Lord." . . .

Then Samuel invited Jesse and his sons to the sacrifice. When they came, he looked at Eliab (Ee-LIGH-uhb) and thought, "This must be the one the Lord has chosen." But the Lord said to Samuel, "Don't look at his appearance or at his height. . . . People look at outside appearance, but the Lord looks at the heart."

Jesse made seven of his sons walk by Samuel [so

111

he could look them over], but Samuel said to Jesse, "The Lord has not chosen these. Are all your sons here?" Jesse said, "There is still the youngest, but he is watching the sheep." "Get him," said Samuel. . . . So Jesse sent for him and had him brought in.

Now, this son had reddish hair and skin and beautiful eyes. He was handsome. And the Lord said, "Anoint him, for he is the one." Then Samuel took the horn of oil and anointed David in the presence of his brothers. And the Spirit of the Lord God became strong in David from that day on.

16:1-7, 10-13

David Plays His Harp for Saul

And the Spirit of God left Saul, and an evil spirit came and made him miserable. . . . So Saul said to his servants, "Get me a man who can play well and bring him to me." One of the young men said, "I have seen a son of Jesse who is skillful in playing." . . . So Saul sent messengers to Jesse, saying, "Send me your son David, who is with your sheep."

David went to Saul and entered his service. And [at first] Saul loved David very much. . . . And whenever the evil spirit was bothering Saul, David took his harp and played it. Then Saul felt better and the evil spirit left him.

16:14-23

David and Goliath (Go-LIGH-ahth)

Now, the Philistines gathered their armies together for a battle against the Israelites. . . . And Saul and the men of Israel lined up for a battle against the Philistines. . . . Out from the camp of the Philistines there came a champion called Goliath. He was about nine feet nine inches tall, and he wore a brass helmet on his head. He was also armed with a metal coat that weighed as much as 5,000 coins. . . .

Goliath stood and shouted to the armies of Israel, "Why have you arranged your armies for a battle? Am

I not a Philistine and aren't you servants of Saul? Choose a man to represent you and let him come down to me. If he is able to fight me and kill me, then we'll all be your servants. But if I win over him and kill him, then you must all be our servants and serve us. . . ."

When Saul and the men of Israel heard these words of the Philistine, they were very much afraid. [For 40 days Goliath came and shouted his dare every morning and evening.]

Now, Jesse said to David [who had returned home when Saul went away to lead his army], "Take this grain and these 10 loaves of bread to your brothers. See how your brothers are getting along." [The three oldest sons of Jesse had gone to fight for Saul.]

So David got up early in the morning, went to where the army was lining up to begin fighting, and ran among the men until he found his brothers. As he was talking with them, the giant Goliath appeared and made his challenge. David heard it. . . .

David said, "Who is this heathen (HEE-then)* that he should be able to dare the armies of God?" And David said to Saul, "Your servant will go and fight this Philistine." But Saul said to David, "You're not able to go out and fight this man. You're only a boy, and he's been a man of war since his youth."

But David said to Saul, "Your servant has killed both lions and bears, and this heathen will be to me like one of them. The Lord who saved me from the paw of the lion and the bear will save me from this Philistine." So Saul said to David, "Go, and the Lord be with you."...

Then Saul armed David with his armor. He put a brass helmet on his head and dressed him with a metal coat. After hanging his sword on his armor, David tried to walk but couldn't. "I can't go with these," he said to Saul, so he took them all off.

Then he took his shepherd's stick and went down to the creek and picked up five smooth stones. Putting these into his shepherd's bag, he took his slingshot and walked toward the giant.

Goliath said to David, "Am I a dog that you come to fight with a stick? And he cursed David and said, "Come; I will give your flesh to the birds and beasts." And David said to Goliath, "You come to me with a sword and a spear, but I come to you in the name of the Lord, the God of the armies of Israel."

Then David ran quickly toward the giant. And David put his hand in his bag and took out a stone and threw it [with his sling]. The stone struck the Philistine on his forehead, and he fell on his face to the ground. . . . Then David ran and stood over the giant and took his sword . . . and cut off his head.

When the Philistines saw that their champion was dead, they ran. And the men of Israel went after them and killed many of them.

17:1-15, 17-23, 26, 32, 36-45,
48-52

David and Jonathan

Saul took David home with him that day and wouldn't let him go back to his father's house. Jonathan, Saul's son, began to love David as his own brother, and they made an agreement of friendship. And Jonathan took off his robe and gave it to David; also his armor and sword and bow.

Saul set David over his soldiers, and he was successful wherever Saul sent him. . . . But as he and Saul were returning from a battle one day, some women came out to welcome their king with singing and dancing. As they played their instruments they sang to each other:

"Saul has killed his thousands,
And David his 10 thousands."

When Saul heard this, he became very angry. He said, "If they think David is 10 times better than I, he will soon want to have the kingdom for himself." From that time on Saul was jealous of David.

The next day David was playing his harp for Saul

as before, and an evil spirit got hold of Saul. Suddenly he picked up a spear and threw it at David. "I will pin David to the wall with it," he said. But David avoided the spear. Then Saul was more afraid of him than ever, because he knew that God was with David and was no longer pleased with him.

One day Saul spoke to his son Jonathan and to all his servants and asked them to kill David. But Jonathan spoke well of David and Saul changed his mind. He said, "As the Lord lives, David will not be put to death." So Jonathan brought David back to the palace, and for a while everything was as before.

But again David won a battle against the Philistines and Saul's jealousy came back. As David was playing his instrument, Saul again tried to pin David to the wall with his spear. But once more David managed to escape and run away.

Later David came to Jonathan and said, "What have I done? What am I guilty of? Why is your father trying to kill me?" . . .

Jonathan said to David, "When I have sounded out my father, I will tell you whether he feels kindly toward you now or still wants to harm you. In three days come and hide yourself behind that heap of stones over there. I will shoot three arrows beside it. And I will tell a boy to go find the arrows. If I say, 'Look, the arrows are on this side of you,' then you may come out. But if I say, 'Look, the arrows are past you,' then go [and run for your life].'"

So David hid himself in that field. . . . And Saul became angry at Jonathan and said, "I know you've chosen to side with that son of Jesse. Shame on you." And he threw his spear at Jonathan. So Jonathan knew that his father was determined to kill David.

The next morning Jonathan went out to the field where David was hiding and took a boy with him. As the boy was running to pick up the arrows, Jonathan shot one past him and shouted, "Isn't the arrow past you? Hurry up. Go." When the boy had collected the arrows, he brought them to Jonathan. Jonathan sent him back to the city with them.

As soon as the boy was gone, David came out from behind the stone heap. He and Jonathan kissed each other and cried, and Jonathan said to David, "Go in peace. . . . The Lord be between me and you and between my children and your children forever." Then David left and Jonathan went sadly back to his city.

18—20

Saul's Death

[After David left Jonathan, he went and lived in a cave in the hills for a while. When others heard where he was, people went and joined him. Soon there were about 400 men following him.]

Saul took 3,000 of his best men and went to look for David and his men. On the way Saul went into a cave to rest himself a bit.

Now, it so happened that David and some of his men were sitting in the farthest part of the cave. When they saw Saul, David's men said to him, "This is the day the Lord said he'd put your enemy into your power."

Then David crept up, and quietly cut a piece off the bottom of Saul's robe. When he came back, he said to his men, "I couldn't kill him since he was chosen by God to be the king."

But after Saul had left the cave, David came out and yelled after him, "My lord the king!" When Saul turned around, David shouted, "Why do you listen to the people who say I'm trying to harm you? Today you have seen how the Lord put you into my power in the cave, but I spared you. See the piece of your robe in my hand! . . ."

Then Saul began to cry and said to David, "You are a better person than I am, because you repaid me with good and I have repaid you with evil. And now I know you will be the king. Promise me that you will not destroy my descendants after me."

David promised and Saul went home. But David and his men went to their hideout in the hills.

[After many more months and happenings] the Philistines again fought against the men of Israel. As the men of Israel tried to get away, the Philistines caught up with Saul and his sons. They killed Jonathan and two of his brothers. When they found Saul, he was badly wounded.

Saul said to the men who carried his armor and weapons, "Draw your sword and shove it through me." But the men wouldn't do it. So Saul took his sword and fell on it. That's how Saul died.

24:2-22; 31:1-6

THE SECOND BOOK OF
Samuel*

Now [after the death of King Saul] David went up to Hebron (HEE-bruhn).* . . . And the men of Judah came to him there and made him the king over the people of Judah. . . . But Abner, the commander of Saul's army, took Ishbosheth (Ish-BO-sheth), the son of Saul, and made him the king over the other Israelites.

[Then there was war for seven and a half years between Abner's army and David's army. When both Abner and Ishbosheth were killed, all the tribes of Israel came to David and made him their king too.]

David Takes Jerusalem

Then the king and his men went to Jerusalem and fought against the people who lived there. They had said to David, "You won't come in here. The blind and the lame will keep you out." They thought David couldn't get into their walled city. But David took the fortress called Jerusalem on Mount Zion and lived in the fort. He called it the City of David. . . .

And David expanded the city and became greater

and greater. [He fought and defeated many enemies.] For the Lord, the God of Israel, was with him. And Hiram, the king of Tyre (TIGHR), sent cedar trees and carpenters and stone-builders to build David a house. David realized that the Lord had made him the king over Israel and had made his kingdom great for the sake of his people Israel.

Then David gathered together all the leaders of Israel, 30,000, and went with them to bring the ark of God to Jerusalem, . . . and David danced with all his might before the Lord [because he was so happy]. . . .

So with shouting and the sound of a trumpet they brought the ark of God to Mount Zion . . . and placed it in a tent that David had made ready for it. There David offered sacrifices of thanks to God and blessed the people in the name of the Lord. . . .

When the Lord had given David rest from all his enemies, the king said to Nathan,* the prophet, "You know, I now live in a house of cedar wood, but the ark of God lives in a tent." [So David wanted to build a more permanent house for God.]

But that same night a message from God came to Nathan. The message was that he should go and tell David, "This is what the Lord said: I will make your name great. When you die, your son will build a house for my name, . . . and your throne will be established forever."

After Nathan had told this to the king, David went into the tent church and sat before the Lord. He said, "Who am I, O Lord God, that you have brought me to where I am? And now, Lord God, you are God, and your words are true, and you have promised this good thing to your servant. So may it please you to bless the family of your servant, that it may continue . . . and be blessed forever."

So David ruled over all the people of Israel and gave justice to all his people.

2—8

David Sins and Repents

Now it so happened, late one afternoon, that David got up from a nap and took a walk on the roof of his palace. From there he saw a very beautiful woman bathing. When David asked who she was, he was told, "She is Bathsheba (Bath-SHEE-buh), the wife of Uriah (Yoo-RIGH-ah), the Hittite (HIT-tight).

[David fell in love with Bathsheba and had her come to see him. And the woman became pregnant.] Then David wrote a letter to Joab (JO-ab).* In it he said, "Put Uriah in the front of the hottest battle. Then draw back from him so that he will be killed." [And that's what happened.]

When Bathsheba heard that Uriah was dead, she cried. But when her sadness was over, David sent for her and she became his wife. However the thing David had done displeased the Lord.

So the Lord sent Nathan [the prophet] to David. Nathan came to David and said, "There were two men in a certain city. The one was rich and the other one was poor. The rich man had many flocks and herds; the poor man had nothing but one little lamb that he had bought and raised. It was like a daughter to him.

"Now, it so happened that a traveler came to the rich man for a visit. The rich man was unwilling to take one of his own flock to prepare a meal for the visitor, but he did take the poor man's lamb and roasted it."

When King David heard this, he became very angry. He said to Nathan, "As the Lord lives, the man who has done this deserves to die!" Nathan said to David, "You are the man! The Lord God of Israel has given you so much. Why have you done this evil? You killed Uriah, the Hittite, and took his wife to be your wife."

David said to Nathan, "I have sinned against the Lord." And Nathan said to David, "The Lord has forgiven you your sin, and you will not die. But because this deed has caused talk among the enemies of God, the child that was born will die."

When the son of Bathsheba and David became sick, David prayed to God and would not eat or drink. But on the seventh day the child died. . . . Then David got up from lying on the ground, changed his clothes, and went into the tent church to worship the Lord.

David said, "As long as the child was still alive, I fasted and cried because I thought God might allow the child to live. But now that he is dead, why should I go on fasting? Can I bring him back to life again?" So David comforted his wife Bathsheba, and in due time they had another son whom they called Solomon.

11:1—12:24

David and Absalom (AB-suh-lohm)*

In the whole country of Israel there was no one as handsome as Absalom, a son of David. From the bottom of his feet to the top of his head there was no mark on him. Whenever his hair became too heavy and he had it cut, it weighed as much as 200 silver coins. [He was noted for his beautiful hair.]

Absalom had chariots and horses and 50 men to serve him. And Absalom used to get up early in the morning and stand by the gate where the king's court was conducted. When anybody came with a case to present to the king, Absalom would say, "See, you certainly are in the right, but there is nobody here to represent you. If I were the judge, any man could come to me and I would give him justice."

When people would bow down to Absalom, he would have none of it. Instead, he would take them by the hand and kiss them. That's how Absalom stole the hearts of the people of Israel.

One day Absalom said to the king, "Please let me go to Hebron (HEE-bruhn)* to keep a promise I made to God when I was in Hebron." The king said to him, "Go in peace." So Absalom went to Hebron. But he sent secret messengers to all the tribes of Israel with this message: "As soon as you hear the sound of a trumpet, then announce that Absalom has become the king in Hebron!"

Absalom took with him 200 men from Jerusalem, and more and more men joined him in Hebron. Finally a messenger came to David and warned him that Absalom was about to try to capture Jerusalem.

So David decided to leave the city with the people who remained loyal to him. He organized his army and sent them to war against his son. But he said, "For my sake, treat the young man Absalom kindly."

The battle was fought in the forest called Ephraim (EE-frah-im). And Absalom's men were defeated there by the army of David. As Absalom was running away on a mule, the mule went under the thick branches of a large oak tree. There Absalom's head got caught in a branch of the tree. When the mule galloped away from beneath him, he was left hanging between heaven and earth.

A man saw Absalom hanging there and told Joab (JO-ab).* Joab went and put three darts into the heart of Absalom. Then his men took Absalom and threw him into a hole in the forest.

When a messenger came to David, the king's first question was, "Is the young man safe?" Hearing that his son was dead, David went to his room crying and saying, "O my son, Absalom, my son, my son. I wish I could have died for you, O Absalom, my son, my son!"

14—19

THE FIRST BOOK OF THE
Kings

David, growing old and knowing that he didn't have much longer to live, spoke to his son Solomon. [David had chosen Solomon to be the next king.] David said, "I am about to go the way that all people on earth must go. Be strong and show yourself to be a man. Keep the commandments of the Lord, your God, and live as he has told you in the writings of Moses. Then you will prosper in all that you do and wherever you go."

When David died, he was buried in Jerusalem, the city of David. And Solomon became the king. Soon the kingdom was firmly in his control.

2:1-4, 10, 12

The Wisdom of Solomon

At first Solomon loved the Lord and followed the ways of his father David. One night God appeared to Solomon in a dream. God said, "Ask what you want me to give you."

Solomon answered, "You have made me the king in place of David, my father, even though I am like a little child....Therefore give your servant an understanding mind with which to rule your people."

God was very pleased that Solomon asked for wisdom. So God said to him, "Because you asked for this and did not ask for long life or riches for yourself, or for the life of your enemies, I will give you a wise and understanding heart. I will also give you what you have not asked, both riches and honor. No other king will equal you all the days of your life."

When Solomon awoke, he knew it was all a dream. But when he went back to Jerusalem, he offered sacrifices before the ark* of the covenant of the Lord and made a feast for all his servants. [He believed that God would do what he had promised in the dream.] And all the people of Israel respected their king, because they soon saw that the wisdom of God was in him and helped him rule his people with justice.

One day two women came to the king. The one woman said, "O my Lord, this woman and I live in the same house. I gave birth to a child in that house. Three days later this woman bore a child too. . . . Her child died in the night. Then she took my child while I slept and laid her dead child in my arms."

The other woman said, "No, the child that is alive is my son, and the dead one is your son." That's how they argued before the king.

Then the king said, "The one says, 'The child that is alive is my son and the dead child is your son.' The other says, 'No, your son is the dead one, and my son is the one that is alive.'" So the king said, "Bring me a sword." When they brought him a sword, he said, "Divide the living child in two and give half to the one and half to the other."

But the mother to whom the living child belonged said to the king, "O lord, give her the child that's alive and don't kill it." She loved her son. But the other woman said, "Make it neither mine nor hers. Divide it." Then the king said, "Give the first woman the living child and don't kill it. She is the mother of it."

God gave Solomon great understanding and wisdom and a big heart. And Solomon was wiser than all the other wise men of Egypt and the east countries. And his fame spread to all the countries around him.

3:3-28; 4:29-31

The Building of the Temple

In the 480th year after the people of Israel had come out of the land of Egypt, in the fourth year of Solomon's rule as king, he began to build a temple of the Lord. The house that Solomon built for God was 90 feet long, 30 feet wide, and 45 feet high. There was a wide porch at the front of the temple, and it had many rooms.

The house was built of stone that was cut before it was brought there. No sound of a hammer or any other tool was heard in the house while it was being built. The walls and floors and ceilings of the house were made with cedar boards, and the whole house was covered with pure gold. The whole altar also was covered with pure gold. . . .

All the walls and the doors were carved with figures of angels and palm trees and flowers and were covered with gold. And in the inside courtyard there were three rows of cut-stone pillars and a row of cedar-wood beams. Solomon also had all the things to be used in the temple made of gold: the candlesticks, the lamps, the bowls and incense burners, even the hinges on the doors.

The temple was completed in seven years. When it was finished, Solomon called together the heads of the families and the heads of all the tribes of Israel and brought the ark of the covenant into the temple. Then Solomon stood before the Lord's altar in the presence of the congregation and stretched out his arms toward heaven.

Solomon said, "O Lord, I have built a house for you to live in. . . . There is no god like you in heaven above or on the earth below. You have kept faith with those who do your will. You have kept the promises you made to my father David."

"But will God really live on earth?" Solomon asked. "The heavens cannot hold you," he said; "how much less will this house that I have built! Still, listen to my prayer, O Lord my God. Look at this house night and day and listen to the prayers I will send toward it. Hear the prayers of your people when they pray toward this place; hear them in your dwelling place in heaven. And when you hear them, forgive the sins we have done."

6:1—8:30

Solomon's Death

Years later, king Solomon began to love many women from other countries. They turned his heart away from the Lord God, and he did wrong in God's eyes. He built places where his wives could worship their gods.

The Lord became angry with Solomon and said to him, "Because you have not kept my covenant, I will tear your kingdom apart. But for David's sake I will not do this until after your death."

Solomon ruled over all the tribes of Israel for 40

years. When he died he was buried in the city of David. And his son Rehoboam (Ree-huh-BO-uhm) became the next king.

11:1, 4, 6-9, 11, 12, 42, 43

Solomon's Kingdom Becomes Divided

Rehoboam went to a place called Shechem (SHEE-kehm), because all the people of Israel gathered there to make him their king. And when Jeroboam (Jair-o-BO-uhm) heard about this, he came back from Egypt and went to the meeting too.

At the gathering Jeroboam and some of the people said to Rehoboam, "Your father made life hard for us. Make it lighter and we will serve you." The king asked the old men how to answer the people. They said, "If you will do what they want and will give them a fair and kind answer, then they will be your servants forever."

But Rehoboam didn't welcome this advice. So he went to the young men who had grown up with him and asked them what he should do. They told him to say, "I will be twice as hard on you as my father was. . . . My father beat you with whips; I will beat you with scorpions (SCOR-pee-ons)."*

So the king didn't listen to the old men and to the people. He gave the answer the young men had suggested. When the people saw that the king was not going to listen to them, they turned against him. "People of Israel, get to your tents!" they said, "Let David look after his grandson!" And off they went to their homes.

That was how 10 of the tribes of Israel rebelled against David's tribe. None of the people accepted Rehoboam as their king except the tribe of Judah and the tribe of Benjamin. The other tribes made Jeroboam their king.

From that time on the people of Israel were divided into two kingdoms. [There was the kingdom of Judah in the southern part of the country, with its capital in

Jerusalem. And in the north the other 10 tribes were united in a kingdom called Israel. Their main city was Shechem. Jeroboam became the king of the tribes in the north. For many years there was war between the two kingdoms.]

12:1-19

Ahab (AY-hab) and Elijah

[After Jeroboam died, there were five other kings who ruled over the 10 tribes in what was called the kingdom of Israel. Then, after about 50 years, came Ahab, the son of Omri (AHM-ree), who had been the king before him.]

Ahab, the son of Omri, ruled Israel in Samaria (Suh-MAR-ee-uh)* 22 years. And Ahab did more things that were wrong in God's sight than any king before him. Besides doing the sins of Jeroboam [encouraging the people to worship idols], Ahab married Jezebel (JEZ-eh-bel), the daughter of the king of Sidon (SIGH-don). She led him to worship Baal (BAY-al),* the god her people worshiped. Ahab built a temple and an altar for the worship of Baal in Samaria.

Now, Elijah (Ee-LIGH-jah),* a prophet who came from Tishbite (TISH-bite), said to Ahab, "As sure as the Lord God of Israel lives, there will be no dew or rain for years unless I say so. [This was to be God's way of punishing Ahab and his country for worshiping idols. And it happened.]

Then the Lord said to Elijah, "Get away from here and go eastward and hide yourself by the brook called Cherith (KEE-rith), which is east of the Jordan. There you can drink from the brook, and I have ordered blackbirds to feed you there."

So Elijah went and did what the Lord told him to do. And birds brought him bread and meat in the morning and again in the evening. And he drank water from the brook. But after a while the brook dried up because there had been no rain for a long time.

Then another message from the Lord came to

Elijah. It said, "Go to a place in Sidon [a nearby country] and live there for a while. I have told a widow there to look after you and feed you." So Elijah went. When he came to the gate of the city, a widow was gathering sticks there.

Elijah called to the woman and said, "Please get me a little water in a cup so that I may have a drink." As she started to go get it, he called to her and added, "Also bring me a little bread, please."

The woman turned to him and answered, "As sure as the Lord your God lived, I have nothing baked. I have only a little flour in a jar and a little oil in a bottle. As you can see, I'm gathering a few sticks to make a fire to prepare a loaf for myself and my son. That will be the last food my son and I will have before we die."

Elijah said to her, "Don't be afraid. Go and do as you said. But first make me a little loaf and bring it to me. After that make some for yourself and your son. For this is God's promise to you; the jar of flour and the bottle of oil will never be empty until rain is sent by God and the famine is over."

So the widow went and did what Elijah had asked, and she and all who lived in her house, also the prophet, had enough food to eat. The jar of flour was never used up, and the bottle of oil was never found empty until the famine was over, as God had promised through Elijah.

16:29—17:16

Baal and God

In the third year of the famine in the country of Israel the Lord God told Elijah to go to Ahab. "I will soon send rain again," God said to him. So Elijah went to meet Ahab. . . . When the king saw him he said, "Is it you, you bringer of trouble?"

Elijah answered, "I am not the one who has brought trouble to Israel, but you have . . . because you failed to keep the Lord's commandments. You have turned to Baal. Now therefore send a message and ask all the families of Israel to meet with me on Mount Carmel (CAHR-mehl), also the prophets of Baal and the prophets of Asherah (AH-shee-rah) who eat at Jezebel's table."

So Ahab sent a message to all the people of Israel and gathered the prophets together at Mount Carmel. When Elijah stood before the people, he said to them, "How long will you go limping between two opinions [as to which God to serve]? If the Lord is the true God, follow him. But if it's Baal, then follow him." The people didn't answer.

Elijah went on and said, "I, and I alone, am a prophet of the Lord, but there are 450 prophets of Baal. So, give us two bulls and let them choose one for themselves. Then let them cut it in pieces and lay it on the wood, but without starting a fire. I will prepare the other bull in the same way. Then, you call on your god and I will call on the Lord. The god who answers us with fire, he is God." All the people answered, "Good; it is well said."

Then Elijah spoke to the prophets of Baal, saying, "Choose one of the bulls and get it ready. You do it first, because there are many of you." . . . So they took a bull and prepared it. And from morning until noon they called to Baal, saying, "O Baal, answer us!" But there was no answer.

When noon came, Elijah began to make fun of them. "Call louder," he said, "for he is a god. He must be thinking or is on a trip or perhaps is asleep and must be awakened." So they shouted louder and cut themselves with daggers and swords . . . until their blood spurted out on them. [They thought this would get Baal to answer.]

Midday passed by and still they went on shouting like crazy until the time for the evening sacrifice. But there was no answer.

Then Elijah spoke to the people. "Come near to me," he said. When the people came closer, he repaired the broken-down altar of the Lord and prepared the wood and the bull.

Then Elijah made a trench around the altar. "Fill four barrels with water," he said, "and pour it on the wood and on the offering." This he had them do a second and third time. Water was running all around the altar, and the trench around it was full too.

Then Elijah said, "O Lord, the God of Abraham, Isaac, and Israel, make it known this day that you are God in Israel and that I am your servant and that I have done all these things at your request. Answer me, O Lord, answer me, so that these people will know that you, O Lord, are the true God."

Suddenly the Lord's fire came with a burst and burnt up the offering—also the wood and the stones and the dust—and licked up the water in the trench. When the people saw this happen, they fell on their knees and put their faces to the ground. "The Lord, he is God," they said. "The Lord is the true God!"

[That evening it rained and the famine ended.]

18:1, 2, 17-39

A Small Quiet Voice

Ahab told Jezebel the whole story of what Elijah had done, also how he had killed all the prophets of Baal. So Jezebel sent a messenger to Elijah with this message: "May the gods do it to me, and more, if by this time tomorrow I do not take your life as you took theirs."

Elijah became afraid and ran for his life. He first went to a place called Beer-sheba (Beer-SHEE-bah). There he left his servant. Then he himself went on to a mountain called Mount Horeb (HOR-eb). There he lived for a time in a cave.

One day the Lord said to him, "Elijah, what are you doing here?" Elijah answered, "I have cared a lot about the Lord God, but the people of Israel have forgotten their covenant with you, O Lord. They have broken down your altars and have killed your prophets. I am the only one left, and now they are trying to kill me."

Then God said to him, "Go and stand before me up on the mountain." So Elijah went, and a strong wind blew against the mountain and broke rocks into pieces. But the Lord was not in the wind. After the wind came an earthquake, and after the earthquake came a fire. But the Lord was not in the fire.

After the fire came a small quiet voice. And when Elijah heard the voice, he wrapped his face in his coat and went back to the opening of the cave. And the voice came to him and asked again, "Elijah, what are you doing here?" Elijah repeated what he had said the first time.

Then the Lord said to him, "Go back through the desert country around Damascus (Dah-MAS-kus).* When you come to him, . . . anoint [and thereby appoint] Elisha (Ee-LIGH-shah) to be a prophet after you. . . . There still are 7,000 people in Israel who have not bowed down to Baal or kissed his statue."

So Elijah left the mountain and found Elisha ploughing in a field. As Elijah passed by Elisha, he threw his coat over him [as a way of showing that Elisha was to be his succesor]. . . . After saying good-bye to his parents, Elisha went with Elijah and became his servant.

19:1-21

THE SECOND BOOK OF THE
Kings

Now when the Lord was about to take Elijah up to heaven in a whirlwind, Elijah and Elisha were on their way from a place called Gilgal (GIL-gal) to Bethel (BETH-el). And Elijah said to Elisha, "Wait here, please, for the Lord has sent me to Bethel." But Elisha said, "As sure as the Lord lives and you live, I will not leave you." So the both of them went to Bethel.

At Bethel the students of the prophets came to Elisha and said to him, "Do you know that today the Lord will take your master away from you?" Elisha said, "Yes, I know."

Later Elijah said to Elisha, "Please stay here, because the Lord has sent me to Jericho (JER-ee-koh)." But Elisha said, "As sure as the Lord lives and you live, I will not leave you." So they went to Jericho. And the students of the prophets at Jericho came to Elisha and said, "So you know that today the Lord will take your master away from you?" And Elisha said, "Yes, I know it."

Then Elijah said to Elisha, "Stay here, please, for the Lord has sent me to the Jordan." And Elisha said, "As sure as the Lord lives and you yourself live, I will not leave you." So the two men went on. And 50 of the students of the prophets went along. They stood at a distance from Elijah and Elisha as they were standing by the Jordan.

Then Elijah took his coat and rolled it up and struck the water with his coat. At once the water parted so that the two of them could cross on dry ground.

When they had crossed, Elijah said to Elisha, "Ask me anything I can do for you before I am taken from you." Elisha said, "Let me receive, I beg you, a double share of your spirit." Elijah answered, "You have asked me a hard thing. But if you will see me when I am taken away from you, you will be given what you asked. If you don't, then it will not be so."

As the two men still went on and talked, suddenly a chariot of fire and horses of fire appeared, and Elijah went up into heaven in a whirlwind. When Elisha saw it, he shouted, "My father, my father! . . ." And he saw Elijah no more. . . .

Then Elisha took Elijah's coat that had fallen off of him and went back to the bank of the Jordan River. There he took Elijah's coat and struck the water with it.

"Where is Elijah's God?" he said. And when he had struck the water with Elijah's coat, the water parted and he went across.

When the students of the prophets saw Elisha coming, they said, "The spirit of Elijah rests on Elisha." So they went to meet him and bowed to the ground in front of him.

2:1-15

Elisha Heals a Leper (LEP-er)*

The commander of the army of Syria (SEER-ee-ah)* was a man called Naaman (NAY-uh-man). He was a very important man and greatly honored because through him God had given victory to Syria. He was a very brave soldier, but he was a leper.

Now, on one of their raids the Syrians had brought back some captives from the land of Israel. Among them was a young girl. She had been given to Naaman's wife as a maid. One day she said to her mistress, "Oh how I wish my lord Naaman could be with the prophet in Samaria (Sah-MER-ee-ah).* He could cure his leprosy."

So Naaman went to Samaria with his horses and chariots and came to the door of Elisha's house. [Instead of coming out to meet him or inviting him in], the prophet simply sent a messenger to Naaman. "Go and wash seven times in the Jordan River," Naaman was told. "Then your flesh will become healthy again and you will be well."

Naaman became angry. He said, "I thought the prophet would surely come out to me and call on the name of the Lord, his God, and wave his hand over the leprosy to cure it. Are not the rivers of Damascus better than all the waters of Israel? Could I not wash in them and become clean?" So he turned and went away in a huff.

But his servants went up to him and spoke to him. One of them said, "My father, if the prophet had ordered you to do something difficult, would you not have done it? Why not, then, do what he told you to do when all he said was 'Wash and be healed'?"

So Naaman went down to the Jordan River and dipped himself seven times in the water, as the man of God had said he should. And to his surprise, Naaman was healed. His flesh became as fresh as a little child's.

Then Naaman went back to the man of God and said, "Now I know there is no God in all the world except in Israel. So I beg you to accept a gift of thanks from your servant Naaman. But Elisha said, "No, I will not take a gift." Naaman urged him to take it, but he refused.

Then said Naaman, "If not, please give me some earth from this land, as much as two mules can carry. From this day on I will not offer sacrifices to any other god than the Lord, the God of Israel."

"But there is one thing I must ask your God to pardon in me," said Naaman. "When my master, the king of Syria, goes into the temple of his god to worship there, I will be attending him. When he will bow down to his god, I must too. May the Lord pardon me for doing this." Elisha said to him, "Go in peace."

5:1-19

The Story of Joash (JO-ash)

When King Ahab's daughter [who ruled the kingdom of Judah, during the boyhood of her son] saw that her son was dead, she saw to it that all his children were murdered. [This she did so she could keep the power for herself.] But the wife of the high priest rescued Joash, a young son of the king, by hiding him and his nurse in a bedroom. In that way he escaped being killed.

For six years the boy was kept hidden in the temple by the high priest and his wife. During that time Ahab's daughter ruled as queen.

In the seventh year the high priest had the chief rulers of the country come to the house of the Lord and made an agreement with them. First he made them

133

swear to keep secret what they would see and hear, and then he showed them the king's son. "This is what you must do," he told them. . . . "You must guard the king by surrounding him with swords drawn as he comes in and goes out. If anyone breaks through your ranks, he must be killed."

The captains did everything exactly as the priest had requested. . . . The soldiers stood on guard with their weapons in hand from one corner of the temple to the other and also by the altar. Then the priest presented the young Joash to them, put the king's crown on his head, and anointed him to be the king. All the people clapped their hands and shouted, "God save the king."

When Ahab's daughter [the wicked queen] heard the noise that the people made, she went to where the meeting was in the temple. Looking in, she saw the young king standing by a pillar, as was the custom at a coronation. She also saw the princes and the people celebrating and the trumpets being played. "Treason, treason!" she screamed.

But the high priest said to the leaders of the army, "Take her away! And if anyone follows her, strike him down with a sword. . . ." So they grabbed her and took her down the road by which horses approached the palace. There she was put to death. . . .

The priest then made a covenant between God, the king, and the people. It was that the king and the people should belong to each other and that both would belong to the Lord. Then the people rushed into the temple of Baal and broke it down. . . . They also took the young king to the king's house and had him sit on the throne. Everybody was very happy, and the city [and country] had peace after the wicked queen was dead.

11:1-20

THE FIRST BOOK OF
Chronicles

[The writer of this book, the "chronicler (KRON-ik-ler),"* believed that when the people of Israel were true to the God Jahweh, whom they called the Lord, then their country was blessed with victories over its enemies; also with peace and prosperity. When they became careless in their worship and in their obedience to the laws of the Lord God, their country had troubles.

To show this, the writer used many stories from the First and Second Books of Samuel and the First and Second Books of the Kings. But the First Book of Chronicles is mainly the story of King David. The following story of David's farewell and death is taken from the last two chapters.]

When David was old, he made his son Solomon the king over the people of Israel. . . . Then David called all the leaders of Israel together at Jerusalem. . . . And David stood up and said, "Listen to me, my brothers and my people! I wanted to build a permanent house for the ark of the covenant of the Lord and a place for our God to live in. I made preparations for the building of it. But God said to me, 'You may not build a house for me, because you are a warrior and have shed blood.'

"Still, the Lord God of Israel chose me from among all my father's family to be king over Israel forever.... And of all my sons [for the Lord has given me many] he has chosen my son Solomon to succeed me on the throne of his kingdom of Israel.

"God said to me," continued David, "'your son Solomon will build my house and my courts, for I have chosen him to be my son and I will be his father. I will make his kingdom last forever if he will continue to obey my commandments as he has until now.' . . .

"And you, Solomon, my son," said David, "get to know the God of your father and serve him happily and eagerly. For the Lord looks at every heart and understands every thought and plan. If you will look for him, you will find him. But if you will leave him, he will get rid of you for good. So be very careful, for the Lord has chosen you to build his house. Be strong and do it."

Then David gave his son Solomon the plan of the temple and of all that he had in mind for the courts and the surrounding areas and rooms. He also gave Solomon the plans for various groups of priests and other ministers in the house of the Lord and instructions about the bowls and furniture that were to be used in the temple. The Lord had given David all these plans.

Again David said to his son Solomon, "Be strong and have good courage and do it. Don't be frightened by the size of the task. The Lord God, my God, is with you. He will not let you down or leave you. He will see to it that all the work for the house of the Lord will be finished. . . . And working with you in all the work will be all kinds of people who have skills of every kind, and the officers of the army and all the people are entirely at your command."

Then King David said to the assembly, "My son Solomon, whom God has chosen to be the next king of Israel, is still young and inexperienced, and the work ahead of him is very great. The palace he will build is not for a man but for the Lord God. So I have provided for the house of my God, as much as I was able, the gold needed for the things of gold, the silver for the things to be made of silver, the needed brass, the iron, the wood, and many precious stones and much marble.

"Moreover," said David, "because I very much want this house for my God, I am giving my own treasury of gold and silver to the building of the house for my God. This is in addition to the materials I have already collected. . . . Who else, then, will willingly give to this building, offering also himself to the Lord?"

Then the heads of the tribes and the commanders of the army and the officers of the king's work gave their offerings. . . . And the people were happy because these men gave willingly and gladly. And King David also was very happy.

That's why David praised the Lord in the presence of the whole assembly. He said, "O Lord, the God of our father Israel, your name will be praised for ever and ever. Yours is the greatness and the power and the glory and the victories. . . . Everything in the heavens and on earth is yours. In your hand is the power to make great and to give strength. And we thank you, our God, and praise your glorious name." . . .

David ruled over the land of Israel for 40 years. Seven of those years he ruled in Hebron and 30 in Jerusalem. He died at a good old age, rich and honored. And his son Solomon ruled in his place after him.

23:1; 28:1-21; 29:1-28

THE SECOND BOOK OF THE
Chronicles

[The Second Book of the Chronicles begins with the story of how King David's son Solomon built the temple his father had wanted to build. It also tells how 10 of the tribes of Israel refused to let Solomon's son Rehoboam (Ree-huh-BO-uhm) be their king and how Solomon's kingdom became divided into a northern kingdom and a southern kingdom.

At first the southern part, called the kingdom of Judah, was ruled by Rehoboam. The northern part, called the kingdom of Israel, was ruled by a man named Jeroboam (Jair-o-BO-uhm).* Here we continue the story of Joash about whom you read in the Second Book of Kings.]

When Joash Rebuilt the Temple

Joash was seven years old when he began to be king, and he ruled 40 years in Jerusalem.... And Joash did what was right in God's eyes during the lifetime of the priest who had raised him. . . .

Joash decided to repair the house of the Lord. He called the priests together and said to them, "Go to all the cities of Judah and collect from all the people of Israel the money you need to repair the house of your God. . . . And hurry the matter."

But the priests didn't hurry to collect the money.... So the king commanded that a large chest be made and that it be set outside the main gate of the temple. Then it was announced all over the country of Judah that the people were to bring to the Lord the tax Moses had commanded.

And all the princes and all the people gladly brought their tax and dropped it into the chest. And whenever the chest was brought to the king's officers and they saw that there was a lot of money in it, the king's secretary and the officer of the chief priest would come and empty the chest and return it to its place. This they did day after day and collected a lot of money.

And the king and the chief priest gave the money to those who were in charge of the work of repairing the temple, and they hired stone workers and carpenters and iron workers to repair the house of the Lord. . . .

When the workers had finished [the work], they brought the rest of the money to the king and the chief priest. With it were made dishes for incense and other bowls of gold and silver for the house of the Lord.

24:1-14

The Prayer of King Hezekiah (Hez-eh-KIGH-uh)

Hezekiah began to rule [the land of Judah] when he was 25 years old. He ruled 29 years in Jerusalem....

And he did what was pleasing to God. . . . He sent letters to all the people of Israel and Judah, asking them to come to the house of the Lord at Jerusalem to keep the Passover. . . . And many people came together in Jerusalem to keep the festival. . . .

After these things the king of Assyria (A-SEER-ee-ah), whose name was Sennacherib (Sen-NACH-er-ib), came [with his armies] and invaded the land of Judah.... When Hezekiah saw that Sennacherib intended to fight against Jerusalem, he . . . stopped all the springs and the brooks that flowed through the land. "Why should the king of Assyria come and find a lot of water?" he said.

Hezekiah also set to work and built up the city wall that was broken down, and outside it he built another wall. . . . He also had many weapons and shields made, and gathered the people together and spoke encouragingly to them. "Be strong and of good courage," he said. "Don't be afraid of the king of Assyria and all who are with him; for there is someone greater with us than with him." . . .

Then Sennacherib sent his servants to Hezekiah and to the people in Jerusalem with this message: "Thus says Sennacherib, king of Assyria, 'On what are you relying? Don't let Hezekiah mislead you, and do not believe him, for no god of any nation or kingdom has been able to save his people from me. . . .'"

Because of this Hezekiah, the king, and Isaiah (Igh-ZAY-ah), the prophet, the son of Amoz (AY-mahz), prayed to heaven. And the Lord God sent an angel, who destroyed all the mighty warriors and officers in the camp of the king of Assyria.

So Sennacherib returned to his own country very much ashamed. And when he went to the temple of his god, some of his own sons killed him there. That is how the Lord God saved Hezekiah and the people of Jerusalem and gave them peace [for a while]. . . .

29:1, 2; 30:1, 13; 32:1-22

139

Josiah, a Good King

Josiah was eight years old when he began to rule, and he ruled 31 years in Jerusalem. He did what was right in the eyes of the Lord and followed in the footsteps of King David. He did not turn aside to the right or to the left. . . .

In the 18th year of his rule, . . . King Josiah sent Shaphan (SHAY-fan) [the secretary of the temple] and the governor of the city to the high priest to have the house of the Lord, his God, repaired. So they came to the high priest with the money that had been brought to the house of God . . . and gave it to the workmen in charge of the temple. They used it for repairing and restoring the temple. . . . And the men did the work faithfully. . . .

While they were bringing the money that had been gathered for the house of the Lord, the priest Hilkiah (Hil-KIGH-uh) found the book of the laws of the Lord given by God through Moses. Then Hilkiah said to Shaphan, the secretary, "I have found the book of the law [of God] in the house of the Lord." And he gave the book to Shaphan. Shaphan brought the book to the king . . . and read it to the king.

When the king heard the words of the law [of God], he tore his clothes and ordered Hilkiah and Shaphan and several of his servants to go and ask what he should do. [He was afraid God was very angry because his people had not kept the words of this book.]

So the priest Hilkiah and the others the king had sent went to a woman prophet called Hulda (HUHL-dah). She told them, "This is what the Lord, the God of Israel, says, 'Yes, I will let evil come upon this place and its people . . . because they have forsaken me and have worshiped other gods. . . . But say to the king of Judah, who sent you: Because you were sorry and you humbled yourself before God when you heard his words against this city and its people, you will die in peace, and your eyes will not see all the evil that will come upon this place and its people.'"

When they brought back this word to the king, he gathered together all the leaders of Judah and Jerusalem. And the king went up to the temple with all the people of Jerusalem and read to them all the words of the book which had been found in the house of the Lord.

And the king made a covenant (KUHV-eh-nuhnt)* with the Lord. He promised to follow his commandments and to do with all his heart what was written in this book that had been found. And he made everyone in Jerusalem agree to do likewise, and they did.

So Josiah removed all the idols from the areas that belonged to the people of Israel. He also required that all who lived in the land of Israel worship the God Jahweh. And throughout the rest of his life the people continued following the Lord, the God of their fathers.

34:1-33

The Last Kings of Judah

[Josiah was killed in a battle with the Egyptians (Ee-JIP-shuhns).] The people of the land chose the son of Josiah to be the king, but he ruled only three months. [He did not obey the Lord God as his father had, so God began to let trouble come upon the land of Judah, as he had said he would. The king of Egypt put Josiah's son in prison and made Eliakim (Ee-LIGH-uh-kim), another son of Josiah, the king.]

Jehoiakim (Jeh-HOY-uh-kim) [changed from Eliakim] was 24 years old when he began to rule, and he ruled 11 years in Jerusalem. He too did much that was evil in God's eyes. So against him came Nebuchadnezzar (Neb-yu-kad-NEZ-ur), the king of Babylon (BAB-i-lahn), and put him in chains and took him to Babylon.

Nebuchadnezzar also took away some of the treasures of the temple and put them in his palace in

Babylon. The rest of the story of Jehoiakim, the terrible things he did, are written in the Book of the Kings of Israel and Judah. His son Jehoiachin (Jeh-HOY-uh-kin) ruled in place of him. . . .

In the spring of the year King Nebuchadnezzar sent some of his men and brought Jehoiachin to Babylon, along with some more treasures from the temple. He also made Jehoiakin's brother, Zedekiah (Zed-uh-KIGH-ah), the king over Jerusalem and over the country of Judah.

Zedekiah was 21 years old when he began to rule, and he ruled 11 years in Jerusalem. He too did what was evil in the eyes of the Lord, his God. . . .

The Lord, the God of their ancestors, often sent his messengers to the king and his priests, because he felt sorry for his people among whom he lived. But they made fun of his prophets. . . .

So God let another king come . . . and gave all the people of Israel into the hand of their enemies. . . . And they burned the house of God and broke down the wall around Jerusalem, and burned all her palaces and destroyed all the treasures. They also killed many men and women, young and old.

This king took all the people who remained alive back with him to Babylon. There the people of Judah [the Jews] became servants of the king and his sons. For 70 years the city lay in ruins, just as the Lord had said through Jeremiah [a prophet] that this would happen.

36:1-21

THE BOOK OF
Ezra

In the first years that Cyrus (SIGH-ruhs) was king of Persia (PUR-shah),* . . . the Lord stirred up the spirit of

Cyrus so that he made a proclamation. He also put this in writing:

"Thus says Cyrus, king of Persia: The Lord, the God of heaven, has given me all the kingdoms on earth, and he has told me to build him a house at Jerusalem, which is in Judah. Whoever belongs to his people, let him go to Jerusalem, which is in Judah, and rebuild the house of the Lord, the God of Israel. . . ."

Then the chief of the leaders of the tribes of Judah and Benjamin and the priests and all whose spirit God stirred decided to go and rebuild the temple in Jerusalem. And all who lived around them helped them by giving them silver and gold and goods of all sorts and animals and precious things.

Cyrus the king also gave them the things that Nebuchadnezzar had taken out of the temple in Jerusalem, and they were brought back to Jerusalem.... Some of the families, when they came to the place in Jerusalem, willingly gave offerings for the building of the house of God on that same site.

1:1-11

The Rebuilding of the Temple

When the people of Israel were back in their towns and cities, they all came together to Jerusalem [to rebuild the house of the Lord]. And the first thing they did was build an altar. On it they gave offerings to the Lord God every morning and evening. They also gave money to the stone builders and carpenters to start the foundation.

In the second year of their coming together to build the house of God in Jerusalem, Zerub-babel (Ze-RUB-bah-bel)* and all who had come back to Jerusalem from Persia put the Levites (LEE-vights)* in charge of the work of building the temple. . . . And when the builders laid the foundation, the priests in their robes came forward with trumpets, and the Levites with cymbals, to praise the Lord.

And the people sang responsively, praising and

giving thanks to the Lord, saying, "For he is good, for his steadfast love endures forever." And all the people shouted with a great shout, because the foundation of the house of the Lord was laid. . . .

Now when the enemies of the people of Judah and Benjamin heard that the returned people were building another temple to the Lord, the God of Israel, they went to Zerub-babel and the other leaders and said, "Let us build with you. We worship your God as you do."

But Zerub-babel and the rest of the leaders said to them, "We don't want you to have anything to do with us in building a house to our God. We alone will build it." Then the people who lived in the land tried to stop the people of Judah from building the temple. [They hired lawyers to keep them from building and wrote letters against them to the king of Persia.]

[At first Darius (Dah-RIGH-uhs),* the king, made a decree that stopped the building. But when the proclamation of King Cyrus was found, King Darius gave another order forbidding anyone to hinder the building of the temple. Furthermore he ordered that the cost of rebuilding the house of God be paid in full from the royal treasury.]

So the elders of the Jews built and finished the temple by the orders of Cyrus and Darius, kings of Persia. And the house was finished in the sixth year of the reign of King Darius. And the people of Israel celebrated the dedication with great joy.

3:1-11; 4:1-6, 17-22
6:1-16

THE BOOK OF
Nehemiah

These are the words of Nehemiah [a Jew who was a trusted servant of Artaxerxes (Arta-ZERK-zees), another king of Persia]:

It so happened that I was in Susa (SOO-sah) when one of my relatives came with some men from Judah. I asked them about the Jews who had escaped being taken away and about the city of Jerusalem. They said to me, "Those who are left there are in great trouble and shame. [Though the temple is rebuilt], the wall of Jerusalem is all broken down, and the gates have been burned."

When I heard this, I sat down and cried, and I fasted and prayed to the God of heaven for several days. . . . [Nehemiah asked God to forgive the sins of his people and to help them as he had promised through Moses.]

Now, I was the cupbearer to the king. In the 20th year of King Artaxerxes I took some wine to the king. And I had never been sad in his presence, so when the king saw me he said to me, "Why do you look so sad? You aren't sick, so you must have a heart sadness."

Then I became very frightened. I said to the king. "May the king live forever! Why shouldn't I be sad when my home city, the place where my ancestors are buried, lies in ruins?" Then the king said to me, "For what are you asking?" So I prayed to the God of heaven and said to the king, "If it pleases the king, . . . send me to Judah, . . . that I may rebuild it."

The king, sitting with the queen beside him, asked, "How long will you be gone and when will you return?" So I set a time, and it pleased the king to send me.

And I said to the king, "If it pleases the king, give me letters to the governors on the other side of the river so that they will let me travel through to Judah. Also please give me a letter to the keeper of the king's forest, so he will give me timber (TIM-ber) to make the beams of the city gates and walls."

The king gave me what I asked, for the good hand of my God was helping me. So I came to Jerusalem and rested there for three days.

Then one night I got up, I and a few men with me, but I told no one what my God had put into my heart to do for Jerusalem. I went on . . . and inspected the walls of Jerusalem that were broken down. . . .

The next day I went to the priests and the rulers and said to them, "You can see the trouble we're in and how Jerusalem lies in ruins with its gates burned. Come, let us build the wall of Jerusalem so we can hold up our heads again."

Then I told them of how God had spoken to me and also what the king had said to me. So they said, "Let's get started and build." And they began immediately to make preparations. But when some of the Arabians living there heard of it, they made fun of us and said, "What are you going to do? Are you planning to revolt against the king?"

I said to them, "The God of heaven will help us and we, his servants, are going to build. But you have no share and no rights in Jerusalem." [The work was then given to the different families. Also women helped in the work of rebuilding the walls.]

When the Arabians and the people of Ammon (AM-mon) heard that the walls of Jerusalem were being rebuilt, they were very angry. They all planned to come and fight against Jerusalem in order to stop the work.

So we prayed to God and set a guard for protection against them night and day. . . . In the lowest spaces behind the wall and in open places I stationed people with their swords and spears and bows. And I said to them, "Don't be afraid of them. Remember the Lord, who is great and terrible, and fight for your brothers and sisters, your sons, your daughters, your wives, and your homes." . . .

From that day on, half of my men worked at building the wall while the other half stood on guard armed with spears and shields. . . . Every builder also carried his sword at his side while he worked. The man who blew the trumpet stood by me.

And I said to the officers and the rest of the people, "The work is great and spread out, and we are separated from each other on the wall. Therefore, wherever you hear the trumpet, run to us there. Our God will fight for us."

So we worked at the job; and half of the men stood on guard from early morning until the stars came out. I also told those who worked by day to spend their nights inside the city to guard us by night."

After 52 days the wall was finished. And when all our enemies heard of it, they were afraid and no longer thought they were so great, because they saw that this work had been accomplished with the help of our God.

1:1-11; 2:1-8, 11-20;
4:6-22; 6:15, 16

THE BOOK ABOUT
Esther

[This book tells about the time when many Jews were living in Persia (PUR-shah).* They had been taken there as prisoners of war. The reading of this story is a regular part of the Jewish festival of Purim (PEEYOOR-im) to this very day.]

King Ahasuerus (Ah-haz-oo-EE-ruhs), who ruled from India to Ethiopia, once gave a banquet for all the army chiefs of Persia and for the nobles and governors of his empire. . . . Queen Vashti (VASH-tee) also gave a banquet for the women in the palace that belonged to King Ahasuerus.

On the seventh day, when the heart of the king was merry with wine, he commanded his servants to bring Queen Vashti to him in order to show the people her beauty. But Queen Vashti refused to come, and this made the king very angry. . . . So he commanded that Vashti should never be allowed to come to him again.

Then the king's servants said [to the king], "Let us look for the most beautiful girls in the land for the king's pleasure. We will appoint men to bring these beautiful young girls to the king's harem in Susa, the capital. Then you can make the girl who pleases you most the queen instead of Vashti." This suggestion pleased the king very much, and he put the plan into action a once.

1:1-12; 2:2-4

The King Chooses Esther

Now there was a Jew living in Susa, the capital, whose name was Mordecai (MOR-deh-kigh). . . . He had raised Esther, the daughter of his uncle. Because her father and mother had died, he had adopted her as his own daughter.

Esther was beautiful and very lovely. So when the king's order was announced, Esther also was taken into the king's palace. . . . Every day Mordecai went to the palace to learn how Esther was getting along. . . . And Esther pleased all who saw her.

When Esther was taken to the king, the king loved Esther more than all the other women. So he set the royal crown on her head and made her the queen instead of Vashti.

Soon after this the king promoted Haman (HAY-muhn) and made him the most powerful person next to the king himself. All the king's servants bowed to Haman. But Mordecai did not. . . . This made Haman very furious. . . . So Haman [who had been told that Mordecai was a Jew] tried to find a way of getting rid of all Jews, throughout the whole kingdom of Ahasuerus.

So Haman said to the king, "There is a certain kind of people among the peoples of your kingdom who do not keep the king's laws. . . . If it please the king, let it be ordered that they be destroyed." . . . So the king took his ring from his hand, gave it to Haman, the enemy of the Jews, and said to him, "You may do with them as seems best to you."

Then an order was written in the name of the king according to Haman's wishes, and it was sealed with the king's ring. . . . When Esther's maids came and told her, the queen was very upset. . . . She put on her royal robes and stood in the inner court of the king's palace.

[In those days it was against the law for a person to go to the king without being called. Anyone who did was put to death unless the king held out his gold scepter to show that he was letting the person live.]

2:5-8, 15-17; 3:1-12; 5:1

Esther Saved Her People

When the king saw Queen Esther standing in the court, he held out his gold scepter. Then Esther approached and the king asked, "What is it, Queen Esther? What is your request? I'll give you whatever it is, up to half of my kingdom."

Esther said, "If it please the king, may the king and Haman come today to a dinner I have prepared for the king."...So the king and Haman came to the dinner....

As they were drinking wine, the king said to Esther, "What is your request? Whatever it is, I will give it." Then Esther answered, "If it please the king, let my life and the life of my people be given to me at my request. For we are to be destroyed, to be killed. . . ."

The king said to Queen Esther, "Who is he and where is he who would try to do this?" Esther answered, "This wicked Haman!"

One of the servants standing near the king said, "Haman has also prepared a gallows (GAL-ohs)* on which he has planned to hang Mordecai." The king said, "Hang him on that." So they hanged Haman on the gallows he had prepared for Mordecai. Then the king's anger died down.

That day the king gave the house of Haman, the enemy of the Jews, to Queen Esther, and Mordecai was brought before the king, because Esther had told him what Mordecai was to her.

And the king took off his ring, which he had taken back from Haman, and gave it to Mordecai. And Esther put Mordecai in charge of Haman's house.

Then Esther went to the king, begging him with

tears to prevent the evil plan that Haman had planned against the Jews. And the king again held out his golden scepter to Esther. As she stood before the king, she said, "If I have found favor in the king's eyes and the thing seems right to the king, let an order be written that will cancel the letters that Haman wrote. [He had ordered all the Jews to be killed.]

The king said to Queen Esther and to Mordecai, the Jew: "You may write as you please in regard to the Jews; you may write in the name of the king and seal it with the king's ring." . . .

So an order was written according to what Mordecai commanded concerning the Jews. . . . By these letters the king allowed the Jews in every city to defend themselves against any people who might attack them. . . . And wherever the king's message came, there was joy among the Jews, a feast and a holiday.

5:2-8; 7:1—8:8, 17

THE BOOK ABOUT
Job

Introduction

There once was a man named Job who lived in the land of Uz. Job was a good man. He worshiped God and had nothing to do with anything evil.

Job had seven sons and three daughters. He owned 7,000 sheep, 3,000 camels, 1,000 head of cattle, and 500 donkeys. He also had a lot of servants. He was the richest man in the East.

Job's sons used to take turns giving a feast for their families. They also invited their three sisters to eat and drink with them. Whenever the feasts were over, Job would get up early the next morning to offer sacrifices [to God] for his children. He did this because he thought, "It may be that my sons have sinned by turning against God in their hearts."

1:1-5

Satan Tests Job's Faith

One day, when the angels of God came into the presence of the Lord, Satan also appeared there. So God asked him, "Where have you been?" Satan answered, "On the earth—going here and there." "Did you happen to notice my servant Job?" God asked. "There is no one on earth as good as he is. He worships me and turns away from anything evil."

Satan replied, "Would Job worship you if he got nothing out of it? You have protected him, his family, and his wealth. You have blessed what he does and have made him rich. But take away what he has, and he will curse you to your face."

The Lord God said to Satan, "Very well, everything the man has is in your power, but leave the man himself alone." So Satan left [to try to turn Job against God].

1:6-12

Job Loses His Wealth and Children

One day [soon after this] Job's children were having a feast at the home of their oldest brother. [Job was home alone.] A messenger came running to Job. He said, "We were out plowing with the oxen. Your donkeys were in a nearby pasture. The Sabeans (Sah-BEE-uhns)* attacked and stole them all. They also killed your servants. I'm the only one who escaped to tell you what happened!"

While he was still talking, another messenger came and said, "Lightning has killed all your sheep and shepherds! I'm the only one who escaped to tell you!"

While he was still talking another came who said, "Three groups of Chaldeans (Kal-DEE-uhns)* attacked us. They took away the camels and killed your

servants. I'm the only one who escaped to tell you."
And before he had finished speaking, another servant
came and said, "Your children were eating and
drinking at your oldest son's house when a tornado
came in from the desert. It blew the house down on the
people in it and killed them all. I'm the only one who
escaped to tell you."

Then Job got up and tore his robe [to show his
feelings]. He also shaved his head and threw himself
face down on the ground. "I came naked from my
mother," he said, "and I'll go back to mother earth
naked. God gave, and God has taken it back. Blessed be
his name!"

In all this, Job did not sin by blaming God for what
had happened. [He never said a word against God.]

1:13-22

Satan Tries Again

Again there came a day when the angels of God
came into his presence. And Satan also was there. And
the Lord God said to Satan, "Well, where have you been
this time?" Satan answered, "Wandering here and
there on the earth."

"Did you notice my servant Job?" God asked.
"There's no one like him on the earth. He's a good man.
He worships me and turns away from anything evil.
You talked me into letting you attack him for no good
reason, but you haven't changed him."

Satan answered, " . . . a man will trade off anything
to stay alive. Touch the man himself, and he'll curse
you to your face!" So the Lord said to Satan, "Very
well, you're free to do whatever you want to do to him—
short of killing him."

Then Satan left the Lord's presence and made sores
break out all over Job's body, from head to foot. And
Job took a piece of broken pottery to scratch himself,
and he went and sat in the ashpit [by the garbage
dump].

His wife said to him, "Are you still trusting and

remaining true to God? Curse him and die!" But he said to her, "You're talking like a foolish woman would speak. Shall we welcome the good things God gives us and complain when he sends us trouble?" Even in all this suffering Job did not say anything sinful against God.

But then came three of Job's friends who had heard how much he was suffering. They had decided to visit him to comfort him.

When the friends first saw Job at a distance, they didn't recognize him. When they did, they began to weep and moan. They tore their clothes and threw dust into the air and on their heads. Then they sat down on the ground with Job for seven days and seven nights. During all this time no one said a word to him because they saw how much he was suffering.

2:1-13

Job's Complaint

Finally Job spoke up and cursed the day he had been born. He said:

Why wasn't I a stillborn baby?
    Why didn't I die when I was born?
I would now be at peace, asleep and resting
    with kings and rulers
        who built what are now ruins,
or with princes who had gold
        and filled their houses with silver,
    or like children born dead.

In the grave the wicked people stop their evil,
    and there the tired people are at rest.
There even prisoners enjoy peace together,
    free from shouts and commands.
Everyone is there, small and great alike,
    and the slave is free at last!

Why let people go on living in misery?
    Why give life to people broken and bitter?

They desire death, but it never comes;
    they hunt for it like hidden treasures.
They are very glad when they find a grave.

3:1, 11, 13-22

Job's Past Life

If only my life could be again as it was
    in the days when God watched over me.
His lamp was shining down on me
    and lighted my way through darkness.
Those were the days when I prospered,
    when God's friendship protected my tent.
The almighty God was with me then,
    and my children were all around me. . . .

When I went to the gate of the city
    and took my seat in the council,
the young men stepped aside when they saw me,
    and old men stood up to show respect.
The leaders of the people stopped talking;
    the most important men became silent.
Everyone who heard about me or saw me
    said good things about me.
I helped the poor and the orphans. . . .
    I was eyes to the blind and feet to the lame.

I thought I would die with my family around me
    after I had lived a long life,
like a tree whose roots always have water,
    with its branches wet with dew, . . .
my strength never failing me.

When I gave advice, people listened to me;
    they had nothing to add after I spoke.
But now younger men make fun of me,
    men whose fathers I wouldn't put with my dogs.

I have never been glad
        when those who hated me suffered,
    or pleased when troubles destroyed them.
I have never sinned
        by praying for their death. . . .

No stranger ever had to sleep in the street;
    my doors have been open to any traveler.

I have never hidden my sins,
    keeping my guilt to myself.
I have never been afraid of public talk,
    holding my tongue and hiding at home.
Oh, if only someone were listening to me!
I am hiding nothing! Let God answer me!

29:1-15, 18-22; 30:1; 31:29-35

God Answers Job

Then the Lord God answered Job out of a windstorm. He said:

Who are you to debate my wisdom
    with ignorant talk?
Pull yourself together like a man
    and answer my questions.
Where were you when I first made the world?
    Tell me if you know so much:
Who decided its shape and size?
    Surely you know.

And tell me—what supports its foundation?
    Or who laid the cornerstone,
when the stars burst into song
    and all the angels shouted for joy?

Where were you when the sea was born
    and came tumbling from out of the earth?
I covered the sea with clouds
    and wrapped it in fog.
I fixed the boundaries of its shores
    and told it, "So far and no farther!"

Do you know where light comes from,
    and where the place of darkness is?
Can you take it to its place
    or follow its paths?
I am sure you can because
    you're so old!

You were already born
    when the world was made!

Have you ever visited the storerooms
    where I keep the snow and the hail,
where I keep them ready for time of trouble,
    for the days of war and of battles?
Do you know the way to where the sun comes up,
    or the place from which the east wind blows?
Can you shout orders to the clouds,
    and make a cloudburst of rain?
And can you send the lightning on errands,
    and will it say to you, "At your service"?

Was it you, Job, who made horses strong,
    and gave them their flowing manes?
Did you make them to leap like a locust,
    and to frighten people with their snorting?

Does a hawk learn how to fly from you
    when it spreads its wings and heads south?
Is it at your command that the eagle goes
    and makes its nest high in the mountains?

38:1-11, 19-24, 34-35;
39:19-20, 26-27

Job Replies

    Job answered the Lord:

What can I say? I am nothing!
I'll not say any more.
I've already said too much.
I knew only what others had told me,
    but now I see you with my own eyes;
so I am ashamed of what I've said
    and repent of my foolish talk.

40:3-5; 42:5-6

A Happy Ending

    Then the Lord God made Job well and rich again. In
fact, he gave Job twice as much as he had had before.

All of Job's brothers and sisters and friends came to visit him and had a dinner with him in his house. They expressed sympathy to him for all the troubles he had gone through, and each of them gave him some money and a gold ring.

The Lord God blessed the last part of Job's life even more than he had blessed the first part. He owned 14,000 sheep, 6,000 camels, 2,000 head of cattle, and 1,000 donkeys.

God also gave Job a second family—seven sons and three daughters. . . . The girls were the most beautiful girls in the whole world. In his will Job gave them an inheritance with their brothers.

Job lived for 140 years after this, long enough to see his grandchildren and great-grandchildren. He was a very old man when he died.

42:10-17

THE
Psalms

The Happy Person
Happy is the person
   who does not follow the advice
      of wicked people,
   who does not hang around sinners,
      or join those who make fun of God.
Such a person loves the Word of the Lord
   and thinks about it day and night.

He [or she] is like a tree
   that is planted near a stream of water;
   it becomes full of fruit in time,
   and its leaves stay fresh and green.

That kind of person succeeds
      in everything he does.

But wicked people are not at all like this;
    they are like straw that a wind easily blows away.

1:1-4

God's Glory and Ours

When I look at the skies
        that your fingers made,
    at the moon and the stars
        you have put in the skies,
[I wonder]: What are human beings
        that you notice them;
    and why [do] you care about them?

Still, you have made us only a little
        less than yourself;
    you have crowned us with glory and honor.
You made us the master
        over all you have made;
    you put human beings over everything else.

You put them over sheep and cattle
    and over the wild animals too;
and over the birds of the air
    and the fish of the sea,
    and over all that lives in the sea.

O Lord, our God,
    how great is your name
        everywhere in the world!

8:3-9

The Word of the Lord

The Word of the Lord is perfect;
    it gives new life.
The truth of the Lord can be trusted;
    it makes simple people wise.
The teachings of the Lord are right
    and make people happy.
The commandments of the Lord are good;
    they help people see what is right.
The worship of the Lord is good;
    it will continue forever.

The laws of the Lord are right;
    they are always fair.
They are more desirable than gold,
    even much gold.
They are sweeter than honey,
    sweeter than the drippings
        from a honeycomb.
By them I am warned,
    and in obeying them I am greatly rewarded.

19:7-11

Our Shepherd

The Lord is my shepherd;
      I'll have everything I need;
    he has me lie down in green pastures.
He leads me to quiet waters;
    he makes my life fresh and new.
He leads me along right paths
    for his name's sake.
Even if I must walk through great darkness,
    I won't be afraid
        that something bad will happen, Lord,
because you are with me;
    your shepherd's rod* and staff
        make me feel safe.

You prepare a banquet for me, Lord,
    where all my enemies can see it,
you pour oil on my head
    and make me someone special;
    my cup is more than full.
I'm sure your goodness and love will be with me
    all the days of my life;
and I will live in the Lord's house forever.

23:1-6

God Lives with Us

God is our protection and our strength,
    an always-present help in times of trouble.

159

Therefore we won't be afraid, even
    if the earth would shift
    and mountains would fall into the middle
        of the sea;
    even if its waters would roar and foam
    and the mountains would shake
        as the sea swells up.

There is a river that brings joy
    to the city of God,
    the holy place of the most high God.
God lives in that city,
        and it will never be shaken.
    God will help it quickly
        whenever it needs help.

God says, "Be still and know that I am God!
    I am the greatest in all the nations;
    I am the greatest in the whole world!"
The Lord of all is with us;
    the God of Jacob is our protection.

46:1-5, 10-11

A Prayer for Forgiveness

Have mercy on me, O God, because
    you have a steady love;
wipe away my sins because
    you have great mercy.
Wash away all that I have done wrong,
    and make me clean from all my sin.

I know what I have done wrong;
    I can't forget it.
It's you I've sinned against—you alone;
    I've done what you think is evil.
So you are right in judging me,
    and can't be blamed
        for what you think of me.
I have been sinful from the time I was born,
    from the time I was in my mother.

You want truth to be deep inside me;
    therefore give me your wisdom
        in my secret heart.
Remove my sin and I will be clean;
    wash me and I will be whiter than snow.
Fill me with joy and gladness;
    so that I can be happy though I am crushed.
Don't look at the sins I have done,
    but wipe all my wrongdoings away.

Give me a clean heart, O God,
    and put a new and right kind of spirit in me.
Please don't sent me away from you,
    and don't take your Holy Spirit from me.
Give me again the joy of being saved by you,
    and make my spirit willing to obey you.
Then will I teach others your ways,
    and sinners will turn back to you.

51:1-13

A Prayer for God's Blessing

God, be merciful to us and bless us
    and look with kindly favors on us,
that your ways may become known on earth,
    your saving power among all nations.

May the people praise you, O God;
    may all people praise you!
O may the nations be glad and sing for joy,
    because you judge people rightly and fairly
    and guide the nations of the earth.
May the people praise you, O God;
    may all people praise you!
Then the land will produce its harvest,
    and God, our God, will bless us.

God has blessed us;
    May all people everywhere honor him.

67:1-7

Safe in God's Care

He who lives in the care
    of the most high God,
who remains under the protection
    of the Almighty,
can say to the Lord, "You are my
    fortress, my God.
    In you I trust."
He will rescue you from every trap
    and from all deadly diseases.
He will cover you with his wings,
    and under his wings you will be safe.
Because you made the Lord your shelter,
        the most high God your dwelling place,
    no harm will come to you,
    no great trouble will come near you.
For God will put his angels in charge of you,
    to guard you wherever you go.
They will hold you up with their hands
    so you won't stub your foot on a stone.

God says, "Because he loves me
    I will rescue him.
    I will protect him because he knows me.
When he calls to me, I will answer him.
    I will be with him in trouble,
    I will rescue him and honor him.
I will give him a long and happy life
    and will show him how I save.

91:1-4, 9-12, 14-16

Praise the Lord

All people everywhere,
        shout with joy to the Lord!
    Worship the Lord gladly,
        and come to him with singing!

Remember that the Lord is God!
    He made us and we are his;
        we are his people, the flock he shepherds.

Enter his temple with thanks,
and go into his courtyard with praise.
Thank him and praise him!

For the Lord God is good;
his love will last forever,
and his faithfulness goes on
from one generation to the next.

100:1-5

Reasons for Praising God

Praise the Lord, O my soul,
and everything in me, praise his holy name!
Praise the Lord, O my soul,
and don't forget what he does for you.
He forgives all your sins,
and he heals all your sicknesses.
He rescues you from the grave
and crowns you with love and mercy.
He fills all your life with good things
and keeps you young and strong like an eagle.

The Lord has set up his throne in heaven,
and he rules over all people.
Praise the Lord, you mighty angels
who listen to what he says,
and do what he wants!
Praise the Lord, all you in heaven,
his servants who do his will!
Praise the Lord, all his creatures
in all the places where he rules!
Praise the Lord, O my soul!

103:1-5, 19-22

God Keeps Us Safe

I look up to the hills;
from where can I get help?
My help comes from the Lord God
who made heaven and earth.

He will not let me fall;
my protector will not fall asleep.
He who takes care of Israel
    will never nap or sleep!

The Lord is your guard.
The Lord stays close beside you to protect you.
The sun will not harm you in the daytime,
    nor the moon at night.

The Lord will protect you from all evil;
he will keep your life safe.
The Lord will keep his loving eye on you
    as you come and go,
        now and forever.

121:1-8

Blessings in Obeying God

Happy are all who worship the Lord God,
    who live in his ways!
You will enjoy the benefits of your work,
    you will be happy,
        and all will go well for you.

Your wife will be like a fruitful vine
      in your house,
and your children will be like young
      olive trees around your table.
This is how people will be blessed
    who worship the Lord God
    and live in his ways!

128:1-4

Give Praise to God

Praise the Lord!

Praise God in his temple!
    Praise his strength in the skies!
Praise him for his mighty acts!
    Praise him for being the greatest!

Praise him with the sound of trumpets!
    Praise him with a harp and guitar!
Praise him with drums and dancing!
    Praise him with string and pipe instruments!
Praise him with the sound of cymbals (SIM-bahls)!*
    Praise him with loud crashing cymbals!

May everything alive praise the Lord!
Praise the Lord!

150:1-6

Proverbs*

The proverbs of Solomon (SAHL-ah-mahn),* son of David and king of Israel (IS-rah-ail).*

To become wise you must first worship God; only fools refuse wisdom and the chances to get it.

Listen to your father and pay attention to what your mother tells you. Their teachings are like a beautiful headband and necklace.

1:1, 7-9

The Happy Person

Trust in the Lord with all your heart,
    and do not rely on what you know.
Think of him in everything you do,
    and he will show you the right way.

Happy is the person who becomes wise,
    and the person who gets understanding.
Wisdom is worth more than silver or gold.
    She [wisdom] is more valuable than jewels.
    Nothing a person could want is worth as much.
Long life is in her right hand,
    and in her left hand are riches and honor.
Wisdom will make your life pleasant
    and will lead you to peace.

165

Wisdom gives life to those who find her
    and makes those who hold on to her happy.

3:5-6, 13-18

Learn from Ants

Learn from the way ants live, you lazy person;
    consider their ways and be wise.
Without having a leader, chief, or ruler,
    they store up food in the summer
        and get ready for winter.
How long will you lie around, O lazy one?
    When will you get up and get going?
A little more sleep,
    a little more folding of your hands in rest,
and soon poverty will attack you
    like an armed robber.

There are six things the Lord hates,
    seven that the Lord cannot stand:
proud-looking eyes, a lying tongue,
    and hands that kill innocent people,
a mind that thinks up wicked plans,
    and feet that hurry off to do evil,
a person who tells one lie after another,
    and the person who stirs up trouble
        among people.

6:6-11, 16-19

More Proverbs

A wise son makes his father glad,
    but a foolish son makes his mother sad.
What you gain by doing wrong
        will not benefit you,
    but doing what's right can save your life.
The Lord does not let good people go hungry,
    but he keeps evil people from getting
        what they want.
Being lazy makes you poor,
    but hard work will make you rich.

10:1-4

The Lord is pleased with good people,
  but condemns those who plan evil.
It is better to be a humble man making a living
    than a man who pretends he's great
        but goes hungry.
A good person takes care of his animals,
  but wicked people are cruel to theirs.
A stupid person thinks he is always right,
  but wise people listen to advice.
The Lord hates liars,
    but is pleased with people
        who keep their word.
A smart person keeps quiet about what he knows,
  but fools show their ignorance.
Worry will weigh a person down,
  but a kind word cheers him up.

12:2, 9, 10, 15, 22, 23, 25

More Wise Sayings

People make plans,
  but God has the final word.
You may think that everything you do
      is all right,
  but the Lord judges your spirit.
Ask God to bless your work,
  and your plans will be successful.
A wise man thinks before he speaks,
  and then what he says sounds right.
Kind words are like honey,
  sweet to the taste and good for one's health.
Some things may seem right to a person,
  but they may lead to death.
An evil man spreads trouble;
  a whisperer separates close friends.
A violent person invites his neighbor
  to join him in doing what isn't good.
People who wink at you often plan something bad,
  and those who press their lips together
    are thinking up something evil.

White hair is a crown of glory;
    it is the reward of a good life.
It is better to be patient than powerful.
    It is better to win control over yourself
        than over a city.
Men roll dice for different reasons,
    but God alone decides what will happen.

16:1-3, 23-25, 28-33

The Lazy Person

I passed by a lazy man's field,
    by the vineyard of a foolish man.
It was all grown over with weeds;
    the ground was covered with thistles.
The stones of the wall had fallen down.
I looked at it and thought about it,
    and I learned a lesson from it.
A little sleep, or a little rest,
    a little folding of the hands,
and poverty will attack you like a robber.

24:30-34

Four Things

There are four things too wonderful
    for me to understand:
the way an eagle flies in the sky,
    the way a snake moves on a rock,
the way a ship goes over the seas,
    and the way a man and woman fall in love.
Four animals on earth are small,
    but they are very very wise:
Ants are weak,
    but they store up their food in the summer.
Rock rabbits aren't strong either,
    but still they make their homes in rocks.
Locusts (LO-kuhsts)* have no king,
    but still they move together.
Lizards (LIZ-urds)* you can hold in your hand,
    but you can also find them in palaces.

There are also four things that walk proudly:
the lion, which is the greatest among animals
    and afraid of none,
strutting roosters, and the he goat,
and a king walking in front of his people.

30:18-19, 24-31

The Good Wife

It's very hard to find a good wife,
    but she is worth far more than jewels.
Her husband trusts her
    and will always be blessed by her.
All the days of her life she does him good
    and no harm.
She is strong and respected,
    and she smiles at the future.
When she speaks, her words are wise,
    and kindness rules her tongue.
She takes good care of her family's needs
    and is never lazy and idle.
Her children appreciate her,
    and her husband praises her.
He says, "Many women have been good wives,
    but you are the best of them all."

A charming manner can fool a person,
    and beauty doesn't last,
but a woman who worships God
    deserves to be praised.

31:10-12, 25-30

Ecclesiastes*

Life Is Empty

These are the words of the preacher, David's son,
who was the king of Jerusalem:

Life is empty and useless, says the preacher; empty and useless! It's all worthless! What does a person get by endless working? Family members are born and family members die, but the world goes on about the same. The sun rises in the east and sets in the west, and then goes back to where it rises again.

The wind blows to the south one day and goes round to the north the next. Round and round goes the wind, turning and returning in its tracks.

All rivers run to the sea, but still the sea is not full. . . . What has been is what will be, and what has been done is what will be done; and there is nothing new under the sun.

Can anybody say about anything, "Look, I've found something new?" No, it has all happened before, long before we were born. No one remembers what happened in the past. In the years ahead no one will remember what happens now!

1:1-11

A Time for Everything

There is a right time for everything:
a time to be born and a time to die;
a time to plant and a time to harvest;
a time to kill and a time to heal;
a time to tear down and a time to build up;
a time to cry and a time to laugh;
a time to be sad and a time to dance;
a time to throw stones
    and a time to collect them;
a time to hug and a time not to hug;
a time to find and a time to lose;
a time to save and a time to throw away;
a time to tear and a time to repair;
a time to keep silent and a time to speak;
a time to love and a time to hate;
a time for war and a time for peace.

3:1-8

Something Better Than Being Alone

I have learned why people work so hard. It is because they want to have as much as their neighbors have. But this is foolish. It is like chasing the wind. A fool folds his hands and won't work. And so he starves. But it's better to have only a little and peace of mind than both hands always busy in trying to catch the wind.

I have noticed something else in life that is foolish. It's a person who is alone, without a son or brother, yet is always working and never thinks he has enough. He never asks, "For whom am I working so hard and giving up my pleasure?" This also is foolish and an unhappy way to live.

Two people together are better off than one, because their life works out better together than alone. If one of them falls down, the other will lift the partner up. But if someone is alone and falls, it's too bad.

There just isn't anyone to help the person who's alone.

4:4-10

Advice to Youth

Remember your creator when you are young. Bad days and years will come when you will say, "I don't enjoy life." That's when the light of the sun and the moon and the stars will be dim for you, and it will continue to seem cloudy even after a rain. . . .

Because the preacher was wise, he taught the people what he knew. He studied proverbs and tested them carefully. . . . The sayings of wise men are like sharp sticks [used to guide sheep]. They are given by the one shepherd of us all. And my son [or daughter], there is one other thing to beware of. There is no end to the making of books, and too much study will wear you out.

There is only one thing more to say: Fear God and obey his commandments, for this is the whole of a

171

person's duty. God will judge everything we do, whether it is good or bad, also the things we do in secret.

12:1-2, 9-14

THE
Song of Solomon

My sweetheart's voice!
　　See he's coming—
　　　　leaping on the mountains,
　　　　running over the hills!

My lover is like a deer,
　　a young male deer.
Now he's standing outside our wall,
　　looking through our windows,
　　peeping through the vines.

My lover speaks and says to me:
"Come, my love, my lovely one,
　　come away with me,
for the winter is over,
　　the skies are clear,
flowers are appearing,
　　the time for singing has come,
and the voice of doves
　　is again being heard.
The fig trees are beginning to bear figs,
　　and vines are in blossom.
They give a sweet smell.

Get up, my love, my lovely one,
　　and come away with me.
O my dove, let me see your face,
　　let me hear your voice;

don't hide like a bird
in the hollow of a cliff,
for your voice is sweet,
and your face is beautiful."

My lover's my very own
and I am his!

2:8-14, 16

THE BOOK OF
Isaiah

In the year that King Uzziah (Uhs-ZIGH-ah) died, I saw the Lord. He was sitting on a throne, very high up, and the temple was filled with his presence and glory.

Above him stood the seraphim (SER-ah-fim).* Each of them had six wings. With two they covered their faces, with two they covered their feet, and with two they flew.

They were all shouting to one another, "Holy, holy, holy is the Lord of Hosts! The whole earth is full of his glory." [What a sound!] It shook the foundations of the place. And suddenly the entire house was filled with smoke.

Then I said, "Woe is me! I'm a gonner (GAWN-er). For I am a man with a sinful mouth, and I live among people with sinful mouths. And I have looked at the king, the Lord of all the armies of heaven."

One of the angels flew over to the altar and picked out a burning coal with a pair of tongs (TAWNGS)* and then flew to me and touched my mouth with it. "See," he said, "now that this has touched your lips, you are no longer guilty. Your sins are all forgiven."

Then I heard the Lord asking, "Whom shall I send [as a messenger to my people]? Who will go for us?" Then I said, "Here I am. Send me." And he said, "Go."

6:1-9

173

The Coming of the Messiah

Someday a shoot will come out of the stump of Jesse (JES-see),* a new branch will grow out of his roots. And the Spirit of the Lord will be in him, the spirit of wisdom, understanding, advice and power, the spirit of knowledge and the fear of the Lord. His delight will be in obeying the Lord.

He will not judge by what he sees; nor will he decide by what he hears. But he will be fair to the poor and defend the weak people on earth. He will rule against the wicked, for he will be wrapped up in rightness and fairness.

[In his kingdom] the wolf will live with the lamb, and the leopard and goat will lie down together. Calves and fat cattle will be safe among lions, and a little child will lead them. The cow and the bear will eat together, and the lion will eat straw like the ox. . . .

Nothing on my holy mountain will hurt or destroy, because the earth will be full of the knowledge of the Lord like the waters fill the sea. In that day the root* of Jesse will be a hope for people. People of all nations will rally to him, because life with him will be glorious.

11:1-10

In that day you will say, "I will give thanks to you, O Lord, for you were angry with me, but now your anger has turned away and you comfort me. See, God is my savior. I will trust him and will not be afraid. For the Lord God is my strength and my song, and he has become my salvation (sal-VAY-shun)."*

You will draw water happily from the wells of salvation. And you will say in that day: "Give thanks to the Lord! Call on him! Make his works known all over the world! Praise his name!"

Sing praises to the Lord, for he has done glorious things. Make this known everywhere. Shout and sing for joy, . . . for the Holy One of Israel who lives among you is great."

12:1-6

Hezekiah's Prayer

In those days King Hezekiah became sick and was about to die. So Isaiah the prophet, the son of Amoz, came to him and told him, "The Lord says, put your house in order, because you will not recover and will soon die."

When Hezekiah heard this, he turned his face to the wall and prayed to the Lord. He said, "Please remember, Lord, how I've always been true to you and have done what you wanted me to do." Then he broke down and sobbed. [He didn't want to die.]

So the Lord sent another message to Isaiah: "Go and tell Hezekiah: The Lord God of your father David heard your prayer and has seen your tears. He will add 15 years to your life. And he will rescue you and this city from attack by the King of Assyria (As-SEER-ee-ah)."

"And here is proof from the Lord that he will do this thing he has promised" [said the message]: "I will make the shadow of the setting sun on the sundial of Ahaz turn back 10 steps." So the sun went back 10 steps on the dial.

When King Hezekiah was well again, he wrote this poem:
It is good for me to have had
    this bitterness;
for you have kept me from death
    and have forgiven me all my sins.
Dead men cannot praise you;
    those who die cannot have hope.
The living, only the living, can
    thank you as I do this day.

38:1-9, 17-19

175

THE BOOK OF
Jeremiah

The Word of the Lord came to me, saying, "Before you were born I knew you and chose you. I appointed you to be a prophet to the nations of the world."

Then I said, "Ah, Lord God! I'm not a good speaker, because I'm still young." But the Lord said to me, "Don't say you're too young. You are to go to whomever I will send you, and you will speak whatever I tell you to say. Don't be afraid of anyone, for I will be with you to keep you and save you."

Then the Lord put out his hand and touched my mouth. "See," he said, "I have put my words into your mouth."

The Lord's Word came to me again, saying, "What do you see?" And I said, "I see a boiling pot, and it's facing away from the north." Then the Lord said to me, "Out of the north trouble will come upon all the people who live in this land."

1:4-9, 13-14

Why God Became Angry

Run up and down through the streets of Jerusalem and take note. Search and see if you can find one man who does what is right and looks for truth. If you can find such a person, I will pardon the city.

Though they say, "Our God is the living God," yet they speak falsely. O Lord, your eyes see the truth. You have punished them, but they have not been sorry. They refuse to receive correction. They have made their faces harder than rock. They have refused to repent.

This is what the Lord, the God of Israel, is saying, "Change your ways, your doing, and I will let you go on living in this place. Don't put your trust in these misleading words: 'This is the temple of the Lord, the temple of the Lord, the temple of the Lord.'

"If you will really change your ways and your doings, if you will really be fair to one another, if you will not harm the stranger, the widow, and the fatherless child, . . . and if you will not harm yourself by worshiping other gods, then I will let you go on living in this place that I gave to your ancestors.

"But look how foolishly you rely on false words. You steal, murder, commit adultery, lie, burn incense to Baal (BAY-ahl),* and go after other gods you don't even know. Then you come and stand before me in this house that has my name and say, 'The Lord has saved us,' but you go on doing all those forbidden things. Has this place that has my name become a den of robbers in your eyes? I myself have seen it," says the Lord.

Then the Lord said to me, "Do not pray for this people. Even if they fast, I will not pay any attention. And if they offer sacrifices to me, I will not accept them. I am going to destroy them with war and famine and sickness."

5:1-3; 7:3-11; 14:11, 12

Jeremiah's Sufferings

When the princes of Judah heard these things, they came over from the king's house to the house of the Lord and sat down at the gate of the temple. Then the priests and the temple teachers said to the princes and to all the people, "This man [Jeremiah] ought to be put to death because, as you yourselves have heard, he has predicted the ruin of this city."

But Jeremiah spoke up to all the princes and the people. "The Lord sent me. He told me to prophesy the ruin of this house and this city and all that you have heard," said Jeremiah. "Change your ways, therefore, and obey the voice of the Lord your God, and the Lord will not do what he has said he will do against you."

Then the princes and all the people said to the priests and the temple teachers, "This man does not deserve to be put to death. He has spoken to us in the name of the Lord, our God." So Jeremiah was not turned over to the people to be put to death.

26:10-13, 16, 24

Then Jeremiah was seen going out of the gate of Jerusalem to a place where he owned some land. A sentry . . . grabbed Jeremiah and said, "You are deserting to the enemy." Jeremiah said, "That's not true. I am not deserting to the enemy." But the sentry would not believe him and brought him to the princes. They beat him and threw him into a prison. . . .

After Jeremiah was in the dungeon many days, the king sent for him. "Is there any word from the Lord?" the king asked him. "There is," said Jeremiah. Then he said, "You will be delivered into the hands of the king of Babylon (BAB-i-lahn)." Jeremiah also said to the king, "What wrong have I done to you or the people? Why have you put me in prison? ..." So the king gave orders that Jeremiah be kept in the guardhouse of the palace.

But when Jeremiah kept telling the people that the city would soon be taken by the army of the king of Babylon, . . . the princes forced the king to give them the prophet. They put him into a well by letting him down with ropes. There was no water in the well, only mud. Jeremiah sank into the mud.

When one of the king's slaves heard that they had put Jeremiah into the well, he went and told the king. "Your Majesty," he said, "these men have done wrong in putting Jeremiah, the prophet, into the well. He will starve to death there, for there is no food left in the city."

So the king ordered the servant to take three men with him and pull Jeremiah out of the well. . . . They pulled Jeremiah out of the well with ropes. . . . After that Jeremiah stayed in the guardhouse until the day that Jerusalem was taken by the king of Babylon and his army.

37:12-21; 38:1-13, 28

THE
Lamentations*
OF JEREMIAH

How lonely is the city
  that was full of people!
She has become like a widow,
  she that was great among nations.

She cries in the night,
  tears are on her cheeks.
Among all her lovers
  she has none to comfort her.

The daughter of Zion has lost
  all her beauty.
Gone are her children;
  they were led away as captives.

The hand of the enemy
  is on all her precious things;
yes, she has seen them
  go into her temples. . . .

All her people groan
  as they search for bread.
They trade their treasures for food
  to get some strength.

Is it nothing to you,
  all you who pass by?
Look and see if there is any sorrow
  like my sorrow.

The Lord in his anger
  brought this upon me.
The Lord is in the right;
  for I disobeyed his Word.

1:1, 2, 6, 10-12, 18

THE BOOK OF
Ezekiel

When I was among the exiles (EG-zighls)* by the river
Chebar (KEE-bahr), the skies opened up and I saw
visions of God. . . . As I looked, a stormy wind suddenly
came out of the north. There was a huge cloud, with
brightness around it and flames darting in and out.
And out of the cloud came four living creatures.

These creatures had the shape of men, but each one
had four faces and four wings. . . . Under their wings, on
their four sides, they had human hands. . . . As for their
faces, each one had the face of a man in front, the face of
a lion on the right side, the face of an ox on the left side,
and the face of an eagle at the back. Such were their
faces.

And their wings were spread out above them. Each
creature had two wings, and each wing touched the
wing of another, while two covered their bodies. . . . In
the middle of these creatures there was something that
looked like burning coals of fire, like torches moving
back and forth among the creatures. The fire was
bright, and out of the fire came lightning. And the
living creatures darted back and forth like a flash of
lightning.

Now, as I looked at the creatures, I saw a wheel
beside each of them. . . . When they moved, they went in
any of four directions without turning as they went.
The four wheels had rims and spokes, and their rims
were full of eyes. And when the living creatures
moved, the wheels went beside them.

And when the creatures rose from the earth, the
wheels rose too. Wherever the spirit would go, there
the creatures went; and the wheels went along with

them; for the spirit of the living creatures was in the wheels. . . .

Above the sky over their heads there was something like a throne, gleaming like a bright blue stone. Seated above this throne was what seemed to be a man. . . . And there was brightness all around him, like the appearance of a rainbow. . . . When I saw it, I fell face downward on the ground. Then I heard a voice of someone speaking to me.

The voice said to me, "Stand up on your feet, man, and I will speak to you." And when he spoke, the spirit entered into me and set me on my feet. "Son of man," he said, "I am sending you to the people of Israel, to a nation of people who have rebelled against me. . . . And you shall say to them, 'This is what the Lord God says.' And whether they listen or refuse to listen, they will know that there has been a prophet among them."

1:1-6, 8-21, 26-28;
2:1-5

The Justice of God

The word of the Lord came to me, saying: "If a man gets a son who sees all the sins that his father has done, and fears God and does not do likewise, who . . . does not do wrong to anyone . . . and walks in my ways, he will not be punished for his father's sins. He will surely live. As for his father, because he . . . robbed his brother and did what is not good among people, you shall see, he will suffer for his sins.

"But you say, 'Why shouldn't the son suffer for the sins of his father?' When the son has done what was right and has been careful to do all my commandments, he will surely live. The person who sins will die. The son will not have to suffer for what the father has done wrong, nor will the father have to suffer for the sins of the son. . . .

"And when a wicked man turns away from all his sins and keeps all my commandments and does what is right, he will surely live. He will not die. None of the

sins he has done will be remembered against him. . . .
But when a good man turns away from his goodness
and does the same terrible things the wicked man does,
should he live? None of the good things he has done
will be remembered. . . .

"Yet you say, 'The ways of the Lord are not just.'
Listen now, you people of Israel: Are my ways not
just? Is it not your ways that are not just? When a good
man turns away from his goodness and does wrong, he
will die for that. . . . Again, when a wicked man turns
away from the wicked things he has done and does
what is right, he will save his life. Because he turned
away from all the sins he had done, he will surely live.
He will not die.

"Therefore I will judge . . . every one according to
his actions, says the Lord God. Turn away from all
your sins so that wrongdoing will not ruin you. Put
them all behind you and get yourselves a new heart
and a new spirit. . . . I do not enjoy seeing anyone die,
says the Lord God. So turn and live!"

18:1, 14-32

The Valley of Dry Bones

The Lord put his hand on me and carried me by his
spirit and put me down in the middle of a valley. It was
full of bones. And he led me around in them. There were
very many, and they were very dry.

Then he said to me, "Son of man, can these bones
live again?" And I answered, "Lord God, you alone
know." Then he said to me, "Speak to these bones and
say to them, 'Dry bones, hear the message of the Lord: I
will cause breath to enter into you and will give you
life. And I will put muscles and flesh on you and will
cover you with skin. And I will put breath into you and
you will live. You will see that I am the Lord.'"

So I spoke as I was commanded, and as I spoke
there was a noise. The bones began to rattle and come
together, one bone to another. And as I looked, muscles

and flesh came on them and skin covered them. But there was no breath in them.

Then the Lord God said, "Say to the breath, 'The Lord God says: Come from the four winds, O breath, and breathe on these dead men and give them life.'" So I called to the wind as the Lord had commanded me. And the breath came into them, and they lived and they stood up on their feet, a very great army.

Then the Lord said to me, "These bones are the whole people of Israel. They say, 'Our bones are dried up; our hope is lost; we are completely cut off.' Tell them, therefore, what the Lord God says to them: I will open your graves, O my people, and I will raise you up out of your graves. And I will bring you back to the land of Israel.... And I will put my spirit into you and you will live. Then you will know that I, the Lord, have spoken these things and have done them," said the Lord.

37:1-14

THE BOOK OF
Daniel

In the third year that King Jehoiakim (Je-HOY-ah-keem) ruled over Judah (JEW-dah), Nebuchadnezzar, the king of Babylon (BAB-i-lon), attacked Jerusalem. And the Lord gave him the victory over the king of Judah. When Nebuchadnezzer returned to Babylon, he took along some of the cups and bowls from the house of God and put them into the treasury of his god.

The king of Babylon also ordered Ashpenaz (ASH-pen-az), who was in charge of his palace, to select certain Jewish youths—young men of the royal families of Israel—to serve in his palace. "Pick healthy, handsome, and bright young men who are well educated and quick to learn," he said. "These I want you to teach the language and wisdom of the Chaldeans (Kal-DEE-uhns)."*

Among the young men chosen were Daniel and three others from the tribe of Judah. The head of the palace gave them Babylonian names: He called Daniel Belteshazzar (Bel-teh-SHAZ-ahr). The other three were called Shadrach (SHAD-rack), Meshack (MEE-shack), and Abednego (A-BED-nee-go). The king said these four could have some of his rich food every day and some of his wine. For three years they were to be taught and trained and then presented to the king.

But Daniel decided he wouldn't eat the king's rich food or drink the wine. He asked the chief of the servants to let him eat and drink other things instead.

Now, God had given the man a special liking for Daniel, but the chief servant said, "I'm afraid the king, who ordered your food and drink, will see you in poorer condition than others of your age. Then I'll be in danger of having my head cut off."

So Daniel said to the man whom the chief had put over the four young men from Judah: "Test your servants for 10 days. Give us vegetables to eat and water to drink. Then look at our faces and the faces of those who eat the king's rich food, and then do with us according to what you see."

The man agreed to this and tested them for 10 days. At the end of 10 days, the four young men looked better and were fatter than all the youth who ate the king's rich food. So the servant took away the rich food and the wine they were supposed to drink and gave them vegetables.

As for these four youths, God gave them knowledge and skill in all kinds of writings and wisdom, and Daniel learned to understand visions and dreams. At the end of the time when the king had said they should be brought to him, the chief servant of the palace presented them to Nebuchadnezzar.

When the king talked with them, he found the four young men 10 times better in wisdom and understanding than all the magicians and astrologers (a-STRAHL-uh-jers)* in his kingdom. So Daniel got to stay as the king's adviser until the first year of the reign of King Cyrus (SIGH-ruhs).

1:1-21

God Saves Three Men

[Some time later] King Nebuchadnezzar made a statue of gold. It was 90 feet high and nine feet wide. He set it up in a plain near Babylon.

Then the king gathered together all the main officials for the dedication of the statue. When they were all standing in front of the statue, a herald shouted out loudly, "You are commanded, O people, to fall down and worship the gold statue when you hear the sound of music. Whoever does not fall down and worship will immediately be thrown into a burning furnace."

So, as soon as the people heard the sound of music, they dropped down and worshiped the gold statue.

But some men of Babylon went to the king and said, "O king, long live the king! You, O king, have commanded that when the music is played, everyone who hears it should drop down and worship the gold statue. You have also said that anyone who refused to do this will be thrown into a burning furnace. But some Jews who have important positions in Babylon—Shadrach, Meshach, and Abednego—these men do not obey you." . . .

The king angrily ordered that these men be brought to him. When they were brought, the king said to them, "Is it true that you do not serve my gods or worship the gold statue I have set up?" The three men answered, "O Nebuchadnezzar, we don't have to answer you in this matter. Our God whom we serve is able to save us from the burning furnace, and he will save us. But whatever may happen, O king, we will not worship the gold statue you have set up."

Then Nebuchadnezzar became furious. . . . He

Daniel

ordered that the furnace should be heated seven times hotter than usual. And he commanded that the three men be tied just as they were—with all their clothes—and thrown into the burning furnace. The furnace was so hot that the fire killed the men who threw Shadrach, Meshach, and Abednego into it.

But Shadrach, Meshach, and Abednego remained unharmed in the burning furnace. When the king came to see, he was amazed. He said to his advisors, "Didn't we throw three tied-up men into the fire?" They answered, "True, O king." He said, "I see four men loose in the middle of the fire. They are walking around unhurt. And the fourth one looks like a son of the gods."

Then Nebuchadnezzar walked up to the door of the burning furnace. "Shadrach, Meshach, and Abednego, servants of the Most High God," he shouted, "come out. Come here to me!" When the three men came out of the fire, the king's men gathered around and saw that not a hair on their heads was burned. Their clothes were not burned, and there was not even the smell of any burning on them.

King Nebuchadnezzar said, "Praised be the God of Shadrach, Meshach, and Abednego. He sent his angel and saved his servants who trusted in him. . . . Therefore I make this law: Any persons, nation, or groups that will say anything against the God of Shadrach, Meshach, and Abednego will be cut in pieces and their houses will be knocked down; for there is no other god who can save in this way."

Then the king promoted Shadrach, Meshach, and Abednego to still better positions in the country of Babylon.

3:1-30

Writing on a Wall

King Belshazzar (Bel-SHAZ-zahr) [the son of Nebuchadnezzar] invited a thousand of his officers to a great feast and drank wine with them. While drinking,

186

the king remembered the gold and silver cups that his father had taken out of the temple in Jerusalem. He ordered them to be brought to him so that he and the people with him could drink from them.

As they drank from the temple cups, they praised the gods of gold and silver. Suddenly they saw the fingers of a man's hand writing on the wall of the king's palace. The king saw the hand as it wrote. As he watched, the color of his face changed and his knees shook, and he became very frightened.

"Bring in my magicians and wise men," shouted the king. When they came he said to them, "Whoever can read this writing and tell me what it means will be made the third ruler of my kingdom." But all the king's wise men could not read the writing or tell the king what it meant. . . .

Then Daniel was brought to the king. . . . He said to the king, "O king, the Most High God gave your father Nebuchadnezzar greatness and glory. Because of that greatness, all people and nations feared him. . . . But when he became proud, he was put off of his throne and his glory was taken from him. His mind became like that of an animal, and he ate grass like an ox. . . .

"And you, his son Belshazzar," said Daniel, "have not humbled yourself, though you knew all this. You and your officers and your wives have drunk wine out of the sacred cups from the Lord's house. You praised the gods of silver and gold, . . . but the God who gives you your breath and governs all your doings you have not honored.

"The hand that wrote and this writing" [Daniel continued] "was sent by this God; and these are the words that were written: MENE (MEE-ni), MENE, TEKEL (TEK-uhl), and PARSIN (PAHR-sin). And this is the meaning: MENE means that God has decided to bring your kingdom to an end. TEKEL means that you have been weighed and found wanting. PARSIN means that your kingdom has been divided and will be given to the Medes (MEEDZ) and the Persians (PUR-shuhnz).

Daniel

When Belshazzar heard all this, he announced that Daniel was to be the third ruler in his kingdom. But that night Belshazzar was killed, and Darius (Dah-RIGH-us),* the Mede (MEED), received the kingdom.

5:1-31

Daniel in the Lion's Den

Darius put 120 governors over the kingdom, and over them he put three presidents. Daniel was one of them. But Daniel soon proved to be a better ruler than all the rest because he had a good spirit in him. So the king planned to put him over the whole kingdom.

This made the other presidents and governors very jealous. They began looking for some reasons to complain about Daniel. But they couldn't find anything to criticize. . . .

Then the rulers decided, "We'll never find any reason to complain about Daniel unless we can find something in connection with his religion." So these men went to the king and said, "King Darius, live forever! All the governors and presidents are agreed that the king should make a law that no one should make any request to any god or man for 30 days except to the king himself. Whoever does so is to be thrown into the den of the lions. . . ." Darius signed the order.

When Daniel heard that the law had been signed, he went to his house and knelt in front of his open window and prayed to God. This is what he had always been doing three times every day. So his enemies found him praying. Then they went back and told the king, "Daniel, who is one of the men from Judah, pays no attention to you, O king, or the new law you have signed. He continues to pray three times a day."

When the king heard this, he was very upset and tried all day to think of ways he could save Daniel. But his enemies came to the king and reminded him that no law made by a king of the Medes and Persians could ever be changed. So the king ordered Daniel to be put into the place where lions were kept. "I hope your God,

188

whom you serve, will save you," the king said to Daniel. . . .

Then the king went to his palace, but he couldn't sleep all night. Very early the next morning he got up and hurried to the den of the lions. When he came near, he called out in a voice full of pain, "O Daniel, servant of the living God, has your God, whom you serve, been able to save you from the lions?"

Daniel answered, "O king, live forever! My God sent his angel and shut the lions' mouths, so they have not hurt me." . . .

When the king heard this, he was very glad. He ordered that Daniel be taken out of the den. . . . He also ordered that those men who had planned against Daniel be thrown into the den. . . . Even before they hit the bottom of the den, the lions leaped up and tore them apart.

Afterward King Darius wrote a message to all the people in his kingdom. It said, "I order that everyone in my kingdom should fear the God of Daniel. For his God is the living, unchanging God. His kingdom and power will never end. . . . He saved Daniel from the power of the lions."

6:1-27

Hosea

Listen to the Word of the Lord, O people of Israel, because the Lord has something against you: There is no faithfulness or kindness and no knowledge of God in the land. There is swearing, lying, killing, stealing, and adultery (uh-DUHL-tur-ree).* The people break all limits, and there is one murder after another.

That is why your country is not producing and all who live in it feel sad and hopeless. Also the animals and the birds and even the fish are beginning to disappear.

4:1-3

God's Love for His People

When the people of Israel were a young nation, I loved them like a son and brought them out of Egypt. But the more I called to them, the more they turned away from me. They kept giving sacrifices to Baals (BAY-ahls)* and burned incense to idols.

It was I who taught the people of Israel when they were young. I took them up in my arms, but they didn't appreciate that I raised them. I led them with ropes of love and was to them like a man who loosens the muzzle so that his animal can eat. I bent down to them and fed them.

Because they refuse to return to me, they must return to [the slavery of] Egypt, and Assyria (A-SEER-ee-ah) will rule them. War will sweep over their cities and will break down their gates. War will destroy them in their fortresses.

My people are set on turning away from me, so I have sentenced them to slavery. No one will set them free.

11:1-7

Hosea's Prayer

Return to the Lord your God, people of Israel. Your sins have made you fall. Return to the Lord and say these words to him: "Forgive all our sins and accept us, and we will give you the fruit* of our lips. Assyria will not save us, nor can our war horses. We will never again say to idols we have made, 'You are our God.' In you, O Lord, the helpless find mercy."

[If you will do this, the Lord will say]:

I will make them faithful;
    I will love them with all my heart;
    I will no longer be angry with them.

I will do to Israel what rain
    does to dry land;
    they will blossom like the lily;
    they will grow roots like trees.

They will spread out with new branches
    and will be beautiful, like olive trees;
    they will smell good, like cedar trees.

My people will return and will live
    beneath my shadow;
    they will be like a watered garden,
    and will blossom like grapes. . . .

May all who want to be wise understand the things I have written. May all who have any sense keep them in mind. For the Lord's ways are right, and good people follow them. But sinners stumble and fall.

14:1-7, 9

Joel

Listen, you old men; everyone listen! Have you ever heard of such a thing in all your born days? Tell your children about it, and have your children tell their children and their children their children.

What the cutting locusts (LO-kuhsts)* left, the swarming locusts ate, and what the hopping locusts left, the stripper locusts ate.

1:2-4

The Coming of the Locusts

Like blackness there spread upon the mountain a great and powerful army. Nothing like it was ever seen before or will ever be seen again. . . . They looked like tiny horses, and they ran like war horses. Leaping along the tops of the mountain, they made a noise like the rumbling of chariots, like the crackling of fire burning a field, and like a powerful army moving into battle.

The people who saw them were terribly frightened; their faces grew pale. These locusts charged like soldiers; like trained commandos they climbed the walls. Straight ahead they marched, never breaking ranks.

They never pushed each other; each one marched in his place. No weapon could stop them. They leaped on the city; they ran over the walls; they climbed into the houses, entering through the windows like thieves.

The earth shook under them and the sky trembled. The sun and moon were hidden by them and the stars stopped shining. The Lord led them with a shout, for they were a very great army; and they followed his orders. Whenever the Lord punishes, it's a terrible happening. Who can stand it?

But even then the Lord says, "Return to me with all your heart. Come with fasting and weeping. But tear your hearts and not your clothes.

"So return to the Lord, your God, for he is gracious and merciful. He is slow in getting angry and is full of kindness. He is sorry when he has to punish. Who knows, he may decide to change what he is doing and give you a blessing."

Then the Lord became concerned about his land and had pity on his people. He said to them, "See, I am sending you again some grain and wine and oil to satisfy your needs. No longer will I make you a disgrace among the nations." . . .

Don't worry, people! Be glad and celebrate, for the Lord has done great things! Don't be afraid, all you animals, for the pastures are green again. The trees bear their fruit, and the fig trees and grape vines are producing a lot.

Be glad, O people of Jerusalem, and praise the Lord, your God. For the rain he sent is a sign of his forgiveness. Once more the rains will come as before. The threshing floors will pile high again with grain, and the barrels will be filled with olive oil and wine.

"I will give you back the crops that the locusts ate—my great destroying army that I sent against you," said the Lord. "Once again you will have all the food you want and will praise the name of the Lord your God, who has treated you so wonderfully well. Never again will my people be treated so severely."

2:2-14, 18-26

Amos

These are the words of Amos, a shepherd from the village of Tekoah (Teh-KO-ah). . . . The Lord's voice will roar from Jerusalem. The pastures of the shepherds will be sad, and the grass on Mount Carmel will turn brown.

The Lord says, "For their many sins I will punish the people of Judah. They have rejected my teachings and have not kept my commands. They have been led astray by the same lies that their ancestors followed. So I will send a fire and will burn down the fortresses of Jerusalem."

The Lord also says, "For their many sins, punishment will come upon the people of Israel, and I will not turn it away. They sell good people into slavery just to get money, and they sell poor people into slavery just because they cannot pay the price of a pair of sandals. They trample the poor into the dust and push aside those in trouble. Young men and old go to the temple prostitutes and disgrace my holy name. At every place for worship they sleep on clothing they have taken from the poor. Even the wine they drink in the house of their God has been taken from people who have been fined.

1:1-2; 2:4-8

The Prophet's Sermon

Listen, people of Israel, to this message that the

Lord has spoken against you and all the people he brought out of Egypt: "Of all the people on earth, you are the only ones I have known [as my children]. That is why I will punish you for all your sins."

[Everything has a reason.] Do two people start traveling together unless they have agreed to meet? Does a lion roar in the forest if he has not found a victim? And does a young lion growl in his den if he has not caught something? Can a bird be trapped unless someone sets a trap? Does a trap spring up unless something sets it off?

Is a warning trumpet ever blown in a city without making people afraid? Does great trouble ever strike a city unless the Lord has sent it? Surely the Lord never does anything without revealing his plans to his servants, the prophets. When a lion roars, who will not be afraid? The Lord God has spoken, so what can his prophet do but prophesy?

Announce to those who live in the palaces of Assyria (Ah-SEER-ee-ah) and Egypt (EE-jipt), "Come to the city of Samaria (Sah-MER-ee-ah)* and see the dreadful things that are happening there, the great disorder and the cruel deeds. They have forgotten how to do right," says the Lord [only adding to and storing up] "what they have won by violence and robbery. Therefore," says the Lord, "an enemy will surround your land. He will destroy your defenses; his soldiers will rob your palaces."

3:1-11

Last Call to Israel

The Lord [still] says to the people of Israel: "Come to me and you will live. But do not go to Bethel (BETH-el) or Gilgal (GIL-gal) or Beersheba (Beer-SHEE-bah) [to worship and to find me], for these places will come to nothing. Look for the Lord and you will live." . . .

He who made the stars and turns darkness to daylight and day into night, who draws up the waters of the sea and pours them down upon the earth, his name is the Lord.

Search for what is good, not for what is evil, so that you may live and so that the Lord God really will be with you, as you say he is. Hate evil and love what is good; and see that justice is done in the courts. Perhaps the Lord God will be merciful to the people who will be left.

The Lord says, "I hate your religious celebrations; I can't stand them! I get no pleasure out of your solemn assemblies. Though you bring me offerings, I will not accept them. Stop your noisy songs; I will not listen to the music of your harps. But let justice roll down like water and righteousness like a river that never dries up."

5:4-8, 14-15, 21-24

Obadiah

This is what the Lord God says about the country called Edom:

"Wait and see, Edom, I will cut you down to size, and you will be looked down on by other nations. You are proud because you live in high cliffs and think, 'Who can reach us up here?' But don't fool yourselves. Though you soar as high as the eagle and build your nest among the stars, I will bring you down," says the Lord.

All your allies have deceived you. They will help drive you out of your land. Your partners will plot against you. Your trusted friends will set a trap under you.

When that day comes, says the Lord, not one wise man will be left in all of Edom, for I will remove their understanding. And the mightiest soldiers will be confused and unable to stop the slaughter.

Why? Because of what you did to the people of

Israel, your brothers and sisters.... For on the day that foreigners entered their gates and carried off their riches, you were like one of them. You didn't lift a finger to help.

And you shouldn't have gloated over your brothers' troubles; you shouldn't have been happy over their being ruined. You shouldn't have gone into the land of Israel and robbed them at the time of their great trouble. You shouldn't have killed those trying to escape, and you shouldn't have turned over survivors to their enemies in that terrible time of trouble.

The day of the Lord's revenge is near. As you have done, it will be done to you. Your acts will return and fall on your head. ... But in Jerusalem there will be a place for escape, and it will be a holy place. And the people of Israel will possess their own possessions.

1:1-4, 7-15, 17

THE BOOK ABOUT
Jonah

One day the Lord spoke to Jonah. He said: "Go to that great city of Nineveh (NIN-eh-vuh) and speak out against it. I know how very wicked those people are."

But in order to get away from the Lord, Jonah went to Joppa, where he found a ship going to Spain. After paying his fare, he went on board and headed for Spain.

1:1-3

The Lord Follows Jonah

On the way the Lord sent a great wind to the sea. The storm was so bad that the ship was in danger of breaking up. The sailors were frightened and each one prayed to his god. ... But Jonah had gone below and was lying down, fast asleep.

When the captain found Jonah asleep, he said to him, "What are you doing, you sleeper? Get up and pray to your god. Maybe he will feel sorry for us and save us." The sailors said to one another, "Let's draw lots* and find the person who has caused us this trouble." When they did this, Jonah's name was drawn.

They said to Jonah, "Tell us, why has this trouble come to us? What is your occupation? What is your country?" And he said to them. "I am a Hebrew. I fear the Lord, the God of heaven, who made the sea and the dry lands." [He probably also told them he was running away from God.]

Then the men were very much afraid. The storm was getting worse. They said to him, "What should we do to you to stop the storm?" Jonah said to them, "Throw me into the sea, and it will calm down. I know it's my fault that you're caught in this storm." . . .

So they picked Jonah up and threw him into the sea. At once the sea calmed down. This made the sailors so afraid of the Lord that they promised to serve him.

1:4-16

Jonah in the Fish

The Lord had a large fish swallow Jonah, and Jonah was inside the fish for three days and three nights. Then Jonah prayed to the Lord, his God, from the belly of the fish, . . . and it vomited Jonah out on the dry land.

Then the Lord spoke to Jonah again. He said, "Go to that great city Nineveh and tell it the message I tell you." That time Jonah obeyed and went to Nineveh. . . . There he shouted, "In 40 days Nineveh will be destroyed."

And the people of Nineveh believed God's message. They decided that everyone should fast,* and all of them, from the greatest to the least important, put on sackcloth.* When God saw what they did, how they gave up their evil ways, he changed his mind. He didn't punish the city as he had said he would.

1:17; 2:1, 10; 3:1-5, 10

A Lesson Jonah Learned

Jonah became very unhappy about God not destroying the city; in fact, he was angry. He said to the Lord, "Isn't this what I said you would do when I was still in my country? This is why I tried to run away to Spain. I knew you are a gracious and merciful God, that you are patient, full of love, and always ready to change your mind and not punish. Therefore, O Lord, take my life, I beg you. I'd rather be dead than alive." But the Lord said, "Jonah, do you have a right to be angry?"

Then Jonah went into the city and made a shelter for himself and sat under it in the shade. He waited to see what would happen to the city. And the Lord had a plant grow up over Jonah, to give him some more shade. Jonah was very pleased with the plant.

But early the next day God had a worm attack the plant so that it withered up. After the sun rose, God sent a hot wind from the east. Jonah was about to faint from the heat, so he wished he were dead. He said, "I'd be better off dead than alive."

God said to Jonah, "What right do you have to be angry for the plant?" Jonah replied, "I have every right to be angry." Then the Lord said, "You pity the plant for which you did nothing. You didn't make it grow. It grew up in one night and disappeared in the next. Shouldn't I pity Nineveh, that great city? It has more than a 120,000 babies in it and also many cattle."

4:1-11

Micah

This is the message that the Lord gave to Micah . . . concerning Samaria (Sah-MER-ee-ah)* and Jerusalem.

The Way It Was

Listen, you leaders and rulers of Israel! Aren't you supposed to know justice? But you hate what is good and love what is evil. You skin my people alive and tear off their flesh from their bones. . . . The time is coming when you will cry out to the Lord, but he will not answer you. He will turn his face away from you because you have done evil.

My people are led by prophets who say "Peace" as long as they have something to eat, but they declare war against anyone who doesn't pay them. To those prophets the Lord says, "Your day is almost over. The sun is going down on you, and darkness will come over you. You will have no more visions (VIZH-uhns)* and you won't be able to predict anything." Those who try will be disgraced by their failures. They will cover their lips because they will get no answers from God.

As for me, I am filled with power. I have the Spirit of the Lord, who gives me right understanding and courage to tell the people of Israel what their sins are.

Listen to me, you leaders and rulers of Israel, you who hate justice and prefer unfairness, you are building God's city with murder and wrongdoing. The city's rulers take bribes. The priests and prophets won't teach and preach unless they're paid. And yet they all claim they are counting on the Lord. They say, "The Lord is with us. No harm will come to us."

Because of you Jerusalem will be plowed like a field and will become a pile of ruins. The hilltop where the temple stands will become a forest.

3:1-12

A Vision of the Future

In the days ahead the mountain where the Lord's house stands will be set high above all the mountains on earth. And people of every land will flock to it. They will say, "Let us go to the mountain of the Lord, to the house of Israel's God. He will teach us his ways and we will follow them." For from Mount Zion in Jerusalem the Lord's message will come.

The Lord will be the judge among the nations, and they will have peace. They will hammer their swords into ploughs and their spears into pruning knives. Nations will not go to war against other nations, nor will they prepare for war any more.

Everyone will live in peace in his own vineyard and under his own fig tree, and no one will make them afraid. The Lord has promised this. All nations worship their own gods, but we will worship and obey the Lord our God for ever and ever.

4:1-5

God Promises a Ruler

The Lord says, "O Bethlehem, you are little among the many towns in Judah. But from out of you I will bring someone who is to be the ruler of Israel. His family line will go back to long ago."

So the Lord will give up his people for a time, until this ruler will be born. . . . When he comes, he will lead his people with the strength of the Lord and in the name of the Lord, his God.

5:2-4

Nahum

The Lord is a jealous God. [He jealously watches over his children.] That is why he gets very angry at his enemies and takes revenge on those who fight against him.

The Lord gets angry very slowly, but when he does, his power is great, and he doesn't just forget about the guilty.

The Lord shows his power in the cyclone and the tornado; the clouds are the dust of his feet.

At his command rivers and seas dry up, green pastures turn brown, and thick forests wither and fade.

In his presence mountains shake and hills melt; the earth crumbles and its people die.

Who can stand before God when he is angry? Who can bear his anger? His fury is like a fire, and rocks are easily broken by him.

The Lord is good. When trouble comes, he is a strong hiding place and helper. And he knows everyone who runs to him for help.

But he will sweep away his enemies like a great flood would, and he will chase them into the darkness of the night.

1:2-8

Habakkuk

O Lord, how long must I call for help before you will listen? How long must I shout "Help!" before you will save me?

Why do you let me see wrongs and troubles? All around me there is quarreling and fighting. Wherever I look there is violence and destruction. The laws are not enforced and so no justice is done. Wicked people outnumber the good. . . .

Are you not the everlasting God, O Lord my God, my Holy One? . . . Your eyes are so pure they cannot look at evil and wrongdoings. Why then are you silent when people hurt people and the wicked destroy people who are better than they?

I will be like a watchman on a tower and will look to see what answer God will give me.

And the Lord said to me, "Write down my answer.

Write it large and clear so that everyone can read it easily and will run to tell others. For the things I plan won't happen right away, but they will surely come to pass. If they seem slow in coming, just be patient. They will happen at the right time.

"Remember, evil people will fail, but the righteous person will live by his faith in me."

1:2-4, 12-13; 2:1-4

A Song of Faith

O Lord, I have heard your report,
    and I fear the things you are going to do.
In your anger remember mercy;
    in these years help us as you did in the past.
Though the fig trees do not blossom
    and no fruit is on the vines;
though the olive crops all fail
    and the fields produce no food;
though the flocks disappear
    and the cattle barns are empty;
I will be glad in the Lord,
    I will be happy that God is my Savior.
God, the Lord, is my strength;
    he makes my feet as
        nimble as a deer's;
    he helps me walk on high places.

3:2, 17-19

Zephaniah

This is the message of the Lord that came to Zephaniah . . . at the time when Josiah (Jo-SIGH-ah) was the king of Judah.
Sing, daughter of Zion (ZIGH-on);*
    shout, children of Israel!

Be glad and celebrate with all your heart,
    people of Jerusalem!
The Lord will forgive you
    and will stop punishing you;
    he will drive away your enemies.
The Lord, the king of Israel,
       will live among you;
    you won't have to be afraid any more.

When that day comes, the good news will be,
    "People of Jerusalem, don't be afraid.
The Lord, your God, is with you;
    He is a warrior who gives victory.
He will be very glad about you;
    He will love you and forgive you.
He will sing about you loudly
    as choirs at a great festival.

I will remove your troubles from you,
    says the Lord. . . .
And I will deal with all
    who have been cruel to you.
I will save the weak and the helpless,
    and will bring together
       those who were driven away.
I will turn their shame into praise,
    and make them known all over the world.

When that time comes,
       I will gather you together;
    I will bring you home again.
Yes, I will make you known
    among all the people on earth.
They will praise you when I will
    restore you to good fortune,
    says the Lord.

3:14-20

Haggai

In the second year of the reign of King Darius (Duh-RIGH-us)* the prophet Haggai went to the governor of Judah and to the chief priest. To both of them he said, "The Lord God has a message for you: These people say it's not yet the right time to rebuild my temple. To that the Lord says, 'Is it right for you to be living in your nice houses while this house of mine lies in ruins?'"

"Now then," the prophet continued, "the Lord says this: 'Consider how things are going for you. You have planted a lot but have harvested very little. You have food but never enough. . . . You have clothes to wear, but still you are cold. The man who earns wages seems to put them into a bag with holes in it.'

"This is what the Lord says," the prophet continued. "Consider what is happening. Then go up to the mountain and bring down wood and rebuild my house. I want to take pleasure in it and want to be seen in my glory there."

"The Lord also says this: You looked for a lot, and it came to very little. When you brought it home, I blew it away. Why? Because my house lies in ruins while every one of you is busy with your own. That is why the sky has kept back the rain and the earth has produced very little."

Then the governor and the chief priest and all the people who were left in Jerusalem listened to the voice of their God and to what the prophet Haggai had said, because the Lord God had sent him to them. . . . And the Lord stirred up their spirit, and they worked on the house of the Lord, their God. . . .

1:1-12

The Lord's Promises

Then the Lord told Haggai to go again to the governor and the chief priest and the people of Judah and to say this: "Who is there left here who saw this house in its former glory? And how does it look to you now? Compared to what it used to be, this is nothing. But be strong and brave," the Lord said to the governor and the chief priest. "Take courage," the Lord said to the people, "for I am with you as I promised I would be when you came out of Egypt. My spirit remains among you, so don't be afraid."

Then the Lord said: "In a little while I will shake the heavens and the earth, the sea and the dry land. And I will shake all the nations, and the treasures of all the nations will flow in and will fill this temple with glory. All silver is mine and all gold is mine! The glory of this temple you will build is going to be greater than the glory of the temple that was destroyed, says the Lord. And in this place I will give peace and prosperity. It is the Lord who promises this."

2:1-9

Zechariah

When I looked up, I saw a man with a measuring line in his hand. "Where are you going?" I asked him. He said to me, "I'm going to Jerusalem. I'm going to measure it to see how long and how wide it is."

Then, as this angel was talking to me, another angel came forward and spoke to him. "Run!" he said. "Tell that young man that Jerusalem will be inhabited again. It will be filled with people and cattle and will be like the villages without walls. I will be like a wall of fire around her, says the Lord, and I will be her glory within her." *2:1-5*

Something Else the Prophet Saw

Again I looked up and this is what I saw: four chariots (CHAIR-ee-ots)* coming out from between two mountains. The mountains were mountains of brass. The first chariot was pulled by red horses. The second by black horses. The third had white horses. The fourth had dapple greys.

Then I asked the angel who had been talking to me, "What is the meaning of these, my lord?" The angel answered, "These are going out to the four winds of heaven after presenting themselves to the Lord of the whole world. The black horses will go north, and the white ones are going to the west country. The grey ones will go toward the south."

When the red horses came out, they were raring to go. They wanted to patrol the whole earth. So the Lord said to them, "Go and patrol the world." They went and patrolled the whole world.

6:1-7

A Message from the Lord

Again the message from the Lord came to me as follows: The Lord says: "I will return to Mount Zion (ZIGH-on),* and I will live in Jerusalem. She will be called the faithful city, and the mountain* of the Lord will be called the holy mountain.

"Old men and old women will again walk about in the streets of Jersualem, all of them so old they will be walking with a stick. And the streets of the city also will be full of boys and girls playing in the streets."

This is what the Lord says: "You'll see. I will rescue my people from wherever they are, and I will bring them back to live in Jerusalem. They will be my people and I will be their God." . . .

8:1-6, 8

The Promised King

Be very happy, O my people!
Shout with joy, O my children!

Look ahead, your king will be coming to you;
　　he will be the victor.
But still he will be humble, riding on a donkey,
　　on a colt, a donkey's colt!
He will banish the war horse from Jerusalem,
　　and will command peace among nations.
His kingdom will reach from sea to sea,
　　from the river to the ends of the earth.

9:9-10

Malachi

"See here, I am going to send my messenger to prepare a way for me. And the Lord you are seeking will suddenly come to his temple. The angel of my covenant (KUHV-ah-nuhnt),* for whom you are waiting, yes, he is coming," says the Lord.

"But who will be able to stand up to him when he comes. For he is like a fire that refines metals and like soap that cleans the dirtiest clothes. He will be like a refiner and purifier of silver and will refine people like gold and silver. Then they will give offerings to the Lord as they ought to be given, and their offerings will be pleasing to the Lord as they used to be."

3:1-4

Worship the Lord

Then those who worshiped the Lord spoke to one another about him. The Lord heard them, and the names of those who worshiped the Lord and thought about him were written in a book of remembrance. "They will be mine," said the Lord, "my special possession. . . .

"And I will take care of them the way a man takes care of his son who serves him. Once again you will see the difference between the good and the bad, between those who serve God and those who do not.

"For a day will come, hot as an oven, when all the proud and all who do evil will be like dry grass in the path of a fire. They will be burned up, and neither roots nor branches will be left.

"But for you who worship me, the sun of righteousness will rise. There will be healing in his wings. And you will leap like calves being let out of their stalls."

3:16-18; 4:1-2

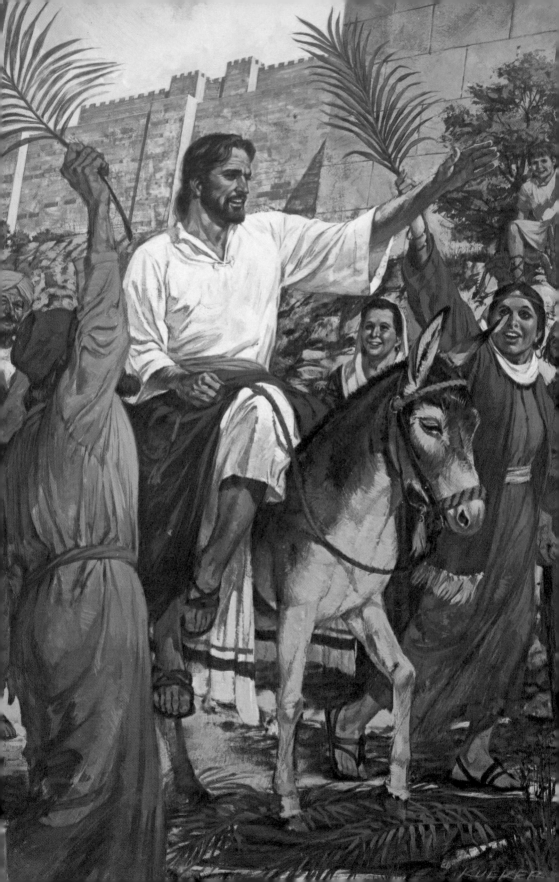

FROM EGYPT TO CANAAN
Entering the Land of Promise

1) The land in Egypt where the Israelites lived
2) The Israelites began their journey here and moved on to Succoth and Eham
3) The Israelites crossed the Red Sea at one of these places
4) The bitter water was made sweet
5) God provided food, manna, and quail
6) God gave Moses the Law on two tablets of stone
7) The first church or tabernacle was built
8) Miriam, sister of Moses, died
9) Moses saw Canaan, died, and God buried him
10) Canaan, the Promised Land, is now Palestine
11) David started this city, and Solomon built the great temple
12) The Israelites, under Joshua, fought their first battle
13) Jacob built an altar and later dug a well
14) Elijah overcomes the prophets of Baal

THE GREAT SEA

Sidon
MT. HERMON
Damascus
Tyre
Dan
BASHAN

14 MT. CARMEL
Sea of Galilee
Megiddo

Shechem
13
Joppa
10
12
Jericho
11
Jerusalem
9 Jahaz
MT. NEBO
Heshbon
Bethlehem
Dibon
Gaza
Hebron
DEAD SEA
MOAB
Beer-sheba
Hormah
Zoar
WILDERNESS OF ZIN
Oboth
Punon
Kadesh-barnea
MT. HOR
8
AMMON
EDOM
Ezion-geber Elath

C A N A A N
JORDAN R.

Sin
Baal-zephon
Succoth
Etham
BITTER LAKES
3
WILDERNESS OF SHUR

SINAI

WILDERNESS OF PARAN

WILDERNESS OF SIN

4 Marah
Elim
5
Hazeroth
7
Taberah
MT. HOREB
Rephidim
6 MT. SINAI

GULF OF SUEZ
GULF OF AQUABA
LAND OF MIDIAN

GOSHEN
EGYPT
2
1

RED SEA

0   20   40   60   80   100

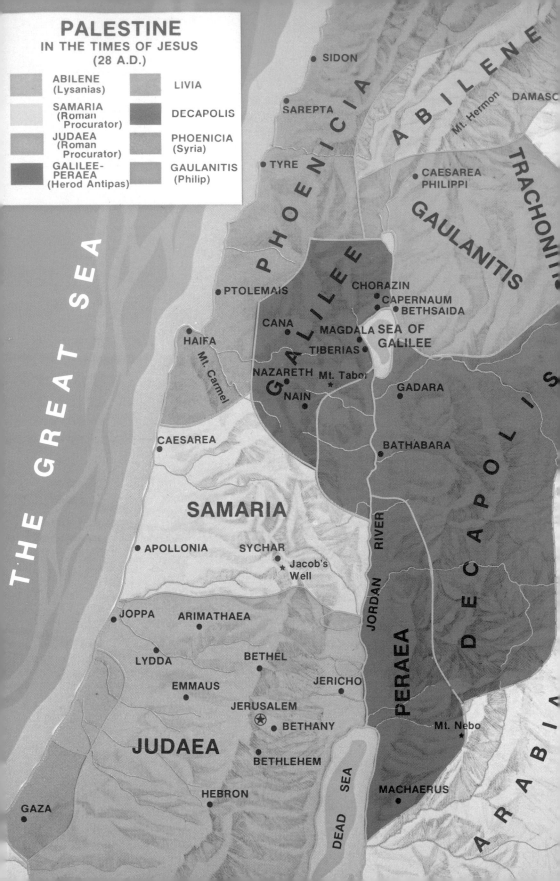

PALESTINE
IN THE TIMES OF JESUS
(28 A.D.)

ABILENE (Lysanias)

SAMARIA (Roman Procurator)

JUDAEA (Roman Procurator)

GALILEE-PERAEA (Herod Antipas)

LIVIA

DECAPOLIS

PHOENICIA (Syria)

GAULANITIS (Philip)

THE GREAT SEA

SIDON

SAREPTA

PHOENICIA

ABILENE

DAMASC

Mt. Hermon

TYRE

CAESAREA PHILIPPI

TRACHONIT

GAULANITIS

PTOLEMAIS

GALILEE

CHORAZIN

CAPERNAUM
BETHSAIDA

CANA

MAGDALA SEA OF
GALILEE

HAIFA

TIBERIAS

Mt. Carmel

NAZARETH

Mt. Tabor

NAIN

GADARA

BATHABARA

CAESAREA

DECAPOLIS

SAMARIA

APOLLONIA

SYCHAR

Jacob's Well

JORDAN RIVER

JOPPA

ARIMATHAEA

LYDDA

BETHEL

PERAEA

EMMAUS

JERICHO

JERUSALEM

BETHANY

JUDAEA

BETHLEHEM

Mt. Nebo

HEBRON

DEAD SEA

MACHAERUS

GAZA

ARABIA

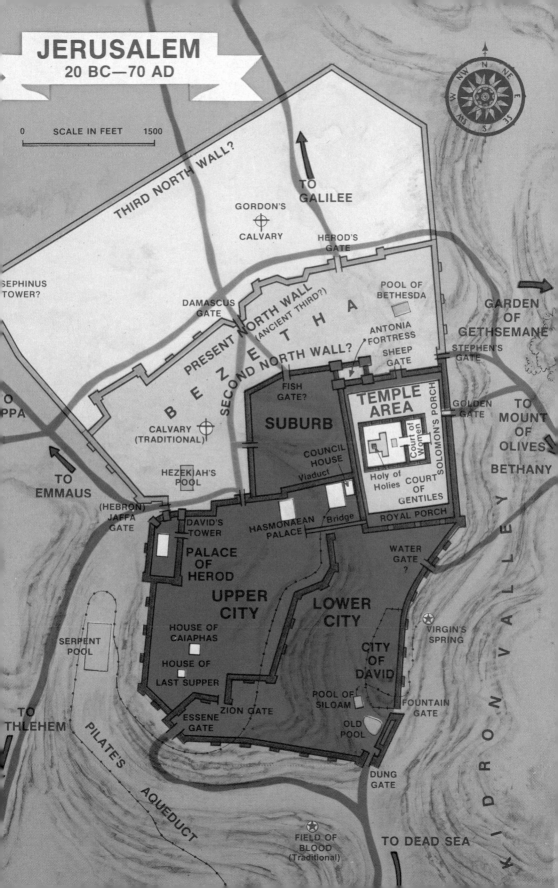

JERUSALEM
20 BC—70 AD

SCALE IN FEET
0   1500

THIRD NORTH WALL?

TO GALILEE

GORDON'S CALVARY

HEROD'S GATE

SEPHINUS TOWER?

DAMASCUS GATE

PRESENT NORTH WALL (ANCIENT THIRD?)

POOL OF BETHESDA

GARDEN OF GETHSEMANE

SECOND NORTH WALL?

ANTONIA FORTRESS

SHEEP GATE

STEPHEN'S GATE

B E Z E T H A

FISH GATE?

SUBURB

TEMPLE AREA

TO JOPPA

CALVARY (TRADITIONAL)

Court of Women

SOLOMON'S PORCH

GOLDEN GATE

TO MOUNT OF OLIVES

COUNCIL HOUSE

Holy of Holies

CORT OF GENTILES

BETHANY

HEZEKIAH'S POOL

Viaduct

TO EMMAUS

(HEBRON) JAFFA GATE

DAVID'S TOWER

HASMONAEAN PALACE

Bridge

ROYAL PORCH

WATER GATE ?

PALACE OF HEROD

SERPENT POOL

UPPER CITY

LOWER CITY

VIRGIN'S SPRING

HOUSE OF CAIAPHAS

CITY OF DAVID

HOUSE OF LAST SUPPER

TO THLEHEM

POOL OF SILOAM

FOUNTAIN GATE

ZION GATE

ESSENE GATE

OLD POOL

PILATE'S AQUEDUCT

DUNG GATE

TO BETHLEHEM

FIELD OF BLOOD (Traditional)

TO DEAD SEA

KIDRON VALLEY

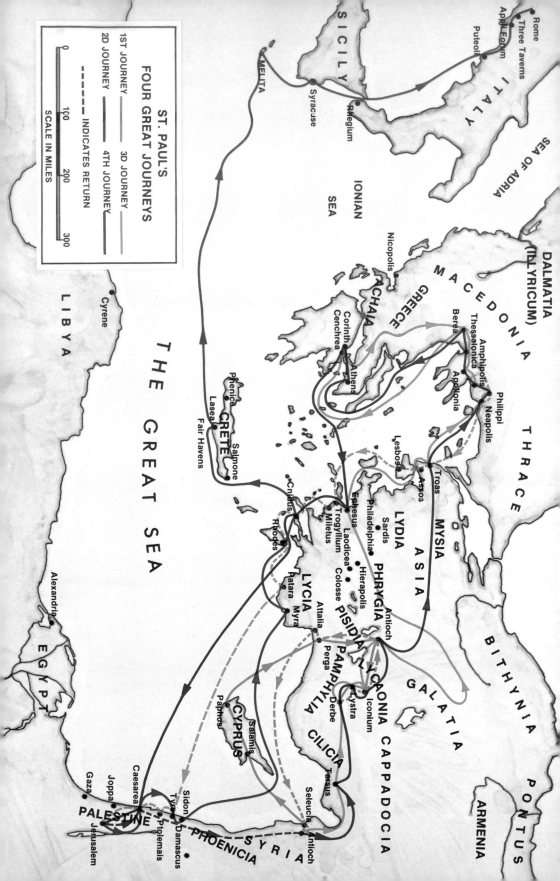

ST. PAUL'S
FOUR GREAT JOURNEYS

1ST JOURNEY
2D JOURNEY
3D JOURNEY
4TH JOURNEY
INDICATES RETURN

SCALE IN MILES

0   100   200   300

SICILY

ITALY

Rome
Three Taverns
Appii Forum
Puteoli

MELITA

Syracuse

Rhegium

SEA OF ADRIA

DALMATIA
(ILLYRICUM)

THRACE

MACEDONIA

IONIAN
SEA

Nicopolis

GREECE
ACHAIA

Corinth
Cenchrea
Athens

Berea
Thessalonica
Amphipolis
Apollonia

Philippi
Neapolis

BITHYNIA

PONTUS

Lesbos

Assos
Troas

MYSIA

ASIA

GALATIA

CAPPADOCIA

ARMENIA

LYDIA

Sardis
Philadelphia

Ephesus
Trogyllium
Miletus

Laodicea
Colosse

Hierapolis

PHRYGIA

Antioch

PISIDIA

Iconium
Lystra
Derbe

LYCAONIA

CILICIA

Tarsus

Seleucia
Antioch

SYRIA

Damascus

PHOENICIA

Sidon
Tyre
Ptolemais

Caesarea

PALESTINE
Jerusalem
Joppa
Gaza

EGYPT

Alexandria

LIBYA

Cyrene

CRETE
Phenice
Lasea
Fair Havens
Salmone

Cnidus

Rhodes

Patara
Myra
LYCIA
Attalia
Perga
PAMPHYLIA

CYPRUS
Salamis
Paphos

THE GREAT SEA

THE
NEW TESTAMENT

THE GOSPEL AS WRITTEN BY
Matthew

The Birth of Jesus

The birth of Jesus happened this way: His mother Mary was engaged to Joseph. But before they began living together, Mary learned that she was going to have a baby by the Holy Spirit.

Now, her husband Joseph was a man who always wanted to do what was right. He didn't want to disgrace Mary publicly, so he made plans to break the engagement secretly.

While Joseph was thinking about this, an angel of the Lord appeared to him in a dream. The angel said, "Joseph, descendant of David, don't be afraid to take Mary as your wife. The baby in her was created by the Holy Spirit. Mary will have a son, and you will name him Jesus, because he will save his people from their sins."

All this happened so that what the Lord had said through his prophet would come true: "Listen! A virgin will conceive and have a son, and he will be called Emmanuel (E-MAN-yu-el)" [which means, God with us].

So when Joseph woke up, he did what the angel of the Lord had told him to do. He took Mary to be his wife. But he had no sex relations with her until after her son was born. Joseph named the child Jesus.

1:18-25

Wise Men Come to See Jesus

Jesus was born in the town of Bethlehem in Judea (Jew-DEE-ah)* during the time when Herod was the king. Soon after that some Wise Men came to Jerusalem from the East. They asked, "Where is he who is born to be the king of the Jews? We saw his star in the east and have come to worship him."

When King Herod (HAIR-ed) heard about this, he became very upset. And so did all the people in Jerusalem who heard this. The king immediately called a meeting of the chief priests and the teachers of the Scriptures. "Where will the Messiah (Meh-SIGH-ah)* be born?" he asked them. "In the town of Bethlehem in Judea," they told him; "for this is what the prophet wrote:

> You, O Bethlehem, in the land of Judah, you are
> by no means the least important among the
> towns of Judah; for from you will come a ruler
> who will rule my people Israel (IS-rah-ail).*"

Then Herod called the Wise Men to a secret meeting with him. At this meeting he asked them the exact time the star had appeared. Then he told them, "Go to Bethlehem and search for the child. When you have found him, come and tell me where he is so that I can go and worship him too."

As the Wise Men went on their way, they again saw the star they had seen in the East. It lead them to the place where the child Jesus was.

When the Wise Men saw where the star had stopped, they became very excited and went into the house. Seeing the boy with his mother, Mary, they knelt down and worshiped him. Then they opened up their treasures and offered him gifts—gold, frankincense, and myrrh (MER).

Later, in a dream, God warned them not to go back and report to King Herod. So they returned to their own country by another way.

2:1-12

The Boyhood of Jesus

After the Wise Men had gone home, an angel of the

Lord appeared to Joseph in a dream. The angel said, "Get up and take the child and his mother to Egypt. Remain there until I tell you to leave because Herod will be searching for the child. He wants to kill him."

So Joseph got up in the night and left for Egypt with the child and his mother; they stayed there until Herod died. This happened so that what the Lord had said through his prophet would come true, "Out of Egypt I called my Son."

When King Herod saw that he had been tricked by the Wise Men, he became furious. He sent his soldiers to Bethlehem and the surrounding area with orders to kill all the baby boys two years old and younger, because the Wise Men had said the star had first appeared two years earlier. . . .

Joseph and his family stayed in Egypt until Herod died. When Herod was dead, an angel of the Lord appeared to Joseph in a dream in Egypt. The angel said, "Get up, take the child and his mother, and go back to the land of Israel (IS-rah-ail). Those who tried to kill the child are dead." So Joseph got up and took the child and his mother back to the land of Israel.

There, in another dream, God warned Joseph not to go to Judea (Jew-DEE-ah) because Herod's son was the new king there. So Joseph took his family to the district called Galilee (GAL-i-lee). There he made his home in a town called Nazareth (NA-zah-reth). This happened so that what the prophet had said would come true, "He will be called a Nazarene (Na-zah-REEN)."

2:13-23

The Baptism of Jesus

In those days John the Baptizer came and started preaching in the desert of Judea. He said, "Turn away from your sins because the kingdom of heaven is coming soon!" John was the person the prophet Isaiah was talking about when he wrote,

There will be a voice shouting in the desert,

"Prepare the way of the Lord; make his paths straight."

John wore a coat made from camels' hair and a leather belt around his waist. His food was grasshoppers and wild honey. People came to hear John from Jerusalem (Je-ROO-sah-lem) and from the whole district of Judea and all along the Jordan River. When they confessed their sins, John baptized them in the River Jordan.

At that time Jesus came to John from Galilee to be baptized by him. At first John didn't want to do it. He said, "I need to be baptized by you, and you come to me?" But Jesus answered, "Do it, because in this way we will be doing all that God requires." So then John agreed to baptize Jesus.

After his baptism Jesus came out of the water. Then he saw the heavens open and the Spirit of God coming down on him like a dove. And a voice from heaven said, "This is my very dear Son, with whom I am well pleased."

3:1-6, 13-17

The Temptations of Jesus

Then the Spirit of God led Jesus into the desert to be tempted by the devil. For 40 days and 40 nights Jesus ate nothing, so he became very hungry. Then the devil came and said to him, "If you are the Son of God, order these stones to become loaves of bread." But Jesus replied, "It is written [in the Scriptures], 'Man cannot live on bread alone, but by every word that comes out of the mouth of God.'"

Then the devil took Jesus to Jerusalem, to the highest point of the temple. There he said to him, "If you are the Son of God, throw yourself down to the ground. For it is written [in the Scriptures],

For God will put his angels in charge of you ...
they will hold you up with their hands so you
won't stub your foot on a stone."

Jesus said, "It is also written, 'You must not tempt the Lord your God.'"

Next the devil took Jesus to the top of a very high mountain. There he showed him all the kingdoms of the world and all their glory. "All these I will give you," he said to Jesus, "if you will kneel down and worship me." But Jesus said to him, "Get away from me, satan! It is written, 'You should worship the Lord your God and serve only him.'"

Then the devil left Jesus and angels came and served him!

4:1-11

Jesus Begins His Work

When Jesus heard that John had been put into prison, he went back to Galilee. But he didn't settle down in Nazareth. He moved to Capernaum (Ka-PER-nah-um), a town by the Sea of Galilee. From that time on Jesus began to preach the message John had preached. "Turn away from your sins and turn to God," Jesus told the people, "because the kingdom of heaven is coming soon!"

One day as Jesus walked along the shore of the sea, he saw two brothers. One of them was Simon, later called Peter; the other was his brother Andrew. They were fishing with a net because they made their living by fishing. Jesus went up to them and said, "Follow me and I will make you men who fish for people." Right away Simon and Andrew left their nets and went with Jesus.

A little farther on Jesus saw two other brothers, James and John. They were sitting in a boat with their father Zebedee (ZEH-beh-dee), mending their nets. Jesus called to them to come with him. Right away they left the boat and their father and went with Jesus.

Jesus traveled all over Galilee, teaching in the synagogues (SIN-ah-gogs). Wherever he went he preached the gospel and healed people who had every kind of sickness. Soon his fame spread through the whole country. So people brought to him their sick and crippled and persons with devils in them. Jesus healed them all. And wherever he went, huge crowds followed him.

4:12, 13, 17-25

A Sermon Jesus Preached

One day when Jesus saw the crowds gathering, he went up a hillside and sat down, and his disciples (dis-SIGH-puls)* came and gathered around him. These are some of the things Jesus said to them there:

"Blessed (BLEH-sed)* are the poor in spirit, because the kingdom of heaven belongs to them.

"Blessed are those who mourn, because they will receive comfort.

"Blessed are the meek, because they will finally win the whole world.

"Blessed are those who are hungry and thirsty for righteousness (RIGH-chus-ness), because they will be satisfied.

"Blessed are the merciful, because they will receive mercy.

"Blessed are the people whose hearts are pure, because they will see God.

"Blessed are the peacemakers, because they will be called sons [and daughters] of God.

"You are the salt of the world. But when salt loses its flavor, how can it be made salty again? It is no longer good for anything, and so it is thrown away.

"You are the light of the world. A city built on a hill cannot be hidden. And no one lights a lamp to put it under a basket. No, it is put on a stand so that it will give light to all in the house.

"Let your light shine so people will see the good things you do and will praise your Father in heaven."

"You heard that it was said, 'Love your neighbor and hate your enemy.' But I say to you, 'Love your enemies and pray for those who hate and hurt you.' In that way you will be the sons [and daughters] of your

216

Father in heaven. For he lets his sun shine on the bad as well as the good people and gives rain to those who do evil as well as to those who do good.

"If you love only people who love you, why should anyone praise or reward you for that? Even rascals do that! And if you greet only your friends, what more are you doing than others do? Even people who aren't Jews do that! You are to be perfect, just as your Father in heaven is perfect."

5:1-9, 13-16, 43-48

Jesus Teaching How to Pray

"When you pray, you must not be like the people who just act religious. They love to stand and pray in the synagogues and in public places so that others will see them. I'm telling you the truth, they get what they want.

"But when you pray, go to your room and shut the door; then pray to your Father secretly there. And your Father, who sees what you do secretly, will bless you.

"And in praying do not just use a lot of words as some people do. They think that God will listen to them because they pray long prayers. Do not be like them, because your Father already knows what you need before you ask him. This is how to pray:

Our Father in heaven,
Hallowed be your name.
Your kingdom come,
Your will be done,
    on earth as it is in heaven.
Give us this day our daily bread;
And forgive us our sins,
    as we forgive those who sin against us;
And lead us not into temptation,
    but deliver us from evil.

"For if you forgive other people what they do wrong, your heavenly Father will also forgive you. But if you don't forgive others what they do wrong, then

217

your heavenly Father will not forgive what you have done wrong."

6:5-15

Mighty Miracles of Jesus

When Jesus came down from the mountain, large crowds followed him back to his town. Along the way a leper (LEP-er)* came up to Jesus and knelt down in front of him. The leper said, "Sir, if you want to, you can make me clean."

Jesus reached out and touched the leper. He said, "I do want to. Be clean!" Right away the man's leprosy disappeared. Then Jesus said to him, "See that you don't say anything about this to anyone, but go straight to a priest. Have him examine you . . . for proof that you are clean."

As Jesus arrived at Capernaum (Ka-PER-nah-um), a Roman army officer came to him and begged for some help. "Lord," he said, "my servant is lying at home sick in bed. He can't move and is suffering great pain." Jesus said to him, "I will come and heal him."

But the army officer said, "Lord, I'm not good enough to have you come into my house. Just give the order and my servant will get well. I know you can do this because I'm a man with soldiers under me. When I say to one of them, 'Go,' he goes, or to another, 'Come,' he comes. And when I say to my slave, 'Do this,' he does it."

When Jesus heard this, he was amazed, and he said to the people who were following him, "I tell you, I have never found faith like this anywhere in Israel." Then to the officer Jesus said, "Go on home. What you believe will be done for you." And the officer's servant became well that very moment.

At Peter's house Jesus found Peter's mother-in-law in bed with a high fever. He took her hand and the fever left her. She got up at once and began to serve him some food.

That evening people brought to Jesus many who

had bad spirits in them. Jesus drove the evil spirits away with a word and healed all who were sick. This was what the prophet Isaiah had said the Messiah would do.

8:1-10, 13-17

Jesus Shows His Power

One day the disciples (dis-SIGH-puls) of John the Baptizer came to Jesus. They said to him, "Why do we and the Pharisees (FAIR-i-sees)* go without eating but your disciples do not?" Jesus answered, "Do you expect the guests at a wedding party to be sad as long as the bridegroom is with them? The day will come when the bridegroom will be taken away from them. Then they will not feel like eating."

While Jesus was still speaking to them, a ruler of the town came to him and knelt down in front of him. The man said, "My daughter just died. But come and lay your hand on her and she will live."

Jesus got up at once and followed the man to his house. His disciples went with him. On the way a woman who had been bleeding for 12 years came up behind Jesus. She said to herself, "If only I can touch his coat, I will get well." So she touched a tassle on the bottom of his coat.

Jesus turned around and, seeing her, said, "Cheer up, daughter. Your faith has made you well." From that moment on the woman was well.

When Jesus came to the ruler's house and saw the players for the funeral music and the crying people, he said, "Everybody get out! The girl is not dead; she's just sleeping!"

At first the people laughed at Jesus. But as soon as the crowd had been put out of the house, Jesus went in. When he took hold of her hand, the girl got up. In no time the news of this traveled all over that part of the country.

9:14-15, 18-26

The Ruler over Rules

At about that time Jesus was walking with his disciples through some grain fields on a sabbath (SA-bahth)* day. The disciples were hungry, so they began to pick and eat some grain. When the Pharisees saw this, they said to Jesus, "Look, your disciples are breaking the law. They are picking grain on the sabbath."

Jesus answered, "Haven't you ever read what David did when he and his men were hungry? He went into the house of God and ate the bread offered to God. It was against the law for them to eat this bread; only the priests were allowed to eat it.

"And haven't you read in the law how the priests (PREESTS)* in the temple work on the sabbath but still are not guilty. . . . God says, 'I want kindness and not sacrifices.' If you know what this means, you would not judge people who are not guilty. The Son of Man is ruler of the sabbath day."

From there Jesus went to one of the synagogues (SIN-a-gogs). And now note, there was a man there who had a crippled hand. And there were some other men there who wanted to catch Jesus doing or saying something wrong. So they asked him, "Is it against our law to heal on the sabbath?"

Jesus said to them, "What if one of you had a sheep, and it fell into a hole on the sabbath? Wouldn't you take hold of it and lift it out? Think of how much more a human being is worth than a sheep! So our law does allow us to do good on the sabbath."

Then Jesus said to the man with the withered hand, "Stretch out your arm." When the man did this, the hand became well, just like the other hand. But instead of being glad, the Pharisees left and talked over ways to get rid of Jesus.

Jesus knew what his enemies were planning, so he left that place. But many people followed him. And he healed all who were sick.   *12:1-15*

The Parable (PER-ah-buhl)* of a Sower (SO-er)*

That same day Jesus went and sat by the sea. There a large crowd gathered around him. The crowd was so large that he got into a boat and sat in it. There he told the people standing on the beaches many things by parables.

He said: "A sower went out to his field to sow some seeds. As he sowed, some seeds fell on a hard path. Soon the birds came and ate them. Other seeds fell on places where there was only a little soil on top of rocky ground. These seeds started to grow quickly, because they had stayed near the top of the ground. But when the sun became hot, they soon died, because they had no roots to give them water.

"Other seeds that the sower sowed fell among weeds. The weeds grew up around the seeds and choked them. But some seeds fell into good ground. And some of these seeds grew into 100 times as much, some 60, some 30. He who has ears better hear," said Jesus.

Later Jesus said to his disciples, "Listen now and learn what the parable of the sower means. When anyone hears the Word about the kingdom [of God] and does not understand it, the devil comes and takes away the good seed from his heart. This is like the seed that was sown along the path. The seed that fell on rocky ground is the person who hears the Word of God and at first is happy about it. But it doesn't sink in deeply. So when troubles come, he stops believing that God loves him.

"The seed that fell among weeds is like the person who hears and learns the Word of God but worries and loves money. This keeps the Word of God from producing any good results in his life.

"As for what was planted on good ground, that's like the person who hears the Word of God and understands it. In such people the seed produces a lot of good fruit."

13:1-9, 18-23

221

Matthew

Jesus Explains His Church

Now when Jesus was on his way to a place called Caesarea Philippi (Seh-za-REE-ah Fill-IP-igh), he asked his disciples, "Who do people say I am?" They answered, "Some say you are John the Baptizer, some say Elijah, and others say Jeremiah or one of the other prophets."

"But who do *you* say I am?" asked Jesus. Simon Peter replied, "You are the Christ, the promised Messiah, the Son of the living God." Jesus said to Peter, "God has blessed you, Simon, son of John. No human being gave you this knowledge. It was given to you by my Father who is in heaven."

"And I tell you," said Jesus, "you are Peter,* and on this kind of rock I will build my church. And not even the forces of death will be able to win against it. I will give you the keys to the kingdom of heaven."

From that time on Jesus began to tell his disciples plainly that he had to go to Jerusalem to suffer many things and that he would be killed and raised from the dead on the third day. Then Peter took Jesus aside and said, "God keep you from all this, Lord! This must never happen to you." But Jesus turned on Peter and said, "Get behind me, devil! You are getting in my way. Your thoughts are human thoughts, not God's way of thinking."

Then Jesus told his disciples, "If anyone wants to come with me, he will have to forget himself and carry his cross and follow me. Whoever tries to save his life will lose it. But whoever will lose his life for my sake will find it."

16:13-19, 21-25

The Greatest in God's Kingdom

At that time the disciples of Jesus came to him and asked, "Who is the greatest in the kingdom of heaven?" Jesus called a young child over to him and had him stand by them. Jesus said, "I'm telling you the truth," said Jesus, "unless you change and become like children, you will never get into the kingdom of heaven. The greatest is the person who humbles himself and becomes like this child."

"And," Jesus continued, "whoever loves such a child in my name loves me. But if anyone causes one of these little ones to stop believing in me, it would be better for that man to have a large stone tied around his neck and that he be drowned in the deep sea."

"See that you don't ever think that these little ones don't matter. Their angels are always in touch with my Father in heaven," said Jesus.

"And what do you think?" asked Jesus. "If a man has a 100 sheep and one of them wanders away, doesn't he leave the 99 in the hills and go and look for the one that is lost? When he finds it, I tell you, he feels happier over it than over the 99 that never went away. In the same way my Father in heaven does not want any of these little ones to be lost."

Then Peter came and asked Jesus, "Lord, how often do I have to forgive my brother who sins against me? Seven times?" Jesus said to him, "I don't say to you just seven times, but seventy times seven."

18:1-6, 10-14, 21-22

The Unforgiving Servant

"The kingdom of heaven," said Jesus, "is like a king who decided to check on what his servants owed him. When he started to do this, a man was brought to him who owed far more than he could ever pay back. So the king said, 'Sell this man and his wife and children and all that he has as a part payment of the debt.'

"When the servant heard this, he got down on his knees and, begging, said, 'Lord, please give me a little more time, and I will pay you everything I owe you.'

"The king felt pity for the man, so he forgave the man everything he owed and let him go free. But that same servant, as he went out, met a fellow servant who

Matthew

owed him just a little. Grabbing the other servant by the throat, he said, 'Pay me what you owe me!'

"Well, the fellow servant knelt down and, begging, said, 'Please give me a little time, and I will pay you.' But the servant refused to wait. He went and had his fellow servant put into jail until he would pay the debt.

"When the other servants saw what had happened, they were very upset. They went and reported to the king what had happened. When the king heard what the unforgiving servant had done, he ordered the man brought to him. 'You wicked servant!' the king said. 'I forgave you everything you owed me just because you begged me to do so. Shouldn't you have had mercy on your fellow servant the way I had mercy on you?'

"Then the king put the unforgiving servant in jail until he would pay back all that he owed." To this Jesus added, "That is how my Father in heaven will treat every one of you if you do not forgive with all your heart."

18:23-35

Children and a Young Man

Then some people brought their children to Jesus. They wanted him to put his hands on them and pray for them. The disciples scolded the people for bothering Jesus. But Jesus said, "Let the children come to me, and don't try to stop them. The kingdom of heaven belongs to people like these."

Then a young man came up to Jesus with a question. "Teacher," he asked, "what good deed must I do to get eternal life?" Jesus said to him, "Why do you ask me about what is good? There is only one who is good. If you want to enter life, keep the commandments."

"Which one?" the young man asked. Jesus answered, "You must not kill. You must not commit adultery.* You must not steal. You must not lie. Honor your father and mother. And love your neighbor as yourself." The young man said, "All these com-

224

mandments I have obeyed. What else must I do?" Jesus said to him, "If you want to be perfect, go and sell everything you own and give the money to the poor. Then you will have riches in heaven. After that come and follow me."

But when the young man heard this, he went away very sad because he was very rich. Then Jesus said to his disciples, "I tell you the truth, it will be very hard for a rich man to enter the kingdom of heaven. And I'll say it again, it is easier for a camel to go through the eye of a needle than for a rich man to enter the kingdom of God."

When the disciples heard this, they were very surprised. "Who, then, can be saved?" they asked. Jesus looked them straight in the eye and said, "It is impossible for anyone to save himself, but with God all things are possible."

19:13-26

On the Way to Jerusalem

As Jesus was leaving Jericho, a large crowd followed. And now note this: two blind men were sitting by the roadside. When they heard that Jesus was passing by, they began shouting: "Son of David, have mercy on us!"

The crowd told the two blind men to be quiet. But they yelled all the louder. "Son of David, have mercy on us!" So Jesus stopped and called to them. "What do you want me to do for you?" he asked them. They answered, "Lord, please open our eyes." Then Jesus, who pitied them, went over and touched their eyes. Right away they were able to see, and they too followed him.

As they came near to Jerusalem, at the Mount of Olives, Jesus sent two of his disciples ahead. "Go to the next village, and you will find a donkey tied there and a colt with her," he said to them. "Untie the animals and bring them to me. If anyone says anything to you, just say, 'The Lord needs them,' and he will let you take them."

All this happened so that what the prophet had said would come true. He had said:

Tell the city of Zion,
Your king is coming to you.
He is humble and rides on a donkey,
On a colt, the foal of a donkey.

The two disciples went and did what Jesus had told them to do. And they brought the donkey and the colt and put their robes on them. And Jesus got on the colt. And many of the people spread their coats on the road. Others cut branches from the trees and spread them on the road.

Then the crowds walking in front of Jesus and behind him began shouting, "Hosanna (Hoe-ZAH-nah)* to the Son of David! Blessed is he who comes in the name of the Lord! Hosanna in the highest!" And when Jesus entered Jerusalem (Je-RUH-sah-lem), the whole city was excited. "Who is this?" the people asked. And the crowds answered, "This is the prophet Jesus from Nazareth up in Galilee."

20:29-34; 21:1-11

Events in the Temple

Jesus went into the temple and drove out all who sold and bought in the temple. He also tipped over the tables of the money changers and the chairs of those who sold pigeons. He said to them, "It is written, 'My house is to be called a house of prayer.' But you are making it a place for thieves."

While Jesus was in the temple, the blind and the crippled came to him there. And he healed them. When the priests and the teachers in the temple saw the wonderful things Jesus was doing and heard children shouting the praises of Jesus, they became angry. They said to him, "Don't you hear what these children are saying?" Jesus answered, "Yes. Haven't you ever read this: Out of the mouths of babies and children you have received perfect praise?"

[When he entered the temple the next morning], Jesus spoke to the people again in parables. He said: "The kingdom of heaven is like a king who prepared a wedding feast for his son. Then he sent his servants to tell the invited guests to come to the feast. But the people would not come. So he sent some other servants. He said to them, 'Tell those who have been invited: My dinner is ready; my steers and fat calves have been roasted, and everything is ready. Come and enjoy the feast!'

"But the invited people didn't take the invitation seriously. They went about their business as usual. One went to his farm, another to his business. Others grabbed the king's servants, mistreated them, and even killed them.

"Well, the king became very angry. He sent his soldiers to kill those murderers and burn down their city. Then he said to his servants, 'My wedding feast is ready, but the people I invited did not deserve it. Now go to the main roads and invite whoever you will find.'

"The servants went out into the street and brought in all the people they could find, both bad and good. So the wedding hall was filled with guests.

"But when the king came in to take a look at the guests, he saw a man who wasn't wearing a wedding robe. The king said to him, 'Friend, how did you get in here without having on a wedding robe?' The man had no answer. Then the king told his servants, 'Tie him up hand and foot and throw him out into the dark. There men will cry and grind their teeth.'"

At the end of his story Jesus said, "Many are called, but few are chosen."

22:1-14

Events Leading to Jesus' Death

When Jesus had finished teaching the people, he said to his disciples, "You know that in two days it will be the Passover celebration. Then I will be handed over to be crucified (KREW-si-fighd)."

The chief priests and the rulers of the people met in the palace of Caiaphas (KAY-a-fuhs), the high priest. They made plans to arrest Jesus and put him to death. "But," they said, "we must not do this during the festival because the people may riot."

While Jesus was at the house of Simon in Bethany, a woman came in with a jar of very expensive perfume. As he sat at a table eating, she poured the perfume on Jesus' head. When the disciples saw this, they became angry. "Why such waste?" they asked. "This perfume could have been sold for a lot of money. That could have been given to the poor!"

Jesus knew what his friends were saying. So he said to them, "Why are you talking about this woman? She has done a good thing to me. You will always have poor people around you, but you won't always have me. She poured this perfume on my body to prepare it for my burial.". . .

Then one of the disciples—the one called Judas Iscariot (JEW-das Iss-CAR-ee-aht)—went to the chief priests and said, "What will you give me if I hand Jesus over to you?" They gave him 30 pieces of silver. From then on Judas looked for a chance to betray Jesus.

26:1-16

The Lord's Supper

On the first day of the Passover celebration the disciples asked Jesus, "Where do you want us to get the Passover meal ready for you?" He said to them, "Go to this man in the city and say to him, 'The Teacher says: My time is near. I will celebrate the Passover with my disciples at your house.'"

The disciples did as Jesus told them. They went and

prepared the supper. That evening Jesus sat at a table with his 12 disciples, and as they were eating, he said, "I'm telling you the truth, one of you will betray me."

The disciples became very upset. They all began to say to him, "Lord, am I the one?" He said, "One who is dipping his bread in the dish with me will betray me." . . . Then Judas, who betrayed Jesus, said, "Master, am I the one?" Jesus said to him, "You have said it."

While they were eating, Jesus took the bread, said a prayer of thanks, broke the bread into pieces, and gave it to his disciples. "Take this and eat it," he said; "this is my body." Then he took a cup, gave thanks to God [for the wine], and gave it to his disciples. "Drink from it, all of you," he said; "this is my blood. It will be poured out for many people for the forgiveness of their sins. . . ."

Then they all sang a hymn and went out to the Mount of Olives. There Jesus said to them, "This very night all of you will leave me. It is written, 'God will strike the shepherd, and the sheep of the flock will be scattered.' But after I am raised back to life, I will go to Galilee ahead of you."

Then Peter spoke up and said to Jesus, "I will never leave you, even if all the rest do." Jesus said to him, "The truth is, Peter, this very night, before the rooster crows, you will say three times that you don't know me." Peter said, "Even if I have to die with you, I will never say I don't know you." And all the other disciples said the same thing.

26:17-35

Jesus in Gethsemane (Geth-SEH-mah-nee)

Then Jesus went with his disciples to a place called Gethsemane. There he said to them, "Sit here while I go and pray." But he took Peter and James and John with him. Then he began to get very sad. He said to them, "The sadness in my heart is so heavy, it's about to kill me. Please stay here and watch with me."

After going a little farther by himself, Jesus threw

himself face down on the ground and prayed. "My Father," he said, "if it is possible, take this cup [of suffering] away from me! But I want you to do what you want, not what I want."

When Jesus returned to the three disciples, he found them asleep. He said to Peter, "Couldn't you watch with me one little hour? You'd better watch and pray so you won't fall into temptation. The spirit is willing but the flesh is weak."

Then Jesus went away a second time. "My Father," he prayed, "if I must drink this cup [of suffering], let your will be done." When he returned, he found the three disciples sleeping again. They couldn't keep their eyes open.

So Jesus went and prayed a third time, saying the same thing. When he returned, he said to the disciples, "Are you still sleeping? Look! The time has come for me to be put into the hands of sinners. Get up and let us go. The man who is betraying me is near."

When Jesus was still speaking, Judas arrived. With him was a large crowd of people carrying swords and clubs. . . . Judas had given the crowd a signal. "The man I will kiss is the one you want. Arrest him," he had said.

So now Judas went straight to Jesus and said, "Hello, Teacher!" Then he kissed Jesus. Jesus said to Judas, "Friend, do what you have come to do." Then the soldiers came up and grabbed Jesus.

One of those who was with Jesus pulled out his sword and started swinging at the high priest's servant, cutting off his ear. Jesus said to him, "Put your sword back in its place. People who use swords will get killed by a sword. Don't you realize that I could call on my Father and that he could send me more than 12 armies of angels at once? . . . But all this is happening to make come true what the prophets wrote in the Scriptures." Then all the disciples left Jesus and ran away.

26:36-56

Jesus on Trial

Those who arrested Jesus took him to the house of Caiaphas, the high priest. There the teachers and the rulers of the people had come together. Peter followed at a distance and went into the yard of the high priest's house. . . . He wanted to see how it would all come out.

The whole group tried to find some reason they could use for putting him to death. But they couldn't find any, even though many people came and told lies about him. Finally two men stepped forward. They said, "This fellow said, 'I am able to destroy the temple of God and to build it up again in three days.'"

The high priest stood up and said to Jesus, "Have you nothing to say to this?". . . But Jesus kept quiet. Then the high priest said, "In the name of the living God I demand that you tell us whether you are the Messiah, the Son of God." To that Jesus answered, "Yes, I am. And I'll tell you this: From now on you will see me sitting at the right side of the almighty God and coming on the clouds of heaven."

Then the high priest tore his robe and said, "Why do we need any more witnesses? You have heard his awful words. What do you think?" They all shouted, "He deserves death." Then they spit in his face and beat him. . . .

All the while Peter was sitting in the courtyard. There a maid came up to him and said, "You also were with Jesus." But he denied it, saying, "I don't know what you're talking about." When he went out to the porch, another maid saw him. She said to those nearby, "This man was with Jesus of Nazareth." Again Peter denied it. He swore and said, "I don't know the man."

After a little while the men standing there came over to Peter. "Of course you are one of them," they said. "The way you speak gives you away." Peter began to curse and swear some more. "I don't even know the man," he said. And then a rooster crowed, and Peter remembered what Jesus had told him: "Before the rooster crows, you will say three times that you don't know me." Peter left the yard and cried and cried.

26:57-77

The Death of Jesus

Early the next morning all the chief priests and rulers of the people made their plans to put Jesus to death. They tied him up and took him to Pilate, the Roman governor.

When Jesus stood before the governor, the governor asked him, "Are you the king of the Jews?" Jesus said, "So you say." . . . Then Pilate said to him, "Don't you hear how many things they are saying against you?" But to that Jesus gave him no answer. The governor was very much surprised at that.

When Pilate saw that he was getting nowhere and that a riot was beginning, he took some water and washed his hands in front of the crowd. "I won't be responsible for putting this man to death," he said. "Do it yourselves." The crowd shouted, "His blood be on us and our children." Then Pilate handed Jesus over to be whipped and crucified (KREW-si-fighd).

As they were going out of the city to crucify Jesus, they met a man named Simon (SIGH-mun) and forced him to carry Jesus' cross. When they came to a place called Golgotha (GUHL-gah-thah), they offered him wine to drink, mixed with vinegar. But after tasting it, he wouldn't drink it.

When they had nailed him to a cross, the soldiers divided his clothes among them by throwing dice. Then they sat around and watched him hanging there. Above his head they had put a written notice that said, "This is Jesus, the king of the Jews."

Two robbers were crucified with Jesus, one on his right side and one to his left. And the people passing by shook their heads and said, . . . "If you are the Son of God, come down from the cross." The chief priests and rulers of the people also made fun of Jesus. They said, "He saved others, but he cannot save himself.". . .

From noon until about three o'clock darkness covered the whole country. At about three o'clock Jesus shouted, "My God, my God, why have you left me?" Some of the people standing nearby said, "That man is calling for Elijah (Ee-LIGH-jah)." One of them ran, and took a sponge, soaked it in cheap wine, put it on a long stick, and tried to make him drink it. The others said, "Wait, let's see whether Elijah will come to save him." Then Jesus gave a loud cry and died.

27:1-2, 11-14, 24-26, 32-50

The Resurrection (Re-zur-RECK-shun) of Jesus

When evening came, a rich man named Joseph went to Pilate and asked for the body of Jesus. This Joseph also was a follower of Jesus. Pilate gave an order that the body be given to Joseph. So Joseph took the body, wrapped it in a clean linen cloth, and laid it in his own grave that he had cut out of rock. Then he rolled a large stone across the door of the grave and went away. Both Mary Magdalene (MAG-dah-leen) and the other Mary were sitting nearby and watching.

On the next day the chief priests and the Pharisees went to Pilate. "Sir," they said, "we remember that while that liar was still alive he said, 'After three days I will become alive again.' So give an order that the grave be guarded until the third day. This will keep the disciples from stealing his body and telling the people, 'He rose from the dead.' This last lie would be worse than the first one." Pilate said to them, "You have soldiers. Go and guard the grave as well as you can."

The day after the sabbath, as the first day of the week was dawning, Mary Magdalene and the other Mary went back to the grave. Suddenly there was a big earthquake. An angel of the Lord came down from heaven and rolled aside the stone from in front of the grave and sat on it. His appearance was like lightning, and his clothes were white like snow. The guards shook with fear when they saw him and became like dead men.

Then the angel spoke to the women. "Don't be afraid," he said. "I know you are looking for Jesus, who was crucified. He is not here; he has risen, as he said he would. Come and see the place where his body was. Then go quickly and tell his disciples that he has risen from the dead. He is going to Galilee ahead of you. There you will see him!"

The women left the grave quickly, very frightened but also full of joy. They ran to tell the disciples the angel's message. On the way Jesus met them and said, "Peace!" And the women went up and took hold of his feet and worshiped him. Jesus said to them, "Don't be afraid. Go and tell my brothers to go to Galilee. There they will see me."

The 11 disciples went to Galilee to the hill where Jesus had told them to go. When they saw him there, they worshiped him, even though some of them couldn't believe it was really Jesus. Then Jesus came nearer to them and said, "The right to rule everything in heaven and on earth has been given to me. Therefore go to people everywhere in the world and make them my disciples. Baptize them in the name of the Father and of the Son and of the Holy Spirit. And teach them to do everything I have commanded. And remember this: I am always with you, and I will be to the end of time."

27:57-66; 28:1-10, 16-20

THE GOSPEL AS WRITTEN BY
Mark

This is the beginning of the news about Jesus Christ, the Son of God. As the prophet Isaiah had written, . . . John the Baptizer appeared in the desert, telling people to turn away from their sins and to be baptized for the forgiveness of sins. And people from all over the country of Judea (Jew-DEE-ah) and many from

Jerusalem came to John. They confessed their sins and he baptized them in the Jordan River.

In those days Jesus came from Nazareth (NA-zah-reth) in the country of Galilee (GAL-i-lee). He too was baptized by John in the Jordan River. When he came out of the water, he saw the heavens open up and the Spirit of God coming down on him like a dove. Then a voice from heaven said, "You are my very dear Son. I am well pleased with you."

Right after that the Spirit of God sent Jesus out into the desert [to be by himself]. For 40 days he was there and was tempted by the devil. There were wild animals around, but the angels of God took care of him.

1:1-5, 9-13

Jesus in Galilee

After John was put into prison, Jesus went to Galilee to preach God's good news. He said, "The time has come for the kingdom of God to appear. Turn away from your sins and believe the gospel."

One day, walking along the Sea of Galilee, Jesus saw two fishermen, Peter and his brother Andrew. They were fishing in the lake with a net. Jesus said to them, "Follow me and I will make you men who fish for people." Right away they left their nets and went with Jesus.

A little farther on Jesus saw James, the son of Zebedee (ZEH-beh-dee), and his brother John. They were in their boat, mending their nets. Jesus called to them. Right away they left their father with the men working for him on the boat and went with Jesus.

When they came to the town called Capernaum (Ka-PER-nah-um), the very next sabbath day Jesus went to the synagogue (SIN-ah-gog) and taught the people. The people who heard him were amazed at the way he taught. He taught them as though he had the right to say what he said. He didn't talk like the scribes (SKRIGHBS) [the teachers of the Scriptures].

At that time there suddenly appeared in the

synagogue a man who had a bad spirit. He began to shout at Jesus, "What do you want with us, Jesus of Nazareth? Did you come to destroy us? I know who you are. You are the holy Son of God." Jesus ordered, "Be quiet and come out of him!" The evil spirit first shook the man and then came out of him with a loud scream.

The people who saw what happened were amazed. They said among themselves, "What is this? Some kind of new teaching? Why, this man gives orders to evil spirits and they obey him!"

When Jesus left the synagogue, he went to the home of Peter and Andrew, taking James and John with him. Peter's mother-in-law was sick in bed with a fever, so they told Jesus about her as soon as he arrived. He went to her, took her by the hand, and helped her get up. Right away the fever left her, and she began to prepare a meal for them.

That evening, at sundown, people brought to Jesus all who were sick or who had evil spirits in them. The whole town came together outside Peter's house. Jesus healed many who were sick, people who had every kind of disease. And from many others he drove out evil spirits. But he wouldn't permit the devils to talk, because they knew him.

The next morning, long before it was daylight, Jesus got up and went to a place where he could be alone. There he prayed. But later Peter and those who were staying with him looked for Jesus. When they found him, they said to him, "Everybody is looking for you." Jesus said to them, "Let's go on to the next towns, so that I can preach there too. That's the reason I came."

So Jesus went all over Galilee, preaching in the synagogues and driving away evil spirits.

1:14-39

Jesus' Troubles Begin

When Jesus returned to Capernaum a few days

236

later, the news got around that he was at home. Soon so many people came to see and hear him that there was no more room, not even outside the door.

As Jesus spoke the word of God to the people, four men came carrying a man who couldn't move his body. When these men couldn't get near to Jesus because of the crowd, they made a hole in the roof above Jesus. Then they let down the bed with the man on it. When Jesus saw their faith, he said to the man on the bed, "Son, your sins are all forgiven."

Now, some teachers of the Old Testament were sitting there. They thought to themselves, "Why does this man talk that way? He's talking as though he's God. Only God can forgive sins."

Jesus knew at once what the teachers were thinking. So he said to them, "Why do you question what I said? Which is easier to say to this man, 'Your sins are forgiven,' or to say, 'Get up, pick up your bed, and start to walk'? I will show you that I have the power to forgive sins on earth." Then he said to the man who couldn't move, "I say to you, get up, pick up your bed, and go home." With that the man got up, picked up his bed, and walked out in front of them all. They were all amazed and praised God. "We have never seen anything like this," they said.   *2:1-12*

Jesus Teaches the People

On another day Jesus again went to the synagogue. And there was a man there who had a crippled hand. Some people who were there watched to see whether Jesus would help the man on a sabbath day. [There were laws against doing things on that day.]

Jesus said to the man with the crippled hand, "Come up here." Then he said to the people who were watching, "Do our laws allow us to do good on sabbath days or to do harm, to save lives or to destroy them?" But the people just looked at him and said nothing.

Jesus looked around at them. He was angry and sad over the way they thought. Then he said to the man,

"Put out your hand." When he held it out, the hand was healed. Right away the strict religious law keepers left the synagogue and had a meeting on how they might kill Jesus.

Jesus and his disciples went away to the Sea of Galilee. A big crowd of people followed him. People from Jerusalem and from the other side of the Jordan River also heard what Jesus was doing and came to him. Jesus told his disciples to get a boat ready to rescue him because sick people kept pushing toward him to try to touch him. And whenever the people who had evil spirits in them got near him, they would fall down and scream, "You are the Son of God."

Afterwards Jesus went up into a mountain and invited the men he wanted for his work to join him there. They came, and he chose 12 to be with him to preach the good news of God's love and to drive away devils.

When Jesus returned to the house where he stayed, the crowds came again. Jesus and his disciples couldn't even find time to eat. When his family heard about this, they went to get him because people were saying he was out of his mind. And the religious teachers who came from Jerusalem said, "He has the devil in him!" Others said, "He gets the power to drive away devils from the chief of the devils."

So Jesus called some of them to him and asked them, "How can the devil drive away the devil? If a country divides itself into parts that fight each other, it cannot last. And if members of a family fight each other, that family won't last. And if the devil fights against himself, he cannot last."

Then the mother and brothers of Jesus came and, standing outside his house, they sent a message to him. There were many people around him in the house. They told him, "Your mother and your brothers are outside, asking for you."

Jesus said to them, "Who are my mother and my brothers?" Then, looking around at those who were sitting there with him, he said, "Here are my mother and my brothers! Whoever does what God wants him to do is my brother and my sister and my mother."

3:1-15, 20-26, 31-35

More Miracles of Jesus

One day, when evening had come, Jesus said to his disciples, "Let's go across to the other side [of the lake]." So they left the crowd [to which Jesus had been talking] and took Jesus with them in a boat. . . . Soon a very strong wind came up, and waves began splashing into the boat. The boat started filling up with water.

Jesus was in the back of the boat, sleeping with his head on a pillow. The disciples were scared. They woke him and shouted, "Teacher, don't you care that we're about to die?" Jesus got up at once and told the wind to stop blowing. Then he said to the sea, "Be still!" And the wind stopped and everything became calm.

Then Jesus said to his disciples, "Why are you so afraid? Don't you have any faith?" They . . . said to one another, "Who is this man? Even the wind and the sea obey him!"

When Jesus had crossed back to the other side of the lake, a big crowd again gathered around him. While he was still by the sea, one of the officers of the synagogue came to Jesus. His name was Jairus (Jah-EYE-rus). He threw himself down at Jesus' feet and begged him for help. He said, "My little daughter is about to die. Please come and touch her so that she'll get well and will live." Jesus went with him, and the big crowd followed Jesus, crowding around him on the way.

In the crowd there was a woman who had been bleeding for 12 years. She had had many doctors and had spent all the money she had. But instead of getting better she grew worse. Because she had heard about Jesus, she came up behind him in the crowd and touched his robe. You see, she had thought to herself, "If I just touch his clothes, I'll get well."

Well, the bleeding stopped at once, and she could feel that she was rid of her trouble. Jesus, knowing that some power had gone out of him, turned around and said, "Who touched my coat?" His disciples answered, "You can see how many people are pushing around you. And still you ask, 'Who touched me?'" But Jesus kept looking around to see who had done it.

The woman, knowing what had happened to her, came shaking with fear. She knelt down at his feet and told him the whole truth. He said to her, "Daughter, your faith has made you well. Go in peace and be rid of your trouble."

While Jesus was saying this, some people came from Jairus' house. They told him, "Your daughter is dead. Why bother the teacher anymore?" But Jesus paid no attention to what they said. He told Jairus, "Don't be afraid; only believe." Then he allowed only Peter and James and his brother John to go on with him.

When they came to the house of the officer of the synagogue, Jesus saw the people crying and making a lot of noise. "Why all this noise and crying? The child is not dead; she's only sleeping," he said. Well, the people laughed at him [for saying that]. So he sent them all out of the house.

Then Jesus took the child's father and mother and the three disciples whom he had brought with him and went in where the child was. Taking her by the hand he said to her, "Little girl, get up, I tell you!" At once the girl got up and started walking around. She was 12 years old.

The people were very amazed at what Jesus had done. But Jesus gave them strict orders not to tell anyone. "Give her something to eat," he said.

4:35-41; 5:21-43

Jesus Visits His Hometown

Soon after Jesus left the house of Jairus, he went back to his hometown. His disciples went with him.

And on the sabbath day he began to teach in the synagogue. Many people were there.

When the people heard him, they were surprised. They said, "Where did this man get to know all this? What wisdom has been given to him! What mighty works are done by him! But isn't he the carpenter, the son of Mary and the brother of James and Joseph, Judas and Simon? And aren't his sisters living here with us?" So they didn't think he was the promised Savior.

Then Jesus said to them, "A prophet is never without honor except in his own hometown and among his relatives and in his own house." And Jesus was not able to do any miracles there, except that he laid his hands on a few sick people and healed them. And he wondered about their lack of faith. Then he went to other villages near there, teaching the people [about God and life with him].

6:1-6

The Work of the 12 Disciples

Then Jesus called his 12 disciples to him and began to send them out two by two. He gave them the right to rule over evil spirits, and he told them to take nothing along with them on their trips except a walking stick. They were to take no food and no money. And they were told to wear sandals but not an extra coat. "When you are invited to stay in a house," said Jesus, "stay there until you leave that town. If in any place you are not welcomed and the people refuse to listen to you, leave and shake the dust off your feet.". . .

So the 12 disciples went and preached that people should turn away from their sins. And they drove away many devils and rubbed oil on many people who were sick and healed them.

When the disciples returned, they met with Jesus and told him everything they had done and taught. But there were so many people coming and going, they didn't even have time to eat. So Jesus said to them,

"Let's go off by ourselves to some place where we can be alone and you can rest awhile." So they went away in a boat to a place where they could be by themselves.

But many people saw them leave and knew who they were [and where they were going]. So they ran on foot and got to the place ahead of Jesus and his friends. When Jesus came to the shore and saw the large crowd, he felt sorry for them because they were like sheep without a shepherd. So he began to teach them many things they needed to know.

When the day was almost over, the disciples of Jesus came to him and said, "It's already late and this is a lonely place. Send the people away to the villages near here to buy something to eat." But Jesus said to them, "You give them something to eat." They said to him, "Do you want us to go and buy enough bread and give it to them?" Jesus said, "How many loaves of bread do you have here? Go and see." When they found out, they came and said, "Five, and two fish."

Then Jesus told his disciples to make all the people sit down in groups on the green grass. So they sat down in groups of 100 and groups of 50. And taking the five loaves and the two fish, Jesus looked up to heaven and gave thanks to God for them. Then he broke the bread and gave it to his disciples to give to the people. He also divided the two fish among them all.

And all the people ate and had enough. The disciples even collected 12 basketfuls of what was left of the bread and the fish. The number of men who ate was 5,000.

6:7-13, 30-44

Jesus Walks on Water

Right after that Jesus made his disciples get into a boat and go ahead of him to the other side of the lake. He sent the people away. After saying good-bye to his disciples, he went up the mountain to pray.

When evening came, the disciples in the boat were half way across the lake. Jesus was still on the land, but he saw that his disciples were having trouble rowing the boat. The wind was blowing against them.

So about three o'clock in the morning Jesus came to them. He walked on the water. At first he was going to walk past them. When they saw him walking on the water, the disciples thought it was a ghost and screamed. And when they saw it was Jesus, they were very frightened.

But Jesus came and talked to them. He said, "Don't be afraid. It is I." Then he came over and got into the boat with them. At once the wind stopped. And they were completely amazed. They had not understood what they should have learned from the loaves of bread; their minds were closed.

When they finally crossed the lake, they tied up the boat on the shore. As they left, people recognized Jesus. So they ran at once through the whole neighborhood and began to bring sick people to him on their mats.

And wherever Jesus went—to villages, cities, or country places—people would bring the sick to the marketplaces and beg him to let the sick at least touch the bottom of his robe. And all who touched it were made well.

6:45-56

Jesus Feeds the Hungry

Again a big crowd of people came together to hear Jesus. When they had nothing left to eat, Jesus called his disciples to him. He said to them, "I feel sorry for these people. They have been with me three days and have nothing left to eat. If I send them home hungry, they will faint on the way. Some of them have come a long distance."

The disciples said, "How can anyone feed all these people here in the desert?" "How much bread do you have?" Jesus asked them. They said, "Seven loaves."

Jesus told the people to sit down on the ground. Then he took the seven loaves of bread and thanked

God for them. After breaking the bread into pieces, he gave them to his disciples to give to the people.

The disciples also found a few small fish. Jesus first gave thanks also for these. Then he had his disciples give the fish to the people too. Everybody ate and had enough. There were about 4,000 people. And when they collected the leftovers, there were seven basketfuls. Then Jesus sent the people away and got into a boat with his disciples and went to another part of the country. . . .

When they came to a town called Bethsaida (Beth-SAY-ee-dah), some people brought a blind man to Jesus. They begged him to touch and heal the man. Jesus took the blind man by the hand and led him outside the town.

After putting some spit on the man's eyes, Jesus laid his hands on them. Then he asked, "Can you see anything?" The man looked up and said, "Yes, I can see people, but they look like trees walking around."

Again Jesus put his hands on the man's eyes. This time the man looked hard and his eyes were healed. He could see everything clearly. As Jesus sent him home he told him, "Don't even go back into the town."

8:1-10, 22-26

The Greatness of Jesus

Then Jesus and his disciples went on to some towns in another part of the country. On the way he asked his disciples, "Who do people say I am?" They answered, "Some say you are John the Baptizer; others say you are Elijah; and others think you are one of the prophets."

"But who do you say I am?" Jesus asked them. Peter answered, "You are the Christ." Jesus ordered them not to tell anyone [yet].

And Jesus began to teach them that the Savior would have to suffer many terrible things. . . . He also told them he would be killed but that after three days he

244

would become alive again. This Jesus said plainly to them.

So Peter took Jesus aside and began to scold him [for saying things like that]. But Jesus turned and looked at his disciples. Then he said to Peter, "Get behind me, Satan (SAY-tun).* Your thinking is not God's thinking; it's human thinking."

Then Jesus called the crowd and his disciples over to him. "If anyone wants to come with me," he told them, "he must forget himself and carry his cross and follow me. Whoever wants to keep his own life safe will lose it. But whoever gives up his life for my sake and for the sake of the gospel will save it. . . ."

Six days later Jesus took Peter, James, and John with him to the top of a mountain to be by themselves. There, as they were looking at him, he changed, and his clothes became very shiny white, whiter than anyone on earth could ever make them. Then the three disciples also saw Moses and Elijah talking with Jesus.

Peter said to Jesus, "Teacher, it's good to be here. Let us make three shelters, one for you, one for Moses, and one for Elijah." Peter really didn't know what else to say. All three were very frightened.

Then a cloud came over them and a voice from the cloud said, "This is my much-loved Son. Listen to him." They quickly looked around, but they no longer saw anyone with them except Jesus.

As they were coming down the mountain, Jesus ordered them not to tell anyone what they had seen. They were to wait until he had risen from the dead. So they kept the matter to themselves, but they often asked each other what Jesus meant by saying he would rise from the dead.

8:27-35; 9:2-10

Who Is the Greatest?

When they came to Capernaum (Ka-PER-nah-um) and were settled in the house where they stayed, Jesus asked his disciples, "What were you talking about on the way?" But they wouldn't answer him, because on the way they had been arguing over who the most important person was in their group.

Well, Jesus sat down and called the 12 disciples around him. He said to them, "Whoever wants to be first [or the greatest] must be last and must be the servant of all." He also called a little child who was in the house and had him stand in front of them. Then he put his arms around the child and said, "Whoever welcomes a child like this for me welcomes me; and whoever welcomes me, not only welcomes me, but also my Father who sent me."

When they left that place, they went to the country called Judea (Jew-DEE-ah)* and crossed over to the other side of the Jordan River. . . . There some people brought children to him. They wanted Jesus to touch [and bless] their children.

But the disciples scolded the people for wanting to bother Jesus and tried to chase them away. When Jesus saw this, he was very angry. He said to them, "Let the children come to me. Don't try to stop them. The kingdom of God is made up of people like these children. I'm telling you the truth, whoever does not come to God as a little child would cannot enter his kingdom." Then he took the little children into his arms, placed his hands on their heads, and kissed them.

9:33-37; 10:1, 13-16

A Rich Young Man

As Jesus was starting again on his trip, a young man ran up to him and knelt down in front of him. He said to Jesus, "Good Teacher, what must I do to have a life that will last forever?" Jesus said to him, "Why do you call me good? No one is good except God. You know the commandments: Do not kill. Do not commit adultery. Do not steal. Do not lie. Do not cheat anyone. Honor your father and mother."

The young man said to Jesus, "Teacher, I have

obeyed all these commandments ever since I was young." But Jesus looked at him with love and said, "There is still one thing for you to do. Go and sell everything you have and give the money to poor people, and you will have riches in heaven. Then come and follow me."

When the young man heard this, his face fell. He turned and went away very sad because he was very rich. Jesus looked around at his disciples and said to them, "How hard it is for rich people to enter the kingdom of God."

The disciples were surprised to hear Jesus say this. So Jesus continued to talk about it. He said, "My children, it is very hard to get into the kingdom of God. It is easier for a camel to go through the eye of a needle than for a rich man to get into God's kingdom."

On hearing this the disciples were completely surprised. "Then who can be saved?" they asked. Jesus looked straight at them and said, "It is impossible for human beings to save themselves, but all things are possible for God. God can save people."

Then Peter spoke up and said, "Look, we have left everything and followed you." To that Jesus replied, "I tell you the truth, anyone who leaves his home or brothers or sisters or mother or father or children for me and for the sake of the gospel will receive 100 times more in this life—houses and brothers and sisters and mothers and children and lands—and also some troubles. And in the world to come he will receive eternal (ee-TER-nal)* life."

10:17-30

Jesus Comes to Jerusalem

As they were going to Jerusalem, Jesus was walking ahead. Those who followed were afraid [of what was ahead]. So Jesus again took the 12 disciples aside and told them what was going to happen to him. He said, "Listen, we are going to Jerusalem, and the Savior will be handed over to the leaders and teachers of the church. They will say he must be put to death. And they will hand him over to people who are not Jews, and they will make fun of him and will beat him and spit on him and kill him. But three days later he will rise from the dead."

When they were near Jerusalem, by the Mount of Olives, Jesus sent two of his disciples on ahead. He said to them, "Go to the village just ahead of you. As soon as you arrive, you will find a colt tied there, one on which no one has ever sat. Untie it and bring it to me. If anyone asks you, 'Why are you doing that?' say, 'The Lord needs it. He will send it right back.'"

So the two disciples went, and they found a colt out in a street. It was tied to the door of a house. As they were untying it, some men who were standing there said, "Why are you untying that colt?" They answered what Jesus had told them to say, so the men let them go.

When the disciples brought the colt to Jesus, they put their coats on the animal's back. Then Jesus got on. As he went riding down the road, many people laid their coats on the road in front of Jesus; others cut branches and laid them down on the road.

The people who went in front of Jesus and those who followed behind began to shout. "Hosanna! Great and blessed is he who comes in the name of the Lord! Blessed [by God] is the coming kingdom of our father David," they shouted. "Praise [be to God] in the highest heaven!"

As soon as Jesus entered the city of Jerusalem, he went to the temple and looked around. But because it was already late, he went out to the town of Bethany [to spend the night there] with his 12 disciples.

10:32-34; 11:1-11

Jesus in the Temple

The next day, when they returned to Jerusalem, Jesus went back to the temple. There he began to chase out all those who sold and bought things in the temple.

He turned over the tables of the money changers and the chairs of those who sold pigeons. And Jesus wouldn't let anyone carry things into the temple grounds.

Jesus said to the people, "Isn't it written [that God said], 'My house will be called a house of prayer for all people'? But you have made it a place for thieves!" Then the chief priests and the religion teachers began looking for a way to kill Jesus. They were becoming more and more afraid of him because so many people were becoming interested in his teachings. When evening came, Jesus and his disciples left the city.

The next morning they came back to Jerusalem. As Jesus was walking in the temple yard, the chief priests and other officers of the temple came to him. "What right do you have to do these things?" they asked him. "Who gave you the right to do them?" Jesus answered, "First I'll ask you a question. If you will answer me, I'll tell you what right I have to do what I do. Tell me, where did John's right to baptize come from? From heaven or from people?"

Then they argued between themselves. They said, "If we say, 'From heaven,' he will say, 'Then why didn't you believe him?' But how can we say, 'From people'?" They were afraid of the people because everyone thought John had been a prophet of God. So their answer to Jesus was, "We don't know." Jesus said to them, "Then I won't tell you by what right I do the things that I do."

11:15-19, 27-33

The Most Important Commandments

One of the teachers of religion, seeing that Jesus answered well, asked, "Which commandment is the most important of all?" Jesus answered, "The first one is, 'Listen, Israel! The Lord our God is one Lord, and you must love the Lord your God with all your heart, with all your soul, and with all your mind, and with all your strength.' The second most important commandment is this: 'You must love your neighbor as yourself.' There is no other commandment greater than those two."

Then the teacher said to Jesus, "You are right. It's true, as you said, that only the Lord is God and that there is no other god. And to love him with one's whole heart and with all of one's understanding and with all of one's strength, and to love one's neighbor as himself—that is much more important than to offer animals and other sacrifices to God."

When Jesus saw that the man answered wisely, he said to him, "You are not far from the kingdom of God." After that no one dared to ask Jesus any more questions.

Then Jesus went and watched the people put their money into the boxes for the temple. Many rich people put in large amounts. But a poor widow (WI-doh)* came along and only put in two small coins worth about a penny.

Seeing this, Jesus called his disciples over to him and said to them, "I tell you the truth, this poor widow put more into the box than all the others who gave to the temple. The others only gave what they could easily spare, but she put in all she had, all she had to live on."

12:28-34, 41-44

Getting Ready for the End

As Jesus was leaving the temple, one of his disciples said to him, "Look, Teacher, what wonderful stones and wonderful buildings!" Jesus said to him, "Yes, you see those great buildings? The time is coming when there will not be one of those stones left on another. They will all be torn down."

Later, as Jesus sat on the Mount of Olives opposite the temple, Peter, James, John, and Andrew asked him, "When will all this happen?" Jesus said, "No one knows when that day or hour will come. Not even the angels in heaven know this, nor the Son, but only the heavenly Father knows."

Two days before the Passover celebration Jesus was in the home of a man who had been a leper. His name was Simon. While they were eating, a woman came in with a jar of very expensive perfume. She broke open the jar and poured the perfume on Jesus' head.

Some of the people there thought to themselves, "Why was all this perfume wasted? It could have been sold, . . . and this money could have been given to the poor!" So they scolded her. But Jesus said, "Let her alone. Why give her trouble? She has done a beautiful thing to me. You will always have poor people around you, and anytime you want to you can be good to them. But you will not always have me with you," said Jesus.

"She did what she could," Jesus continued. "She poured perfume on my body to make it ready to be buried. And I tell you the truth," he said, "wherever the gospel will be preached all over the world, what she did will be told."

Then Judas (JEW-dahs), one of the 12 disciples, went to the chief priests and offered to help them capture Jesus. They were very glad to hear what he was willing to do and promised to give him some money. So Judas started to look for a way to betray Jesus.

13:1-4, 32; 14:1-11

The Lord's Supper

On the first day of the Passover* celebration, the day the lambs for the meal were killed, the disciples of Jesus asked him where he wanted them to go and prepare the Passover (PASS-over)* meal. Jesus sent two of the disciples to Jerusalem.

He said to them, "Go into the city. There you will see a man carrying a pot of water coming toward you. Follow him. At the house he enters, say to the owner, 'Our teacher says: Where is the room where I am to eat the Passover meal with my disciples?' He will show you a large upstairs room, fixed up and ready. Prepare the meal for us there."

So the two disciples went to the city and found what Jesus had told them. There they prepared the Passover meal. When it was evening, Jesus came with his other disciples. While they were eating at the table, Jesus said, "I tell you the truth, one of you will betray me, one who is eating with me."

The disciples became very upset and all asked him, one after the other, "Am I the one?" He said to them, "It will be one of you 12, one who is dipping his bread in the dish with me. The Son* of Man will die as the Scriptures said he would, but it will be very sad for that man who will betray him. It would have been better for that man if he had not been born!"

And while they were eating, Jesus took the bread and gave a prayer of thanks for it. Then breaking it, he gave it to his disciples. "Take and eat it," he said, "this is my body." Then he took the cup and gave thanks to God for the wine. Then he passed the cup to his disciples, and they all drank from it. "This is my blood, which will be poured out for many people," he said. "My blood seals God's covenant (KUHV-eh-nuhnt)."* . . . Then they sang a hymn and went out to the Mount of Olives.

14:12-26

In the Garden

They went to a place called the Garden of Gethsemane (Geth-SEH-mah-nee). There Jesus said to his disciples, "Sit here while I go and pray." And he took with him Peter and James and John, and he began to feel very sad. He said to them, "The sadness in my heart is almost killing me. Stay here and watch."

Then Jesus went a little farther and threw himself on the ground. He prayed that, if it were possible, his time of suffering might pass. He said, "Abba (AH-bah),* Father, for you all things are possible. Please take this cup [of suffering] away from me. But don't do what I want; only what you want."

When Jesus returned, he found the disciples asleep. He said to Peter, "Simon, are you asleep? Couldn't you stay awake for just one hour?" . . . Then Jesus went away once more and prayed, saying the same words. When he came back, he found them sleeping again. They just couldn't keep their eyes open. And they didn't know what to say to Jesus.

When Jesus came back a third time, he said to them, "Are you still sleeping and resting? Enough of that! The time has come when the Son of Man will be put into the power of sinful men. Get up and let us go. See, the man who is handing me over to my enemies is near."

While Jesus was still speaking, Judas, one of the 12 disciples, arrived. With him was a crowd of people carrying swords and clubs. They had been sent by the chief priests and the rulers and teachers of the temple. Judas had given them a signal. "The man I will kiss is the one you want," he had told them. "Grab him and take him away." As soon as Judas arrived, he went up to Jesus and said, "Master!" and kissed him.

Then the mob grabbed Jesus and held him. But one of the disciples standing nearby pulled out his sword and swung at the high priest's servant, cutting off his ear. Jesus said to the crowd, "Did you have to come with swords and clubs to capture me, as though I'm a robber? Many a day I was with you in the temple, teaching, and you did not arrest me. But what the Scripture said would happen must happen." Then all the disciples left Jesus and ran away.

14:32-50

Jesus on Trial

The crowd took Jesus to the high priest's house, where all the chief priests and rulers were meeting. . . .

These men tried to find some report against Jesus that they could use as a reason for killing him. But they couldn't find any. Many people told lies against Jesus, but their stories didn't agree.

Finally some men stood up and told this lie against Jesus: "We heard this man say, 'I will tear down this temple that was made with human hands, and in three days I will build another not made with hands.'" But not even they could get their stories to agree.

Then the high priest stood up and asked Jesus, "Haven't you any answer to what these men say against you?" But Jesus kept silent and gave no answer. Then the high priest asked him, "Are you the Christ, the Son of God?" To that Jesus said, "I am; and you will someday see me sitting at the right side of God and coming on the clouds of heaven."

When the high priest heard this, he tore his robe [to show his anger] and said, "Why do we need any more witnesses? You all heard what he said. What is your decision?" And they all voted that he should be put to death. Some of the people began to spit on him. Others covered his face and hit him and asked him to tell who had hit him. . . .

As soon as it was morning the chief priests and the other rulers had another meeting. They decided to take Jesus to Pilate (PIGH-lught).* Pilate asked Jesus, "Are you the king of the Jews?" Jesus answered, "You have said so." But the leaders of the people said many things againt Jesus. So Pilate asked him, "Don't you have anything to say? Listen to all the things they are saying against you!" Jesus remained silent, and Pilate was surprised at that.

Now, at every Passover celebration Pilate set free any prisoner the people chose. Among the men in prison at that time was a man called Barabbas (Bah-RAB-bus). He had killed some people in a riot. So when a crowd came and asked Pilate for the usual favor, he asked them, "How about me freeing the king of the Jews?" He knew the chief priests had handed Jesus over to him because they were jealous. But the priests got the people to ask Pilate to set Barabbas free instead of Jesus.

Pilate said to the crowd, "What do you want me to do with the man you call the king of the Jews?" They shouted, "Nail him to a cross!" "Why! What wrong has he done?" asked Pilate. They only shouted louder, "Nail him to a cross." So Pilate, wanting to please the crowd, set Barabbas free. And after having his soldiers whip Jesus, Pilate ordered that Jesus be nailed to a cross.

The soldiers first took Jesus into the yard of the governor's palace and called together the rest of their company. There they put a purple robe on Jesus and made a crown out of thorny branches and put it on his head. Then they began to salute him, saying, "Hail, king of the Jews!" They also beat him on the head with a stick, spit on him, and knelt down in front of him.

When they got tired of making fun of him, they took off the purple robe and put his own clothes on him. Then they took him out to crucify (KREW-si-figh)* him. On the way they forced a man named Simon from Cyrene* to carry Jesus' cross. Simon had been coming into the city from another country.

14:53-65; 15:1-21

The Death of Jesus

They brought Jesus to a place called Golgotha (GUHL-gah-thah), which means the place of a skull. There they first tried to give him some wine mixed with a pain-killer, but he refused to drink it. So they nailed him to a cross and divided his clothes among them by throwing dice to see what each one would get. It was nine o'clock in the morning when they nailed him to the cross. . . .

About noon the whole country became dark, and it stayed that way for three hours. At three o'clock Jesus shouted loudly, "My God, my God, why have you left me?" Some of the people who heard him said, "Listen, he is calling Elijah (E-LIGH-jah)."* One of them ran and filled a sponge with vinegar, put it on a long stick, and gave it to Jesus for a drink. He said, "Let us see whether Elijah will come to take him down from the cross."

But Jesus gave a loud cry and died. At that moment the curtain hanging in the temple split in two from top to bottom. And when the army captain who was standing there facing Jesus saw how he died, he said, "This man really was the Son of God!"

Toward evening, since it was the day before the sabbath, Joseph of Arimathea (Air-ri-mah-THEE-ah) . . . went to Pilate and asked for the body of Jesus. Pilate was surprised to hear that Jesus was already dead. He called the army captain and asked him whether Jesus was dead. When he heard the captain's report, he told Joseph he could have the body.

Joseph bought a linen cloth, took the body down from the cross, wrapped it in the sheet, and placed the body in a grave he had dug out of a rock. Then he rolled a large stone across the door of the grave. Mary Magdalene (MAG-dah-leen) and Mary, the mother of Joses, saw where Jesus' body was laid.

15:22-39, 42-47

Jesus Rises from Death

After the sabbath day was over, Mary Magdalene, and Mary the mother of James, and another woman bought some spices. They wanted to put these on the body of Jesus. Very early the next day, the first day of the week, they went to the grave at sunrise. On the way they said to one another, "Who will roll away the stone from the door of the grave for us!" It was a very large stone. And when they looked, they saw that the stone had been rolled away.

When the women entered the grave, they saw a young man sitting at the right side. He was dressed in a white robe. At first they were frightened. "Don't be frightened," he said to them. "I know you are looking for Jesus of Nazareth, who was crucified. He has risen from death; he is not here. See, here is the place where they laid him. Now go, tell his disciples and Peter that he is going to Galilee ahead of you. There you will all see him, just as he told you."

The women ran from the grave; they were shaking. And they said nothing to anyone. They were too frightened to talk.

After Jesus became alive he appeared first to Mary Magdalene. She went and told his friends, who were sad and crying. When they heard that Jesus was alive and had been seen by her, they wouldn't believe it. Soon after this Jesus appeared to two disciples while they were walking into the country. They went back and told it to the others, but they still wouldn't believe it.

Later Jesus appeared to the 11 disciples as they were eating together. First he scolded them for not believing those who had seen him alive. Then he said to them, "Go to the whole world and preach the gospel to all people. Whoever believes and is baptized will be saved. Whoever does not believe will have to suffer for his sins." . . . Then the Lord Jesus, after he had talked to his disciples, was taken up to heaven. There he sat down at the right side of God. And the disciples went and preached everywhere. And the Lord worked with them.

16:1-20

THE GOSPEL AS WRITTEN BY

Luke

At the time when Herod was king of Judea (Jew-DEE-ah),* there was a priest whose name was Zachariah (Zach-ah-RIGH-ah). . . . His wife's name was Elizabeth (Ee-LIZ-ah-beth). They both lived good lives and obeyed all the commandments and rules of the

Lord. But they had no children because Elizabeth wasn't able to have any. And now both she and Zachariah were very old.

One day, as Zachariah was doing his work as a priest, he was chosen to burn the incense on the altar in the temple. During the time the incense was burned, a crowd of people prayed outside. As Zachariah was burning the incense, an angel of the Lord appeared to him at the right side of the altar. When Zachariah saw him, he was upset and felt afraid.

But the angel said to him, "Don't be afraid, Zachariah! God has heard your prayer. Your wife Elizabeth will give you a son, and you are to call him John. You will be very happy, and many others will be happy when he is born, for he will become a great man in the sight of God. He will drink no wine or strong drink, and he will be filled with the Holy Spirit even before he is born. He will bring many people of Israel back to the Lord their God . . . and he will make the Lord's people ready for him."

Zachariah said to the angel, "How will I know if this is so? I am an old man and my wife is old too." The angel answered, "I am Gabriel (GAY-bree-el). I stand in the presence of God. It was he who sent me to speak to you and to bring you this good news. Because you have not believed my message, which will come true at the proper time, you will be unable to speak until the day that these things will happen."

The people who were waiting outside for Zachariah to appear began to wonder why he stayed so long in the temple. When he finally came out, he couldn't speak to them. Unable to speak, he made motions to them with his hands. So they realized he had seen something in the temple.

When his time of service in the temple was over, Zachariah went back home. Soon after that his wife Elizabeth became pregnant. . . . "This is the way the Lord has taken away my disgrace," she said.

1:5-25

An Angel Speaks to Mary

Six months [after Elizabeth knew she was going to be a mother], God sent the angel Gabriel (GAY-bree-el) to a city in Galilee called Nazareth (NA-zah-reth). There he came to a woman whose name was Mary. This Mary was engaged to be the wife of a man named Joseph, who was a descendant of King David. When the angel came to her, he said, "Greetings, O favored woman. The Lord is with you!" But Mary was puzzled by the angel's message. She wondered what his words meant.

The angel went on to say, "Don't be afraid, Mary. God is being especially good to you. Soon you are to become a mother and will have a son. You are to name him Jesus. He will be very great and will be called the Son of the Most High God. The Lord God will make him a king, . . . and his kingdom will never end!"

Mary asked the angel, "How can this happen since I have no husband?" And the angel said to her, "The Holy Spirit will come to you, and the power of the Most High God will come over you. Therefore your child will be holy, the Son of God."

The angel also said, "And listen to this: Your relative Elizabeth will have a son in her old age. . . . There is nothing that God cannot do." Then Mary said, "I am the servant of the Lord. May it happen to me as you said." And then the angel disappeared.

1:26-38

The Birth of John

When the time came for Elizabeth to have her baby, it was a boy. Her neighbors and relatives all were happy with her when they heard how good the Lord had been to her.

And when the baby was eight days old, they came to the house and wanted to name him Zachariah, his father's name. But his mother said, "No; he must be called John." They said to her, "Why? You don't have

---

any relative with that name." Then they asked his father what name he would like to give the boy. Zachariah motioned for a writing pad and wrote, "His name *is* John." They all were surprised at that.

All at once Zachariah was able to speak again and praised God for what was happening. And all the neighbors became afraid. The news about this spread through all the hill country of Judea. And everyone who heard about this wondered about it and asked, "What will this child turn out to be?" They could see that he was already receiving the power of God.

And the little boy grew and became strong in his spirit. [When he left home], he lived in the desert until the day he started to preach to the people of Israel.

1:57-66, 80

The Birth of Jesus

In those days the Roman ruler Augustus (Uh-GUHS-tuhs) sent out a royal command. All the people in his empire were to register for taxing. This happened when Quirinius (Quigh-REEN-ee-yus) was the governor of Syria. So everyone went to his own town to register.

And Joseph also went from the town of Nazareth in Galilee to a town in Judea called Bethlehem. This was where King David had been born. Joseph went there because he was a descendant of David. He went there with Mary, who was going to be his wife. She was pregnant.

And while they were in Bethlehem, the time came for her to have her baby. So there her first son was born. And she wrapped him in clothes and laid him in a manger (MAYN-ger).* You see, there had been no room for them in the inn.

Not far away there were some shepherds out in the fields. They were watching over their sheep. Suddenly an angel of the Lord appeared to them, and the glory of the Lord shone around them. At first they were very afraid. But the angel said to them, "Don't be afraid. I am bringing you good news that will give great joy to all people. This very day, in King David's town, the Savior, Christ the Lord, was born."

The angel also said, "This is the way you will know him. You will find the baby wrapped in cloths and lying in a manger." Then suddenly there was with the one angel many many more. They were praising God, saying, "Glory to God in the highest, and on earth peace among people with whom he is pleased."

When the angels went back to heaven, the shepherds said to one another, "Let's go over to Bethlehem and see this thing that the Lord has made known to us." So they hurriedly went and found Mary and Joseph in a place where animals were kept. They also saw the baby lying in a manger.

When they told Mary and Joseph and others what the angel had said about this child, all who heard them were amazed. But Mary kept in her heart the things the shepherds had said, and she thought about them a lot. When the shepherds returned to their work, they praised God for what they had heard and seen. It was just as the angel had told them it would be.

2:1-20

Jesus Presented in the Temple

When Jesus was just a few weeks old, Mary and Joseph took him to Jerusalem to present him to God in the temple. The Old Testament law of God said, "Every woman's first boy child is to be presented to the Lord." This is what the law of God required in those days. . . .

Now, there was a man in Jerusalem whose name was Simeon (SIM-ee-on). He was a good man and very religious. He was hoping the time would come when the people of Israel would be saved. The Holy Spirit was in him and had told him that he would not die before he had seen the Savior God had promised.

Led by the Holy Spirit, Simeon went to the temple that day when Jesus' parents brought him to the temple. Seeing them, Simeon took the child into his arms and thanked God. He said:

Lord, now let your servant die in peace, as you said you would.
For with my own eyes I have seen the one you have sent to save all people.
He will be a light to show your way to the people who are not Jews, and he will bring glory to your people Israel.

The child's father and mother were amazed at what Simeon said about their baby. . . .

And there was also a woman named Anna in the temple. . . . She was a teacher of God who was very old. She was a widow who worshiped God day and night by fasting and praying. She came [just as Simeon was telling Mary how her heart would someday be broken by what people would do to her son].

Anna also gave thanks to God for sending the promised Savior and spoke about the child to all who were waiting for God to save his people. When Mary and Joseph finished doing what the law required them to do, they returned to their hometown Nazareth in Galilee. And the child grew and became strong and full of wisdom. And the love of God shone on him and blessed him.   2:22-40

When Jesus Was 12

Every year Jesus' parents went to Jerusalem to celebrate the Passover.* When Jesus was 12 years old, they went as they always did and took him along. When the holiday was over and they started to go back home, the boy Jesus stayed behind in Jerusalem. But his parents didn't know this. They thought he was somewhere with the group.

So Mary and Joseph traveled a whole day before they started looking for Jesus among their relatives and friends. When they didn't find him, they went back to Jerusalem to look for him.

After three days of looking they found Jesus in the temple. He was sitting with the teachers, listening to them and asking them questions. All those who heard him were amazed at his understanding and his answers.

When his parents saw him, they didn't know what to think. His mother said to him, "Son, why have you done this to us? Your father and I have been very worried in looking for you." Jesus said to them, "Why did you have to look for me? Didn't you know I had to be in my Father's house?" But they didn't understand what he said to them.

Then Jesus went back with his parents to Nazareth and was obedient to them. And his mother kept in her heart all these things that had happened. And Jesus grew wise as well as tall, and was loved by God and people.

2:41-52

John the Baptizer

In the fifteenth year that the Roman Emperor Tiberius (Tigh-BEER-ee-uhs) ruled, Pontius Pilate (PON-shus PIGH-luht) was the governor of Judea and Herod (HAIR-ahd) was ruler of Galilee (GAL-i-lee). . . . It was at this time that a message from God came to John, the son of Zachariah, in the desert. John went up and down both sides of the Jordan River, preaching that people should turn away from their sins and be baptized in order to receive God's forgiveness of sins. It was like the prophet Isaiah had written in his book:

A voice is shouting in the desert: "Make a way ready for the Lord; make a straight path for him. . . . All people will soon see God's salvation."*

Large crowds came to be baptized by John. He said to them, "You snakes! You are trying to escape God's anger without turning to God. Do the things that will show you have turned away from your sins. And don't start saying to yourselves, 'We have Abraham as our father.' I can tell you that God is able to make children of Abraham out of these stones.". . .

So the people asked John, "What should we do?" He answered, "If you have two coats, give one to him who has none; and he who has food ought to share it with the hungry."

When some tax collectors came to be baptized, they said to John, "Teacher, what should we do?" He said to them, "Don't collect any more money from people than you're supposed to." Some soldiers also asked him, "What about us? What should we do?" He said to them, "Don't take anything from anyone by force or by wrongly accusing anyone. And be satisfied with your pay."

Everybody was expecting the Messiah to come soon, so people began to wonder about John. They hoped he might be the promised Savior. But John said to all of them, "I baptize you with water, but someone much greater than I is coming. I am not good enough even to untie his sandals. He will baptize you with the fire of the Holy Spirit." . . .

In many other ways John preached good news to the people. But John spoke against Herod, the governor, because he had married his brother's wife and had done many other wrong things. So Herod did another sin by putting John in prison.

When all the people were being baptized by John, Jesus also came to him and was baptized. While Jesus was praying, heaven opened, and the Holy Spirit came down on him in the shape of a dove. And a voice that came from heaven said, "You are my very dear Son. With you I am well pleased."

3:1-22

The Devil Tempts Jesus

When Jesus left the Jordan River full of the Holy Spirit, he was told by the Spirit to go into the desert.

There he was tempted by the devil for 40 days. During all that time he ate nothing, so he was very hungry when that time was over.

Then the devil said to him, "If you are the Son of God, tell this stone to turn into bread." But Jesus replied, "It is written [in the Scriptures], 'People cannot live on bread alone.'" So the devil took Jesus in a flash and showed him all the kingdoms of the world. "I will give you all this power and glory," the devil said to him. "It has all been given to me, and I can give it to anyone I wish. If you will worship me, it will all be yours." But Jesus answered, "It is written, 'You should worship the Lord your God and serve only him.'"

Then the devil took Jesus to Jerusalem and put him on the highest part of the temple. There he said to him, "If you are the Son of God, jump down from here. The Scripture says, "God will put his angels in charge of you,' and 'they will hold you up with their hands so you won't stub your foot on a stone.'" But Jesus answered, "The Scriptures also say, 'You must not test the Lord your God.'"

When the devil had finished tempting Jesus in every way, he left him until another chance would come.

Then Jesus returned to Galilee full of the power of the Holy Spirit. And he taught in the synagogues (SIN-ah-gogs), and reports about him spread all over that part of the country. All who heard him praised him.

When Jesus came to Nazareth, where he had grown up, he went to the synagogue on the sabbath day (SA-bahth), as he usually did. When he stood up to read, he was handed the book of the prophet Isaiah. Opening the book, he found the place where it said,

The Spirit of the Lord is on me, because he has chosen me to preach good news to the poor. He has sent me to tell people who are captives that they can be free and to tell blind people that they will see again. He wants me to free all who are mistreated and to announce the time when the Lord will save his people.

Then Jesus closed the book and gave it back to the man in charge of the service and sat down. The eyes of all in the synagogue were on him. And Jesus said to them, "This Scripture reading happened today as you heard it being read." And all who were there spoke well of him and were amazed at the words he spoke. But they said, "Isn't he the son of Joseph?"

4:1-22

The First Disciples

One day when Jesus was standing on the shore by the Sea of Galilee, many people were pushing to get near him. They wanted to hear the word of God. Nearby Jesus saw two boats up on the beach. The fishermen who had left them were washing their nets. So Jesus got into one of the boats. It belonged to Simon. Jesus asked Simon to push the boat out a little way from the land. Then he sat down and taught the people from the boat.

When he had finished speaking, Jesus said to Simon, "Go out to the deep water and let down your nets for a catch." Simon said, "Master, we worked hard all night and caught nothing. But because you have told us to do so, I will let down the nets." When Simon and his partners did this, they caught a big school of fish. There were so many the nets began to break. So they called to their partners in the other boat to come and help them.

When they came, they filled both the boats so full of fish that they began to sink. When Simon Peter saw what had happened, he knelt down in front of Jesus and said, "Go away from me, Lord! I'm a sinful man." Simon and all the others with him were amazed at all the fish they had caught. The same was true of Simon's partners, James and John, the sons of Zebedee (ZEH-bed-dee). Jesus said to Simon, "Don't be afraid. From now on you will be catching people." So when they had put their boats back on the beach, they left everything and followed Jesus.

5:1-11

Jesus Heals a Paralyzed Man

One day when Jesus was teaching a crowd of people, some Pharisees and teachers of the Scriptures were present. They had come from towns all over Galilee and Judea. And some men brought on a bed a friend who was paralyzed. At first they tried to bring him into the house to lay him in front of Jesus.

When the friends could find no way to bring the paralyzed man into the house because of so many people, they carried him up to the roof of the house. There they made a hole in the roof and let the man down on his bed into the middle of the crowd and in front of Jesus. When Jesus saw how much faith the friends had in him, he said to the man, "Friend, your sins are forgiven."

Now, when the religion teachers and the Pharisees heard what Jesus had said, they began to say to themselves, "Who is this man who talks as though he's God? Only God can forgive sins!" Jesus knew what they were saying, so he said to them, "Why do you doubt I can do such things? Which is easier, to say 'Your sins are forgiven' or to say 'Get up and walk'? I will show you that I have the right and power to forgive sins."

Then Jesus said to the paralyzed man, "I say to you, get up, pick up your bed, and go home." At once the man got up, picked up what he had been lying on, and went home, thanking God as he went. And all who saw this were surprised. They praised God, saying, "We have seen some strange things today!"

5:17-26

Jesus Chooses Levi (LEE-vigh)*

After this Jesus went out and saw a tax collector

sitting at the place where he collected taxes. His name was Levi. Jesus said to him, "Follow me." Levi got up, left everything, and went with Jesus.

Later Levi had a big dinner for Jesus at his house. At the dinner there were a number of tax collectors and other friends of Levi. When some Pharisees and teachers of the Scriptures heard about this, they complained to Jesus' disciples. "Why do you eat and drink with tax collectors and other sinners?" they asked. Jesus answered, "People who are well do not need a doctor, but those who are sick do. I have not come to call perfect people to repent, but the sinners."

5:27-32

Lessons Jesus Taught

One sabbath day Jesus was walking through some grain fields. His disciples [who were with him] began to pick some of the grain, rubbed it in their hands, then ate it. Some of the Pharisees who saw this said to Jesus, "Why are you doing what you're not supposed to do on the sabbath?"

Jesus answered, "Haven't you read what David did when he was hungry, he and those who were with him? He went into the house of God, took the bread used for the worship of God, and ate it. He also gave some to the men who were with him. And it is against our law for anyone to eat this bread except the priests." Then Jesus added, "The Son* of Man is the Lord* also of the sabbath."

On another sabbath day, when Jesus went into a synagogue and taught the people, a man with a dried-up right hand was there. Some Bible teachers and Pharisees were watching Jesus to see if he would heal anybody on the sabbath.* They wanted something they could say against Jesus.

Jesus knew what they were thinking. So he said to the man who had the dried-up hand, "Come and stand here." The man got up and went and stood by Jesus. Then Jesus said to his enemies, "Now I ask you: does our law want us to do good on a sabbath or do harm? To save life or to kill it?"

Then, after looking around at them all, Jesus said to the man, "Stretch out your hand." When the man did so, his hand became well. But the Pharisees and Bible teachers became very angry and began to talk among themselves about what they could do to Jesus.

Soon after that Jesus went up on a mountain to pray. He spent the whole night there praying to God. In the morning he called his disciples to him and chose 12 of them and called them his apostles (ah-PAH-suhls).*. . .

When Jesus came down from the mountain to a level place, a large crowd of people came to hear him and be healed by him. Those who were bothered by bad spirits also came and were healed. And all the people tried to touch him, because power was going out from him, healing them all.

Then Jesus looked at his disciples and said: "Why do you call me 'Lord, Lord,' and do not do what I tell you? Everyone who comes to me and hears my words and does them, I will show you what he is like: He is like a man who built a house and dug deep and put the foundation on a rock. And when a flood came and the river ran against that house, it did not shake it because it was well built.

"But the person who hears my words and does not do them," said Jesus, "is like a man who built a house on the ground without a foundation. When the river hit that house, it fell at once. What a crash that was!"

6:1-13, 17-20, 46-49

Jesus Heals a Man's Servant

When Jesus finished speaking to the people, he went back to Capernaum (Ka-PER-nah-um). A Roman army captain who lived there had a servant who was very dear to him. This servant was sick and about to die.

When the captain heard about Jesus, he sent some

of the Jewish rulers of the city to Jesus to ask him to come and heal his servant. They went to Jesus and begged him to do this favor for the Roman captain. They said, "This man deserves to have you do this for him because he loves our people. He even built a synagogue for us."

So Jesus went with the men who had come to him. But just before arriving at the captain's house, the captain sent some friends to tell Jesus not to come. He said, "Sir, I don't deserve to have you come into my house. Nor am I good enough to come to you in person. Just give an order from where you are and my servant will get well."

The captain also said, "I have soldiers under me; and when I say to one, 'Go,' he goes; and when I say to another, 'Come,' he comes. And when I say to my slave, 'Do this,' he does it." When Jesus heard this, he turned and said to the crowd that was following him, "I tell you, I have never found such faith, not even in Israel."

When those who had been sent by the captain returned to his house, they found his servant well.

7:1-10

Jesus at the Home of Simon

One of the Pharisees asked Jesus to have dinner with him, so Jesus went to his house and took his place at a table. When a very sinful woman of that town heard that Jesus was eating at the Pharisee's house, she came and brought with her a beautiful jar of perfume.

Standing behind Jesus, by his feet, the woman began crying. She cried so much that her tears wet his feet. Then she dried his feet with her hair, kissed them, and poured the perfume on them. When the Pharisee who had invited Jesus saw this, he thought to himself, "If this man really were a prophet, he would have known what kind of woman this is who is touching him, for she is a sinner."

Jesus said to the Pharisee, "Simon, I have

something to say to you." And he said, "What is it, Teacher?" Then Jesus told this story: "There were two men who owed money to a banker. One owed 500 silver pieces and the other owed 50. When they could not pay him back, the banker canceled the debts of both. Which one of them will love him more?" asked Jesus. Simon answered, "The one, I suppose, who was forgiven the most."

Jesus said to Simon, "You have answered correctly." Then turning toward the woman Jesus said to Simon, "See this woman? I came into your home and you gave me no water to wash my feet. But she has washed my feet with her tears and dried them with her hair. You didn't welcome me with a kiss, but she hasn't stopped kissing my feet since I came in. You didn't cool my head with oil, but she has covered my feet with perfume."

Then Jesus said, "I tell you, Simon, her sins, which are many, are forgiven. Her great love shows that. But he who is forgiven only a little shows only a little love." Then Jesus said to the woman, "Your sins are all forgiven."

Those who were at the table with Jesus began to say to one another, "Who is this man who even forgives sins?" Jesus said to the woman, "Your faith has saved you. Go in peace."

7:36-50

The Story of a Sower

Soon after [what happened at Simon's house], Jesus went on to many other cities and towns, preaching the good news about the kingdom of God. His 12 disciples went with him, and so did some women who had been healed by Jesus. Mary Magdalene (MAG-dah-leen) . . . was one of them. Joanna, the wife of one of Herod's helpers, was another. Susanna and many others also helped take care of Jesus and his disciples with their money.

People kept coming to Jesus from one place after another. One day when a big crowd had come together, Jesus told this parable (PER-ah-buhl):*

"A farmer went out to plant his seed. As he sowed it, some of it fell on the path, where it was stepped on, and birds came and ate it up. Some of it fell on rocky ground. When it grew, the plants dried up because the ground had no moisture. Some of the seed fell among thorns that grew up with the plants and choked them. And some seeds fell into good soil and grew and produced 100 times as much grain as was sown."

When Jesus finished his story, he said, "Whoever has ears to hear with ought to listen." When his disciples asked him what this parable meant, he said, "The secrets of the kingdom of God have been given to you, but for others they are in parables.". . .

Then Jesus said, "This is what the parable means: The seed is the word of God. The seed that fell on the path is like those who hear. But the devil comes and takes away the word from their hearts to keep them from believing and being saved. The seed on the rock is like those who hear the message and at first receive it gladly. But because they have no deep roots, they believe only for a while. When they are tested they wither up."

"The seed that fell among thorns," said Jesus, "is like the people who hear, but as they go on their way, their faith is choked by worries and riches and pleasures. So their fruit never ripens. And the seed that fell into good ground is like those who hear the word of God and keep it in a good and honest heart. They produce fruit.". . .

Then his mother and his brothers came to Jesus, but they couldn't get near him because of the crowd. So he was told, "Your mother and your brothers are outside. They want to see you." But Jesus said, "My mother and my brothers are those who listen to the word of God and do it."

8:1-15, 19-21

A Dead Girl Becomes Alive

When Jesus returned [from across the lake], a crowd welcomed him because they had been waiting for him. And a man named Jairus (Jah-IGH-rus), a leader of the synagogue, came and knelt at Jesus' feet. He begged Jesus to come to his house because he had an only daughter, about 12 years old, who was dying.

[On the way] a man from the officer's house came and said, "Your daughter is dead. Don't bother the teacher any longer." But upon hearing this Jesus said to Jairus, "Don't be afraid. Only believe and she will be well."

When Jesus came to the house, he permitted no one to enter with him except Peter and John and James and the father and mother of the child. All the other people were crying and moaning. But Jesus said to them, "Don't cry, the child is not dead. She is only sleeping."

The people all laughed at Jesus because they knew the girl was dead. But Jesus took her hand and said, "Get up, child!" And at once her life returned and she got up. Jesus told her parents to give her something to eat. They didn't know what to think. Jesus told them not to tell anyone what had happened.

8:40-42, 49-56

The Glory of Jesus

Now it happened that one time, when Jesus was praying, his disciples were with him. And Jesus asked them, "Who do people say I am?" They answered, "Some say you are John the Baptizer. But others say you are Elijah. And others say you are one of the prophets of long ago come back to life."

Then Jesus asked them, "But who do *you* say I am?" Peter answered, "You are the Christ sent by God." Then Jesus gave them strict orders not to tell this to anyone. He said, "The Son of Man must suffer many things . . . and be killed and be raised to life on the third day."

And Jesus said to all of them, "If anyone wants to follow me, he must give up his own desires. He must daily take and carry his own cross and follow me closely. For whoever wants to save his life will lose it. But whoever loses his life for my sake will save it. And what good does it do a person if he wins the whole world but loses or gives up his life?"

Jesus also said, "If anyone is ashamed of me and of my words, the Son of Man will also be ashamed of him when he comes in his glory and in the glory of his Father and of the holy angels."

About eight days after these sayings, Jesus took with him Peter and John and James and went up a mountain to pray. While he was praying, the appearance of his face changed and his clothes became shiny white.

And suddenly two men were talking with Jesus, Moses and Elijah. They appeared in glory and spoke of how Jesus would soon die in Jerusalem in order to accomplish God's work. But Peter and those with him had fallen asleep. When they woke up, they saw Jesus covered with brightness and the two men standing there with him. As the men were leaving, Peter said to Jesus, "Master, it's great that we were here. We'll make three shelters, one for you, one for Moses, and one for Elijah." He didn't really know what he was saying.

And while he was speaking, a cloud came and covered them with a shadow. When the cloud came over them, the disciples became afraid. Then a voice coming from out of the cloud said, "This is my Son, my chosen one; listen to him!"

When the voice had finished speaking, Jesus was seen standing there all alone. The three disciples kept quiet about all this. They told no one at that time what they had seen.

9:18-26, 28-36

Jesus' Journey to Jerusalem

As the time came closer when Jesus would be taken

up to heaven, he made up his mind to go to Jerusalem. On the way he sent messengers ahead of him. They went to a village in Samaria (Sah-MER-ee-ah)* to get things ready for his coming. But the people there would not welcome him, because they knew he was headed for Jerusalem [and big trouble].

When James and John heard this, they said to Jesus, "Lord, do you want us to ask that fire from heaven burn them up?" Jesus turned and scolded them, and they all went on to another village.

9:51-55

The Good Samaritan

One day a certain lawyer came and tried to check on Jesus' teachings. "Teacher," he asked, "what must I do to get to live forever in heaven?" Jesus said to him, "What do the Scriptures say? What do you read in them?" The man answered, "You must love the Lord your God with all your heart, and with all your soul, and with all your strength, and with all your mind; and your neighbor as yourself." Jesus said to him, "Your answer is right. Do this and you will live."

But the lawyer, knowing there were some people he didn't love, asked, "And who is my neighbor?" Jesus told him this story:

"A Jew was going from Jerusalem to Jericho when robbers attacked him. They took everything he had, beat him up, and left him half dead.

"It so happened that a Jewish priest was going down that road. When he saw the man, he walked by on the other side. A little later a man who worked in the temple also came there. He went over and looked at the man and then went on by. But a certain Samaritan (Sah-MER-i-tahn)* who was traveling that way, when he came to where the man was lying, and saw him, felt sorry for him. So he went to him, poured some oil and wine on his wounds to clean them, and bandaged them.

"Then the Samaritan put the man on his donkey and brought him to an inn, where he took care of him through the night. The next day the Samaritan gave the innkeeper two silver coins and said, "Take care of the man. When I come back this way, I will pay you whatever more you will spend on him."

Now Jesus asked the lawyer, "Which of the three, do you think, acted like a neighbor to the man who was attacked by the robbers?" The lawyer answered, "The one who was kind to him." Jesus said to the lawyer, "Go and do the same."

10:25-37

Mary and Martha

As they went on their way, Jesus came to a village where a woman called Martha welcomed him into her home. And Martha had a sister named Mary. Mary sat down on the floor next to her Lord's feet and listened to his teaching.

But Martha got upset over all the food she wanted to prepare for her guests. So she went to Jesus and said, "Lord, don't you care that my sister has left me to do all the work by myself? Tell her to come and help me!"

But the Lord answered, "Martha! Martha! You worry and fuss about so many things. Only one thing is really needed. And Mary has chosen that good thing. It must not be taken away from her."

10:38-41

Jesus' Teaching About Prayer

One time when Jesus finished praying in a certain place one of his disciples said to him, "Lord, teach us to pray, just as John taught his disciples." So Jesus said to them, "When you pray, say: "Father, may your name be kept holy. May your kingdom come. Give us each day the bread we need. And forgive us our sins, for we forgive those who sin against us. And do not lead us into hard testing.""

Then said Jesus to his disciples, "Suppose you would go to a friend's house at midnight and would say to him, 'Friend, let me borrow three loaves of bread. A friend of mine who is on a trip just arrived, and I don't have anything to serve him.'

"And suppose your friend would answer from his bedroom upstairs, 'Don't bother me. The door is already locked, and my children and I are in bed. I can't give you anything now. It's too late.' Well, even if he didn't want to get up and give you the bread as a friend, still he would get up and give you what you need if you would keep on asking.

"So I say to you," Jesus continued, "ask, and you will receive; seek, and you will find; knock, and the door will be opened to you. For everyone who asks receives, and he who seeks finds, and to him who knocks the door will be opened. Would any of you fathers give your son a snake when he asks for a fish? Or if he would ask for an egg would you give him a poisonous spider?

"If you who are sinful know how to give good gifts to your children," said Jesus, "then certainly the heavenly Father will give the Holy Spirit to those who ask him!"

11:1-13

Warnings and Other Lessons

[At another time Jesus said to his disciples], "I tell you, my friends, don't be afraid of those who kill the body but can't do any more harm than that. I will tell you whom to fear: fear God, who has the power to kill and to throw into hell. Yes, I tell you, be afraid of him!

"But aren't five sparrows sold for two pennies?" Jesus continued. "Yet not a single one of them is forgotten by God. Why, even the hairs of your head all are numbered. So don't be afraid; you are worth much more than many sparrows!"

"And I tell you," said Jesus, "whoever admits publicly that he belongs to me, the Son of Man will do the same for him before the angels of God. But if someone says he doesn't belong to me, the Son of Man will say the same before the angels of God. . . ."

Then a man in the crowd said to Jesus, "Teacher, tell my brother to divide with me the property our father left us." But Jesus said to him, "Man, who made me a judge or a divider over you?" Then he said to them all, "Watch out and guard yourself against all coveting, because a man's life does not come from all the things he owns."

Then Jesus told the people this parable: "A rich man had land that produced good crops. And he began to think to himself, 'I don't have enough room to store all my crops. What shall I do?' Then he said to himself, 'This is what I'll do. I will pull down my barns and build bigger ones. Then I'll have room for all my grain and other goods. I'll say to myself: Man, you have all you need for many years. Take life easy; eat, drink, and be merry.'

"But God said to this man, 'You fool! This very night you will have to give up your life. Then who will get all these things you have kept for yourself?'"

Jesus ended his story by saying, "This is the way it is with those who pile up riches for themselves but are not rich in God's ways." Then Jesus said to his disciples, "This is why I tell you, 'do not worry about the food you need for staying alive or about the clothes you need for your body. Life is much more than food, and the body is more than clothing.'

"Learn something from the ravens," said Jesus. "They don't plant seeds or gather a harvest. They don't have storerooms or barns. Still, God feeds them! And you are worth so much more than birds!

"Who of you can live a little longer by worrying about it?" asked Jesus. "If you aren't able to do such a little thing as that, why worry about the other things? Look how the lilies grow. They don't work or make clothes for themselves. But I tell you that not even Solomon (SAHL-ah-mahn)* at his best was ever dressed as well as one of these. God dresses the grass, which is alive today and tomorrow may be thrown into an oven. So he certainly will also dress you, you people who have such little faith."

"So don't always be worrying about what to eat and what to drink. For all the people of this world look for these things, and your Father knows that you need them. If you will search for his kingdom, he will give you these other things as well."

12:4-9, 13-31

Teachings in a Synagogue

One sabbath day when Jesus was teaching in a synagogue, a woman was there who had a bad spirit that had kept her sick for 18 years. She was bent over and couldn't straighten herself up. When Jesus saw her, he called to her and said, "Woman, you are free from your trouble." Then he laid his hands on her, and all at once she could straighten herself up. Oh, how she praised God for what Jesus had done for her!

But the man in charge of the synagogue was angry because Jesus had healed the woman on a sabbath day. He said to the people, "There are six days for doing work. Come on those days to be healed and not on a sabbath day."

The Lord answered the man by saying, "You hypocrites! Don't all of you untie your animals on the sabbath day and lead them away from their mangers to water them? And shouldn't this woman, a daughter of Abraham whom the devil kept tied up for 18 years, be freed from her trouble on the sabbath day?" Jesus' words made all his enemies ashamed of themselves. And all the other people were very happy over the wonderful things Jesus did.

Then Jesus asked, "What is the kingdom of God like? To what can I compare it? It is like a grain of mustard seed that a man took and planted in his garden. The plant grew and became a tree, and the birds of the air made nests in its branches."

And again Jesus asked, "To what shall I compare

the kingdom of God? It is like the yeast a woman took and mixed into a bushel of flour until the yeast made the whole batch of dough rise."

13:10-20

Another Healing on a Sabbath

On another sabbath day Jesus went to have dinner at the home of one of the leaders of the Pharisees, and the people there were all watching Jesus very closely. And a man whose legs were very swollen came up to Jesus. So Jesus said to the lawyers and the Pharisees who were present, "Is it all right to heal on the sabbath or not?" But they all remained silent.

So Jesus took the man by the arm, healed him, and told him to go home. Then he said to the people who were at the dinner, "If you had a son or an ox that had fallen into a well, which one of you would not pull him out at once on a sabbath day?" And none of them could reply to this.

Then Jesus noticed how some of the guests were trying to sit near the head of the table. So he told this parable to the people at the dinner: "When you are invited to a wedding dinner, don't take the most important seats. Someone more important than you also may have been invited, and the one who invited both of you may come and say to you, 'Please give your place to this man.' Then you will go ashamed to the least important place.

"Instead," said Jesus, "when you are invited, go and sit in the least important place. Then the one who invited you may come and say to you, 'My friend, come on up to a better place.' This will honor you in front of all who are at the table with you. For everyone who tries to make himself look more important than he is will be humbled. But the person who does not try to get important will be honored."

Jesus also said to the man who had invited him, "When you give a dinner or a banquet, do not invite your friends or your brothers or your relatives or your rich neighbors. They will invite you back, and in this way you will be paid for what you did. But when you give a feast, invite poor people and crippled people and people who are blind. This will make you happy because they aren't able to pay you back."

14:1-14

God's Concern for Lost People

Many tax collectors and people with bad reputations began coming to hear Jesus. When the Pharisees and the religion teachers saw this, they talked about it. "This man welcomes sinners and eats with them," they said. So Jesus told them this story:

"Suppose a man had 100 sheep and lost one of them. What would he do? He would leave the 99 in the pasture and go look for the one that is lost until he finds it. And when he has found it, he puts it on his shoulders happily. And when he comes home with it, he calls together his friends and neighbors. 'Be happy with me,' he says to them; 'for I found my lost sheep.'"

Then Jesus added, "In the same way there is more joy in heaven over one person who is sorry about sinning and turns to living with God than over 99 people who are all right with God and do not have to repent (ree-PENT)."*

"Or suppose a woman had 10 silver coins," Jesus continued. "When she loses one of the coins, doesn't she light a lamp and sweep the house and look carefully for the lost coin until she finds it? When she finds it, she calls her friends and neighbors together and says, 'Be happy with me. I found the piece of money I lost.' Like that, I tell you, the angels of God are happy over any sinner who is sorry about his sins and turns away from them."

Then Jesus told another story to make his point: "There was a man who had two sons. The younger one said to his father, 'Father, give me the share of the property I'm to get later.' So the man divided the family riches between his two sons.

"A few days later the younger son packed up all his possessions and took a trip to a faraway country. There he spent all the money he had in wild and foolish living. When his money was all gone, he began to be in a lot of trouble, because there was a bad food shortage in that country. So he had to go to work for a man in that country, and this man gave him the job of feeding his pigs.

"Well, the young man got so hungry he wished he could eat some of the food the pigs received, but no one gave him anything to eat. At last he began to think about the trouble he was in. He said, 'All my father's workers have more food than they can eat, and I'm about to die from hunger! I'm going back to my father and will say to him: Father, I have sinned against God and against you, and I no longer deserve to be called your son. Make me one of your hired workers.'

"So the young man started back to his father. But when he was still quite a distance from home, his father saw him coming and felt sorry for him. He ran to him and hugged him and kissed him. And the son said to him, 'Father, I have sinned against God and against you. I no longer deserve to be called your son.'

"But the father said to his servants, 'Hurry! Bring the best robe we have and put it on my son; and put a ring on his hand and shoes on his feet. Then go and kill a fat calf and let us eat and be glad. My son was dead and is alive again. He was lost but now he has been found.' So they began to celebrate.

"But the older son had been out in the field when his brother came back. As he came close to the house and heard the music and dancing, he asked one of the servants, 'What's going on here?' The servant told him, 'Your brother has come back, and your father has butchered our best calf to celebrate his being home again safe and sound.'

"When the older brother heard this, he got so angry he wouldn't go into the house. So his father came out and begged him to come in. 'Look,' said the brother, 'I served you for many years and I never disobeyed your orders. But you never even gave me a goat for a party with my friends. But this son of yours wasted your property, and for him you killed the best calf.'

"'Look son,' the father said to him kindly, 'you are always here with me and all that is mine is yours. It is right that we should celebrate and be glad. Your brother was dead and has come back to life. He was lost but now he has been found.'"

15:1-32

Ten Lepers (LEP-ers)*

On his way to Jerusalem Jesus was passing between Samaria and Galilee. As he entered a village there, he was met by 10 lepers. They stood at a distance and shouted, "Jesus! Master! Have pity on us!"

When Jesus saw them, he said to them, "Go and show the priests that you are healed." On the way their leprosy disappeared. So one of them, when he saw that he was healed, came back, praising God with a loud voice. He threw himself down at Jesus' feet and thanked him. That man was a Samaritan.

Then said Jesus, "Weren't 10 men healed? Where are the nine? Is this stranger from another country the only one who turned back to give thanks to God?" And Jesus said to him, "Get up and go on your way. Your faith has made you well."

Asked by the Pharisees when the kingdom of God was coming, Jesus answered, "The kingdom of God does not come in ways that can be observed. Nor can people say, 'Look, here it is!' or 'There it is.' For the kingdom of God is in you."

17:11-21

On Entering the Kingdom

Jesus also told this story to people who thought they were good and better than anybody else:

"Two men went into the temple to pray. One was a

Pharisee; the other was a tax collector. The Pharisee stood apart by himself and prayed, 'I thank you, God, that I am not like other people. I am not like those who steal, who are unfair to others, or who commit adultery.* And I'm not like that tax collector. I go without food two days a week, and I give one-tenth of the money I earn to the temple.'

"But the tax collector stood off by himself and would not even raise his eyes to heaven. Instead, he hit himself on his chest and said, 'God, have pity on me. I am a sinner.'

"I tell you," said Jesus, "this man and not the other went back to his house forgiven and right with God. For everyone who thinks himself better than he is will find out how unimportant he is. But whoever humbles himself will become important."

Then some people brought their babies to Jesus. They wanted him to touch [and bless] them. When the disciples saw them, they scolded the parents [for bothering Jesus]. But Jesus called the disciples to him and said, "Let the children come to me and do not try to stop them. The kingdom of God belongs to such people. I tell you the truth, whoever does not welcome the kingdom of God like a child will not be able to enter it."

And then a young ruler of the people asked Jesus, "Good Teacher, what must I do to receive life that will last forever?" Jesus said to him, "Why do you call me good? No one is good except God alone. You know the commandments: 'Do not commit adultery.* Do not murder. Do not steal. Do not lie. Honor your father and mother.'" The man replied, "Ever since I was young I have obeyed all these commandments."

When Jesus heard this, he said to the young man, "One thing you still haven't done. Sell everything you have, give the money to the poor, and you will have riches in heaven, and come, follow me." But when the young man heard this, he became very sad because he was very rich. Looking at him Jesus said, "How hard it is for rich people to enter the kingdom of God! It is easier for a camel to go through the eye of a needle than for a rich man to enter the kingdom of God."

Those who heard Jesus say this said, "Then who can be saved?" Jesus said, "What is impossible for men is possible for God."

Peter said, "Look, we left our homes and followed you." Jesus answered, "I tell you the truth, anyone who has left his house or wife or brothers or parents or children for the sake of the kingdom of God will receive much more right away. And in time to come he will have life that lasts forever."

18:9-30

On to Jerusalem

Taking his 12 disciples aside, Jesus said to them, "Look, we are going to Jerusalem. There all the things the prophets wrote about the Son of Man are going to happen. He will be handed over to people who aren't Jews, and they will make fun of him and mistreat him and spit on him. They will also beat him and kill him. But on the third day he will rise [come back to life]."

But the disciples didn't understand any of these things Jesus said about himself. The meaning was hidden from them. They didn't know what Jesus was talking about.

As he came near the city of Jericho (JER-ee-ko), a blind man was sitting by the side of the road, begging. When he heard the crowd passing by, he asked what was happening. They told him, "Jesus of Nazareth is passing by." So he began to yell, "Jesus! Son of David! Have mercy on me!"

The people who were at the head of the crowd told the man to be quiet. But he yelled louder, "Son of David! Have mercy on me!" So Jesus stopped and ordered that the man be brought to him. When the blind man came near, Jesus asked him, "What do you want me to do for you?" The man said, "Lord, let me see again." Jesus said to him, "Receive your eyesight! Your faith has made you well."

At once the man was able to see, and he went with Jesus, thanking God. And all the people, when they saw what had happened, praised God.

As Jesus went into Jericho and was passing through it, a rich man named Zacchaeus (Za-KEE-us) tried to see Jesus. He was the chief tax collector there. He couldn't see Jesus because of the crowd and because he was a little man. So he ran on ahead and climbed up into a sycamore (SICK-ah-more) tree because Jesus was going to pass by that way.

When Jesus came to the place, he looked and said to Zacchaeus, "Come down at once, Zacchaeus, because I must stay at your house today." So Zacchaeus hurried down from the tree and gladly welcomed Jesus to his house. But all the people who saw this started grumbling. They said, "He [meaning Jesus] has gone to visit with a man who is known to be a sinner!" [They didn't think anyone should be friendly with a tax collector.]

In his house Zacchaeus said to the Lord, "Look Lord, half of what I own I'm going to give to poor people. And if I have cheated anyone, I will pay him back four times as much." Then Jesus said to him, "Today a person was saved in this house. This man also is a son of Abraham. And I, the Son of Man, came to look for and to save all those who are lost."

18:31-43; 19:1-10

Jesus Goes to Jerusalem

After Jesus had said all this, he went on to Jerusalem. When he was coming to Bethany (BETH-ah-nee),* near the hill called the Mount of Olives, he sent two of his disciples ahead. "Go to the village there ahead of you," he told them, "and as you enter, you will find a tied colt that no one has ever ridden. Untie it and bring it here. If someone asks you, 'Why are you untying it?' say, 'The Lord needs it.'"

So the two men went and found everything just as Jesus had told them they would. As they were untying the colt, its owners said to them, "Why are you untying it?" And they said, "The Lord needs it." When they brought the colt to Jesus, they threw their coats on the animal and helped Jesus sit on it. As he rode along, people put their coats on the rode in front of them.

When Jesus came near to Jerusalem, at the place where the road went down the Mount of Olives, the whole big crowd of his followers began to praise God loudly. They thanked God for all the great things they had seen Jesus do. "God bless the king who comes in the name of the Lord!" they shouted. "Peace in heaven and glory in the highest!"

But some of the Pharisees in the crowd said to Jesus, "Teacher, tell your disciples to stop saying what they are shouting." Jesus answered, "I tell you, if these people would keep quiet, the stones along the road would shout."

When Jesus came closer to the city and saw it, he wept over it. "If only you knew what is needed for peace!" he said. "But now they are hid from your eyes. And the days will come," he said, "when your enemies will surround you and will close in on you from every side. They will crush you, you and the people in you [the city]. They will not leave a single stone above another because you did not know the time when God visited you."

Then Jesus went to the temple and began to chase out those who sold things there. "It is written [in the Scriptures]," he said to them, "'My house is to be a house of prayer,' but you have made it a hangout for robbers."

And every day Jesus taught in the temple. The main priests, the teachers of the Bible, and the leaders of the people wanted to kill Jesus, but they couldn't find a way to do it because all the people hung around him, wanting to hear what he taught.

19:28-48

The Plan Against Jesus

It was almost time to celebrate the Passover.* The chief priests and the teachers of the people were trying to find some safe way of killing Jesus because they were afraid of the people.

Then the devil went into Judas, the one called Iscariot (Is-CAR-ee-ot). He was one of the 12 disciples. Judas went and talked to the chief priests and the officers of the temple about helping them capture Jesus. They were pleased and promised to give him money. So he agreed to do it and began to look for a chance for them to arrest Jesus when there were no crowds around.

Then came the day during the Passover holidays when the Passover lamb had to be killed. So Jesus told Peter and John, "Go and prepare the Passover meal for us, so we can eat it together."

They asked Jesus, "Where do you want us to prepare it?" He said to them, "Remember this! When you have entered the city, a man carrying a jar of water will meet you. Follow him into the house he enters and tell the owner, 'The teacher asks you: Where is the room where I may eat the Passover meal with my disciples?' The man will show you a large room upstairs. There go ahead and get everything ready."

So Peter and John went and found everything just as Jesus had told them they would. And there they prepared the Passover meal.

22:1-13

The Lord's Supper

When the time came to eat the Passover meal, Jesus came and sat down at the table with his disciples. And he said to them, "I have wanted very much to eat this Passover meal with you before I suffer! For I tell you, I will never eat this supper again until it receives its full meaning in the kingdom of God."

Then he took some bread, thanked God for it, broke

it into pieces, and gave it to them. "This is my body which is given for you," he said. "Do this as a way of remembering me." In the same way he gave them a cup of wine after supper. "This cup," he said, "is God's new covenant (KUHV-eh-nuhnt)* sealed with my blood which will be given for you."

"But now," said Jesus, "the one who will betray me is with me here at this table! Everything will happen according to God's plan, but it's too bad for that man who will betray me." So they all began to ask each other which one of them would do this.

They also began to argue among themselves over who was the greatest [or most important] among them. When Jesus heard this, he said to them, "The kings of this world rule their people with power, and the rulers over the people are called their helpers. But this is not the way it ought to be among you. Rather, let the greatest one among you be like the youngest, and the leader ought to be a servant.

"Who is greater," asked Jesus; "the one who sits down to eat or the one who serves him? Is it not usually the one who sits down? But I am among you as one who serves!"

22:14-27

Jesus Arrested

When Jesus left the city, he went, as he often did, to the Mount of Olives. His disciples went with him. When he came to the place, he said to them, "Pray that you will not be tempted." Then he went off from them about the distance one can throw a stone. There he knelt down and prayed. "Father," he said, "if you are willing, take away what is about to happen to me. But don't do what I want; do what you want."

When Jesus got up from praying, he went back to the disciples and found them asleep because they were very sad. He said to them, "Why are you sleeping? Get up and pray that you will not fall when you are tempted."

While Jesus was still speaking, a crowd arrived. The man called Judas, one of the 12 disciples, was leading them. Judas came up to Jesus to kiss him. But Jesus said, "Judas, would you betray the Son of Man with a kiss?"

When those who were with Jesus saw what was going to happen, they said, "Lord, shall we fight with our swords?" One of them swung and hit the high priest's servant and cut off his right ear. But Jesus said, "No more of this!" And he touched the man's ear and healed it.

Then Jesus said to the chief priests and the officers of the temple guard who had come there to get him, "Have you come with swords and clubs as though I were an outlaw? When I was with you in the temple every day, you didn't try to arrest me. But this is your hour and a time when the power of darkness rules."

So they grabbed Jesus and took him away to the house of the high priest. Peter followed at a distance. The soldiers started a fire in the middle of the courtyard, and Peter joined those who sat around it. When one of the maids saw him sitting there at the fire, she looked at him for quite a while. Then she said, "This man was with Jesus!" But Peter denied it. He said, "Woman, I don't even know him!"

A little later someone else saw Peter and said, "You are one of them too!" But Peter answered, "Man, I am not!" About an hour later another man insisted [that Peter was a follower of Jesus]. He said, "This man certainly was one of his disciples because he's from Galilee." But Peter answered, "Man, I don't know what you're talking about!"

As Peter said these words, a rooster crowed. And Jesus [who was being lead across the yard] turned at that moment and looked at Peter. Then Peter remembered how the Lord had said to him, "Before the rooster crows today, you will say three times that you don't know me." Peter left the yard and cried and cried.

Meanwhile the men who were guarding Jesus

made fun of him and beat him. They blindfolded him and asked him to guess who hit him. They also said many other insulting things to him.

22:39-65

Jesus on Trial

When daylight came, the leaders, the chief priest, and the teachers of the Jews met together, and Jesus was brought to their meeting. "Tell us," they said, "are you the Messiah (Meh-SIGH-ah)?"* He answered, "If I tell you, you will not believe me; and if I ask you, you will not answer. But from now on the Son of Man will be sitting at the right hand of God's power."

When they heard this, they all said, "Are you, then, the Son of God?" He said to them, "You're saying that I am." And they said, "What more evidence do we need? We have heard him say this ourselves."

So the whole group got up and brought Jesus to Pilate (PIGH-luht).* There they began to accuse him of many things. "We caught this man misleading our people," they said. "He told them not to pay taxes to Caesar (SEE-zar)* and claimed that he himself is the Christ, a king."

Pilate asked Jesus, "Are you the king of the Jews?" Jesus answered, "You say it." Then Pilate said to the chief priests and the crowds, "I find nothing wrong with this man." But the Jewish leaders tried all the harder to have Pilate order the death of Jesus. They said, "He is starting riots among the people with his teachings all over Judea, from Galilee all the way down to here."

When Pilate heard this, he asked whether the man was from Galilee. When he heard that Jesus was from the country ruled by Herod, he sent him to Herod, who was in Jerusalem at that time. Herod was very pleased to see Jesus, because he had heard about him and had been wanting to see him for a long time. He was hoping to see Jesus do a miracle.

So Herod asked Jesus many questions, but Jesus

didn't answer him anything. The chief priests and the religion teachers who stood by accused Jesus of many things, but Herod and his soldiers just made fun of Jesus. Then, dressing Jesus in a beautiful robe, Herod sent Jesus back to Pilate. And that day Herod and Pilate became friends. They had been enemies before this.

Pilate then called together the chief priests, the rulers, and the people and said to them, "You brought this man to me and said he was misleading your people. I examined him and didn't find the man guilty of any of your charges. Neither did Herod, because he sent him back to us. So, nothing deserving of death has been done by him. I will therefore have him whipped and will let him go."

At each Passover celebration Pilate had to set free one prisoner. But the whole crowd began to shout, "Get rid of this man! Set Barabbas free!" Barabbas (Bah-RAB-bas) was a man who had been put into prison for starting a riot in the city and for murder. Pilate wanted to free Jesus, so he talked to the crowd again. But they all shouted back at him, "Crucify him! Crucify him!"

For the third time Pilate said to them, "Why? What wrong has he done? I found no reason whatever to put him to death. I will therefore have him whipped and let him go." But the people kept demanding that Jesus be put to death on a cross. Finally their loud shouting won. Pilate gave the order that what they wanted should be done.

22:66-71; 23:1-24

Jesus Nailed to a Cross

As the soldiers took Jesus away, they met a man named Simon, who was coming into the city from the country of Cyrene (Sigh-REEN).* The soldiers grabbed Simon and made him carry Jesus' cross. A large crowd followed, among them also some women who were crying and feeling sorry for Jesus. Jesus turned to them and said, "Women of Jerusalem, don't cry for me, but cry for yourselves and for your children.". . .

Two others, who were criminals, also were taken to be put to death with Jesus. When they came to the place called *The Skull*, they nailed Jesus to a cross and also the two criminals, one to the right and one to the left of Jesus. Jesus said, "Father, forgive them! They don't know what they are doing."

The soldiers threw dice to decide who would get Jesus' clothes. And the people stood around, watching. The Jewish leaders made fun of him, saying, "He saved others; now let him save himself if he is the Messiah chosen by God." The soldiers also made fun of him. They came up to him and offered him some cheap wine. "If you are the king of the Jews," they said, "save yourself!" A sign was put above Jesus. It said, "This is the king of the Jews."

23:26-28, 32-38

The Death of Jesus

It was now about 12 o'clock and the sun stopped shining. The whole country became dark until three o'clock. And the big curtain in the temple was ripped in half [by a wind]. And Jesus, shouting loudly, said, "Father, into your hands I put my spirit!" After saying this, he died.

When the captain of the guard saw what happened, he praised God, saying, "Certainly this man was a good man!" And all the people who had come there to watch what was happening went away beating their chests. All the friends of Jesus and the women who had followed him from Galilee stood off at a distance and watched these things.

And there was a man named Joseph. He was from the Jewish town of Arimathea (Air-i-mah-THEE-ah). He was a good man, a man who tried to do what was right. He was a member of the Jewish court, but he had not agreed with what it had done to Jesus. He was looking for the kingdom of God. This man went to Pilate and asked for the body of Jesus.

Joseph took the body down [from the cross] and wrapped it in a linen cloth. Then he laid it in a grave cut out of the side of a rock. This grave had never been used. It was a Friday, and the sabbath day was about to begin.

The women who had come with Jesus from Galilee went with Joseph. They saw the grave and how Jesus' body was put into it. Then they went back to the city and got some spices and perfumes ready [to put around the body]. But on the sabbath day they rested, as the law said they should.

23:44-56

Jesus Alive Again

On Sunday morning, very early, the women went to the grave, taking with them the spices they had prepared. And they found the big rock rolled away from the opening of the grave. But when they went in, they didn't find the body.

While they were standing there and wondering what might have happened, suddenly two men in bright shiny clothes stood by them. The women, very frightened, bowed down to the ground. The men said to them, "Why are you looking for a living person among the dead? Don't you remember what he told you while he was still in Galilee? He said the Son of Man would have to be handed over to sinful men, would be crucified, and on the third day would become alive again."

The women remembered these words. So they returned from the grave and told all this to the 11 disciples and all the rest who were there. The women were Mary Magdalene (MAG-dah-leen) and Joanna (Jo-ANN-ah) and Mary, the mother of James. They and the other women with them told the apostles what had happened. But the apostles did not believe them. It all seemed like foolish talk.

That same day two of the disciples were walking to a village called Emmaus (Em-MAY-us), about seven miles from Jerusalem. They were talking to each other about all the things that had happened. As they talked, Jesus himself came up to them and walked with them. But he kept them from recognizing him.

"What are you talking about to each other as you are walking along?" he asked. They stopped, looking very sad. One of them, named Cleopas (KLEE-o-pahs), said to him, "Are you the only person visiting Jerusalem who hasn't heard the things that have happened there these days?"

Jesus asked, "What things?" They said to him, "The things that happened to Jesus of Nazareth. He was a prophet who did powerful deeds and spoke powerful words in the eyes of God and all the people. But our chief priests and rulers had him sentenced to death and crucified. We had hoped he would be the one who would save Israel (IS-rah-ail).*

"Besides all that," they continued, "this is now the third day since it happened. And some women in our group surprised us. They were at the grave early this morning and didn't find his body. They came back saying they had seen angels who said he was alive. Some of our group went to the grave and found it just the way the women had said it was. But they did not see Jesus."

Then Jesus said to them, "How foolish you are and slow to believe all that the prophets have said! Wasn't it necessary for the Messiah to suffer these things in order to enter into his glory?" Then Jesus explained to them what was said about him in all the Scriptures, beginning with the writings of Moses and all the prophets.

When they came to the town to which they were going, Jesus pretended to be going on. But they said to him, "Stay with us. It will soon be evening. The day is about over." So he went home with them.

As Jesus sat at the table with them, he took the

bread and said a prayer of thanks. Then he broke the bread and gave it to them. And suddenly they knew who it was. Then he disappeared. The two disciples said to each other, "Wasn't it just like a fire burning inside us when he talked to us on the road and explained the Scriptures to us?"

Then they got up and went back to Jerusalem, where the 11 disciples and others were staying together. "The Lord has really risen. He appeared to Simon!" they told the two men from Emmaus. Then the men told what had happened on the road home and how they had recognized Jesus when he broke the bread [in their house].

24:1-35

Jesus Appears

While the two men were telling this, Jesus himself suddenly appeared among them. At first they were frightened and thought they were seeing a ghost. But he said to them, "Why are you upset and why are you doubting that I am alive? Look at my hands and feet and see that it is I myself. Feel me and you will see. A ghost doesn't have flesh and bones as you can see I have."

As he spoke, Jesus showed them his hands and his feet. They were so happy about all this, they still couldn't believe it. So Jesus said to them, "Do you have anything to eat here?" They gave him a piece of baked fish, which he took and ate as they watched.

Then he said to them, "These are the things I told you while I was still with you. Everything written about me in the writings of Moses and the prophets and the psalms had to happen."

Then Jesus helped them understand the Scriptures. He said to them, "This is what was written: That the Messiah must suffer and rise from death on the third day. Also that in his name all people must be told to turn from their sins and receive God's **forgiveness**. You are witnesses of these things. And I will send to you what My father has promised. But stay in the city until you have received God's power.

Then Jesus led them out of the city as far as Bethany. There he raised his hands and blessed them. And while he was blessing them, he left them and was taken up into heaven. The disciples returned to Jerusalem very happy, and for a while they were continually in the temple, thanking God.

24:36-53

THE GOSPEL AS WRITTEN BY
John

This is what John [the Baptizer] said when the Jewish leaders in Jerusalem sent some priests to ask him, "Who are you?" John told them, "I am not the Christ!" So they asked him, "Then who are you? Are you Elijah (Ee-LIGH-jah)?"* He answered, "No."

Then they said to John, "Who are you? Give us an answer for those who sent us? What do you say about yourself?" John said, "I am the voice of a man shouting in the desert, 'Make a straight road for the Lord to come,' as the prophet Isaiah said."

The men had been sent by the Pharisees (FAIR-i-sees).* They asked John, "If you are not the Messiah, nor Elijah, nor the prophet [who was to speak for God], why do you baptize?" John answered, "I baptize with water. But there is someone among you whom you do not know. He is coming after me. And I am not good enough even to untie his sandals." This happened in Bethany, on the other side of the Jordan River, where John was baptizing.

1:19-28

The Baptism of Jesus
The next day John saw Jesus coming toward him.

He said, "Look! There is the Lamb of God who takes away the sin of the world. This is the person I was talking about when I said, 'After me is coming a man who is way ahead of me, because he lived long before me. I myself didn't know him, but I came baptizing with water so that he would become known to the people of Israel.'"

John also gave this report: "I saw the Spirit of God come down like a dove from heaven and stay on him. I still didn't know him, but God, who sent me to baptize with water, said to me, 'The one on whom you see the Spirit come down and remain, he is the one who baptizes with the Holy Spirit.' I saw this happen, and I tell you that this is the Son of God."

The next day John the Baptizer was standing there again with two of his disciples when he saw Jesus walking by. "Look! The lamb of God!" he said. When the two disciples heard him say this, they followed Jesus.

Jesus turned and saw the two men following him. "What are you looking for?" he asked them. They said to him, "Rabbi (RAB-igh),* which means teacher, where do you live?" He answered, "Come and see." So they went with him and saw where he was staying. And they stayed with him all the rest of that day, for it was about four o'clock in the afternoon [when they met him].

One of the two who had heard John speak about Jesus and had gone with him was Andrew, Simon Peter's brother. Andrew then went and found his brother Simon and told him, "We have found the Messiah," which means the Christ. When he took Simon to Jesus, Jesus looked at him and said, "So you are Simon, the son of John? From now on you will be called Cephas (SEE-fas)," which means the same as Peter, a rock.

The next day Jesus decided to go to Galilee. So he found Philip (FILL-up) and said to him, "Come with me!" Philip was from Bethsaida (Beth-SAY-ee-dah), the city where Andrew and Peter lived. Philip found Nathanael (Na-THAN-ay-el) and told him, "We have found the person about whom Moses and also the prophets wrote: Jesus of Nazareth, the son of Joseph." Nathanael said to him, "Can anything good come out of Nazareth." Philip said to him, "Come and see."

1:29-46

A Wedding in Cana

Two days later there was a wedding in the town of Cana (KAY-nah) in the country called Galilee. Jesus was invited to the wedding, along with his disciples. The mother of Jesus was there too.

When all the wine was gone, Jesus' mother said to him, "They have no wine." Jesus said to her, "Woman, what right do you have to tell me what to do? My time [to do things] has not yet come." His mother said to the servants, "Do whatever he tells you to do."

Now, there were six stone water jars standing there. Each one held 20—30 gallons of water. These jars were used for religious washing of tables and dishes. Jesus said to the servants, "Fill the jars with water." So they filled them to the top.

Then Jesus told the servants, "Now draw some out and take it to the man in charge of the dinner." So they took it to him. And when the man tasted the water that had become wine, he called for the bridegroom. He didn't know where this wine had come from, but the servants knew.

The man said to the bridegroom, "Everyone else serves the good wine first. After the people have drunk a lot, then the poor wine is served. But you have kept the good wine until now!" This was the first mighty act that Jesus did and by which he showed his power and greatness. And his disciples believed in him.

After this Jesus went down to Capernaum (Ka-PER-nah-um) with his mother and his brothers and his disciples and stayed there for a few days.

When it was almost time for the Jewish Passover

holiday, Jesus went to Jerusalem. In the temple he found men selling cattle, sheep, and pigeons and also money changers doing their business. Making a whip from ropes, Jesus drove them all out of the temple, along with their animals. He also turned over the tables of the money changers and scattered their coins.

To those who sold pigeons Jesus said, "Take them out of here! Do not make my Father's house a place for buying and selling." Then his disciples remembered that it was written [in the Scriptures], "My love of your house, God, will destroy me."

The Jewish leaders said to Jesus, "What can you do to show us that you have the right to do these things?" Jesus answered, "Tear down this temple and in three days I will raise it up again." The leaders said, "It has taken 46 years to build this temple, and you are going to build it again in three days?"

But the temple Jesus was talking about was his body. So after Jesus later came back to life again, his disciples remembered that he had said this. And they believed the Scriptures and what Jesus had said.

2:1-22

Jesus and Nicodemus

[In Jerusalem] there was a man named Nicodemus (NICK-o-DEE-mus), a Pharisee, and a ruler of the Jews. This man came to Jesus one night and said to him, "Rabbi (RAB-igh),* we know you are a teacher who has come from God. No one could do the things that you do unless God were with him." Jesus answered, "I'm really telling you the truth, unless a person is born again, he cannot see the kingdom [and life] in which God rules."

Nicodemus said to Jesus, "How can a man be born again when he is old? Can he enter a second time into his mother and be born?" Jesus answered, "I'm telling you the truth, unless a person is born through water and the Spirit, he cannot enter the kingdom of God. People born from human beings are just human. Only people born from the Spirit of God have God's spirit.

"Don't be surprised that I said to you, 'You must be born again,'" Jesus continued. "The wind blows where it wants to and you can hear its sound. But you do not know where it comes from or where it goes. That's the way it is with everyone who is born from the Spirit of God."

Nicodemus said to Jesus, "How can this be?" Jesus answered, "You are a teacher of the Jews, and you don't understand this? I'm telling you the truth, we are talking about things we know and we tell what we have seen. Still you do not accept our message. If you do not believe me when I tell you about things on earth, how will you ever believe me when I tell you about things in heaven?"

"No one has ever gone up to heaven except the Son of Man, who came down from heaven," said Jesus. "And as Moses lifted up the snake on a pole in the desert, so will the Son of Man have to be lifted up, so that whoever believes in him will receive everlasting life. God so loved the world that he gave his only son, so that whoever believes in him will not die but will have eternal (e-TER-nal)* life. For God did not send his son into the world to judge [and damn] the world, but so that the world could be saved through him."

3:1-17

The Woman in Samaria

The Pharisees heard that Jesus was making and baptizing more disciples than John. Actually Jesus himself did not baptize anyone; only his disciples did the baptizing. But when Jesus heard what was being said, he left Judea and went again to Galilee.

On the way he had to go through Samaria (Sah-MER-ee-ah).* So he came to a city in Samaria called Sychar (SIGH-car). It was near the field that Jacob had given to his son Joseph. Jacob's well was there, and Jesus, tired out by the trip, sat down by the well. It was about 12 o'clock noon.

As Jesus sat there, a woman came to get some water [from the well]. Jesus said to her, "Give me a drink [of water]." His disciples had gone into the city to buy some food. The woman said to Jesus, "How can you, a Jew, ask me, a woman of Samaria, for a drink?" In those days most Jews wouldn't have anything to do with Samaritans (Sah-MER-i-tahns).* Jesus answered, "If you knew what God gives and who it is that is asking you for a drink, you would ask him, and he would give you living water."

"Sir," the woman said, "you don't have a bucket and the well is deep. Where would you get that living water? Are you greater than our ancestor Jacob who gave us this well?" . . . Jesus said to her, "Everyone who drinks this water will get thirsty again, but whoever drinks the water that I will give him will never get thirsty. The water that I will give him will become in him a spring that will give him eternal life."

"Sir," the woman said, "give me this water so that I'll never be thirsty again. Then I won't have to come here to get water." Jesus said to her, "Go and get your husband and come back here." She said, "I don't have a husband." Jesus said to her, "You are right in saying, 'I don't have a husband' because you have had five husbands. And the man you are living with now is not your husband. You have told the truth."

The woman said, "Sir, I see you are a prophet. I know that the Messiah is coming; he who is called the Christ. When he comes, he will tell us everything." Jesus said to her, "I who am talking to you am he!"

Just then the disciples came back. They were surprised to find Jesus talking with a woman. But none of them said to her, "What do you want?" or asked him, "Why are you talking with her?" So the woman left her water jar there and went back to the city. There she said to the people, "Come and see a man who told me everything I ever did. Could this be the Christ?" So they went out to see Jesus. . . .

And many of the people of that city believed in

Jesus because the woman had said, "He told me everything I ever did." So when the Samaritans came out to him, they begged him to stay with them, and he stayed there two days.

And many more believed because of what he told them. They said to the woman, "It is no longer because of what you said that we believe, but because we ourselves have heard him. And we know that he really is the Savior of the world."

4:1-19, 25-30, 39-42

Jesus Heals a Boy

After two days in that city in Samaria, Jesus left. . . . He went back to Cana in Galilee, where he had turned water into wine. There a man whose son was sick in Capernaum came to Jesus when he heard that Jesus had come back from Judea. The man begged Jesus to go to Capernaum and heal his son, who was dying.

Jesus said to the man, "Unless you see proof and wonderful works, you will not believe." But the man said to him again, "Sir, come with me before my child dies." So Jesus said to him, "Go; your son will live." And the man believed Jesus' words and went.

As he was on his way home, some of his servants met him and told him that his son was going to live. He asked them exactly what time it was when his son started to get better. They said to him, "Yesterday at one o'clock the fever left him." The father knew it was at that very time that Jesus had said to him, "Your son will live." So he and all his family believed [in Jesus].

This was the second great work that Jesus did after coming from Judea to Galilee.

4:43, 46-54

A Healing by the Pool

After this there was a Jewish festival, so Jesus went to Jerusalem. Now, there is in Jerusalem, by the Sheep Gate, a pool with five porches around it. In the

Hebrew language the place is called Bethesda. A large number of people were lying there on the porches—sick, blind, lame, and helpless people. [They were waiting for the water to bubble because every now and then an angel of God stirred up the water. The first person to go into the water after it was stirred up became well.]

One man who was there had been sick for 38 years. When Jesus saw him and knew he had been lying there a long time, he said to him, "Do you want to be healed?" The sick man answered, "Sir, I have no one to put me into the pool when the water is stirred up. While I am trying to get in, somebody else gets in ahead of me."

Jesus said to the man, "Get up, pick up your mat, and walk." Right away the man got well. He picked up his mat and walked away. But the day this happened was a sabbath day. So the Jewish officers said to the man who had been healed, "This is the sabbath, and it's against the law for you to carry your mat." But he answered, "The man who made me well told me to pick up my mat and walk."

Then they asked him, "Who is this man who told you to pick up your mat and walk?" The man who had been healed didn't know who it was because there was a crowd in that place and Jesus had slipped away.

Afterward Jesus found the man in the temple and said to him, "See, you are well! Sin no more, so that nothing worse will happen to you." Then the man went and told the Jewish officers that it was Jesus who had healed him. For this reason they began to hate and hound Jesus, because he did these things on the sabbath day.

Jesus said to them, "My father is still working all the time, so I am working also." This was why the Jewish leaders decided to find a way to kill Jesus—not only because he worked on the sabbath but also because he called God his own father and in this way made himself equal with God.

5:1-18

Jesus Feeds the Hungry

After this Jesus went to the other side of the Sea of Galilee. A large crowd followed him because they had seen his power in healing the sick. Jesus went up into the hills and sat down there with his disciples.

Now, the Passover holiday of the Jews was near. Looking up and seeing the crowd coming to him, Jesus said to Philip, "Where can we buy enough food to feed all these people?" This he said to test Philip, because he already knew what he would do.

Philip answered, "[A year's wages] wouldn't buy enough bread for each one to have even a little." But another one of Jesus' disciples, Andrew, Simon Peter's brother, said to him, "There is a boy here who has five loaves of bread and two fish. But what good will that do for so many people?"

Jesus said, "Make the people sit down." There was a lot of grass there. So the people sat down. There were about 5,000 men. Then Jesus took the boy's loaves of bread, thanked God for them, and gave the bread to the people sitting there. He did the same with the fish. And they all had as much as they wanted.

When they were all filled, Jesus said to his disciples, "Collect the pieces that are left over, so that nothing will be wasted." So they gathered what was left and filled 12 baskets. When the people saw this mighty work that Jesus had done, they said, "This is the prophet (PRAH-fet)* who was to come into the world!"

Then, seeing that the people were about to come and make him their king, Jesus went off into the hills by himself. When evening came, his disciples went down to the lake, got into a boat, and started across the water to Capernaum. By now it was dark, and Jesus still hadn't come back to them.

After they had rowed about three or four miles, the disciples saw Jesus walking on the water and coming to their boat. At first they were frightened, but Jesus said to them, "Don't be afraid. It is I." Then they were willing to take him into the boat. And right away the boat was at the other side where they wanted to go.

6:1-21

Jesus in Jerusalem

After this, Jesus traveled around in Galilee. He didn't travel in Judea because the leaders there wanted to kill him.

But when the Jewish festival of Tabernacles* was near, Jesus' brothers said to him, "Go to Judea so that your followers there will see the works you are doing. No one hides what he is doing if he wants to be well known. Since you are doing these things, show yourself to the rest of the world." Even his brothers didn't believe in him.

Jesus said to them, "The right time for me [to do this] has not yet come. Any time is all right for you. The world cannot hate you. But it hates me because I am saying that its ways are evil. You go ahead to the festival by yourselves. I am not going, because the right time for me is not yet." So, having said this, he remained in Galilee.

But after his brothers had gone, Jesus also went. However, he went secretly. The Jewish leaders were looking for him. "Where is he?" they asked. There was much whispering about him among the people. Some said, "He is a good man." Others said, "No, he is fooling the people." But no one talked openly about Jesus because they were afraid of the leaders of the people.

When the festival was about half over, Jesus went to the temple and began teaching. The leaders were very surprised. They said, "How does this man know so much? He has never studied at a school." Jesus answered, "What I teach is not my teaching, but his who sent me. Whoever is willing to do what God wants will know whether or not my teaching comes from God."

On the last day of the festival, the big day, Jesus stood and said loudly to the people, "If any one is thirsty, let him come to me and drink [the water I give]. Whoever believes in me, as the Scripture has said, 'out of his heart will come rivers of living water.'" Jesus was talking here about the Spirit that those who believe in him would receive. As yet the Spirit had not been given [to his followers] because Jesus had not yet been raised to glory.

When the people heard these words, some of them said, "This is really the prophet [who was expected to come]." Others said, "This is the Messiah." But some said, "Is the Messiah to come from Galilee? The Scripture says the Messiah will be born in Bethlehem, the town where David lived, and [will be] a member of David's family." So there was a disagreement among the people. Some wanted to arrest him, but no one laid a hand on him.

Then the officers went to the chief priests and Pharisees to report. They said, "Why didn't you bring him to us?" The officers answered, "No man ever spoke like this man speaks!" The Pharisees said to them, "Are you being fooled by him too? Have any of the Pharisees and your leaders believed in him? This crowd doesn't know the laws of Moses, and so they will be punished by God."

Nicodemus, who had gone to Jesus one night before this, said to them, "Does our law judge a man without giving him a hearing and learning what he does?" The others said to him, "Are you from Galilee too? Study the Scriptures and you will see that no prophet [of God] ever comes from Galilee."

7:1-17, 37-52

A Man Born Blind

As Jesus walked along [a street in Jerusalem], he saw a man who had been born blind. And his disciples asked him, "Teacher, whose sin was the reason this man was born blind, his or his parents?" Jesus

John

answered, "This man was born blind not because of his sin or his parents' sin, but so that the works of God could be seen in his life."

"We must do the works of him who sent me while it is still daylight," Jesus continued. "The night is coming when no one can work. As long as I am in the world I am the light for the world."

As he said this, Jesus spit on the ground and made some mud with the spit. Then he put the mud on the man's eyes and told him to go and wash [his eyes] in the Pool of Siloam (Sigh-LO-ahm).* So the man went, washed his face, and came back able to see.

His neighbors and those who knew him as a beggar said, "Isn't this the man who used to sit and beg?" Some said, "It is"; others said, "No, but he looks like him." He said, "I'm the man." They said to him, "Then how were your eyes opened?" He answered, "The man called Jesus made some clay, put it on my eyes, and said to me, 'Go to Siloam and wash!' So I went and washed [my eyes] and received my sight."

The people said to him, "Where is this Jesus now?" He said, "I don't know." So they took the man who had been blind to the Pharisees. You see, the day Jesus had made clay and healed the man's eyes was a sabbath day [and there was a strict law against doing anything unnecessary on a sabbath day].

The Pharisees also asked the man how he had become able to see. He said to them, "Jesus put mud on my eyes and I washed them and now I can see." Some of the Pharisees said, "The man who did this is not from God because he didn't obey the sabbath law." But others said, "How could a man who is a sinner do such wonderful works?" So there was a disagreement among them.

Then the Pharisees asked the man once more, "Since he opened your eyes, what do you say about him?" He said, "He is a prophet." But these leaders of the Jews were not willing to believe that the man had been blind and now could see. So they called the

308

parents of the man and asked them, "Is this your son? You say he was born blind? Well, how is it that now he can see?"

The parents answered, "We know that this is our son and that he was born blind. But how he is now able to see we don't know, nor do we know who opened his eyes." The parents said this because they were afraid of those leaders. For they had already decided that if anyone said that Jesus was the Messiah, he would be put out of the synagogue. That is why the parents said, "He is old enough [to speak for himself]; ask him."

So for the second time they called for the man who had been blind and said to him, "Give God the praise; we know that this man is a sinner." He answered, "Whether or not this man is a sinner I don't know. But one thing I do know: though I was blind, now I see!"

"What did he do to you?" they asked him. "How did he open your eyes?" The man answered, "I have already told you, and you wouldn't listen to me. Why do you want to hear it again? Do you also want to become this man's disciples?"

They became angry at him and said, "You are that man's disciple, but we are disciples of Moses. We know that God spoke to Moses. But as for this man, we don't even know where he came from." The man who had been blind said, "My, this is strange. You don't know where he came from but he opened my eyes! We know that God doesn't listen to sinners, but he does listen to people who worship him and do what he wants them to do. Never since the world began had anyone opened the eyes of a man born blind. If this man didn't come from God, he wouldn't be able to do anything [like that]."

The Jewish leaders answered back, "You were born in sin. Are you trying to teach us?" Then they put him out of the synagogue. Jesus heard about this and went and found the man. He said to him, "Do you believe in the Son of Man?" The man answered, "Tell me who he is, sir, so I can believe in him." Jesus said to him, "You have seen him, and he is talking with you right now."

The man said, "Lord, I believe!" and knelt down and worshiped Jesus.

9:1-38

The Good Shepherd

"I am the good shepherd," said Jesus. "The good shepherd is willing to die for his sheep. A hired man who is not a shepherd and does not own the sheep leaves the sheep and runs away when he sees a wolf coming. And the wolf catches the sheep and scatters them. The hired man runs away because he is a hired man and doesn't care about the sheep."

"I am the good shepherd," said Jesus again. "I know my sheep and the sheep know me, just as my Father knows me and I know my Father. And I am willing to die for my sheep. I also have other sheep that are not in this flock. I must bring them to me also, and they will listen to my voice. There will be one flock and one shepherd."

Then the time came to remember and celebrate the building of the temple in Jerusalem. It was winter and Jesus was there, walking in the part called Solomon's Porch. Some Jews gathered around him and said, "How long are you going to keep us in suspense? If you are the Messiah, tell us plainly."

Jesus answered, "I already told you, but you don't believe me. The things I do in my Father's name, they speak for me. You don't believe because you are not my sheep. My sheep listen to my voice, and I know them, and they follow me. And I give them eternal* life. They will never die, and no one can take them away from me. My Father, who has given them to me, is greater than anybody. No one is able to take them away from him, and my Father and I are one."

Then the Jews [who were listening to Jesus] picked up some stones to throw at him. So Jesus said to them, "I have done many good works at my Father's direction. For which one of these are you going to throw stones at me?" The men answered, "It is not for a good work that we stone you, but because you, being a man, make yourself God."

Jesus answered, "Isn't it written in your law that God said, 'You are gods'? If God called them gods, those people to whom the word of God came, how can you say that I, who was sent by the Father, am speaking against God because I said, 'I am the Son of God'? Whatever the Scripture says cannot be changed."

"If I am not doing the works of my Father," Jesus continued, "then don't believe me. But if I do them, even though you do not believe me, you ought to believe the things I do. In that way you would know and understand that the Father is in me and I am in the Father."

Again the Jewish leaders tried to arrest him, but he escaped. He went across the Jordan River to the place where John baptized, and there he stayed for a while. Many people came to him there, and they said, "John didn't do any miracles, but everything that John said about this man was true." And many people believed in him there.

10:11-16, 22-42

Lazarus (LA-zah-rus) Brought Back to Life

A man named Lazarus was sick. He lived in Bethany (BETH-an-nee) the town where Mary and her sister Martha lived. It was this Mary who had put perfume on the Lord and had wiped his feet with her hair. Lazarus was their brother.

The sisters sent a message to Jesus, saying, "Lord, your dear friend is very sick." But when Jesus heard this, he said, "This sickness will not end in death. It has happened so that it will bring glory to God and so that the Son of God will be honored by it."

Now, Jesus loved Martha and her sister and Lazarus. But when he heard that Lazarus was sick, he stayed two more days in the place where he was. Then he said to his disciples, "Let's go back to Judea (Jew-DEE-ah)."* The disciples said to him, "Teacher, not

311

long ago the people there tried to kill you by throwing stones at you. Are you going there again?"

Jesus answered, "If anyone walks during the day, he does not stumble, because he sees the light. But if anyone walks during the night, he stumbles, because the light is not in him." That's the way he spoke.

Then he said to his disciples, "Our friend Lazarus has fallen asleep; I will go to wake him up." The disciples said, "Lord, if he's sleeping, he will get well." Jesus meant that Lazarus was dead, but they thought he meant that Lazarus was resting in sleep.

Then Jesus told them plainly, "Lazarus is dead. But for your sake I'm glad I wasn't there so that you will believe. Come, let us go to him.". . .

When Jesus got there, he heard that Lazarus had already been in the grave four days. The town of Bethany was about two miles from Jerusalem. Many Jews had come to Mary and Martha to comfort them in their sadness over the death of their brother.

When Martha heard that Jesus was coming, she went and met him. Mary stayed in the house. Martha said to Jesus, "Lord, if you had been here, my brother would not have died. But even now I know that God will give you whatever you ask." Jesus said to her, "Your brother will rise again."

Martha said to him, "I know that he will rise again when the dead will be raised on the last day." Jesus said to her, "I am the one who raises the dead and gives them life. Whoever believes in me will live even if he dies. And whoever is living and believes in me will never die. Do you believe this?" Jesus asked. Martha answered, "Yes, Lord; I believe that you are the Christ, the Son of God. You are the one who has come into the world."

After Martha said this, she went and called her sister Mary. "The teacher is here and has asked for you," she said quietly. When Mary heard this, she got up quickly and went to him.

When the people who were with Mary in the house

saw her get up quickly and go out, they followed her. They thought she was going to the grave to cry there. But Mary went to the place where Jesus was. When Mary saw him, she knelt down at his feet and said, "Lord, if you had been here, my brother would not have died."

When Jesus saw her crying, and also the people who had come with her, he was deeply touched. "Where have you laid him?" asked Jesus. They said to him, "Lord, come and see." Then Jesus also cried, and the people said, "See how much he loved Lazarus." But some of them said, "He opened the eyes of a blind man. Couldn't he have kept Lazarus from dying?"

Then Jesus, very sad, came to the grave. It was a cave [in the side of a rock] and had a stone in front of the opening. Jesus said, "Take away the stone." Martha said to him, "Lord, by this time there will be an odor, because he's been dead four days!" Jesus said to her, "Didn't I tell you that if you would believe, you would see the glory of God?"

So they took the stone away. Then Jesus looked up and said, "Father, I thank you for hearing me. I know that you always hear me. But I have said this for the people standing here, so they will believe that you have sent me."

After saying this, Jesus called with a loud voice, "Lazarus, come out!" And the dead man came out. His hands and feet were still tied with grave cloths, and a white cloth was tied around his face. Jesus said to the people. "Unwrap him and let him go."

11:1-44

Jesus' Death Planned

Many of the Jews who had come with Mary, when they saw what Jesus had done, believed in him. But some of them went to the Pharisees and told them what Jesus had done. So the chief priest and the Pharisees called a meeting of the council. "What will we do?" they said. "This man is doing many wonderful works.

If we let him go on this way, everyone will believe in him. And the Romans will have their soldiers destroy our temple and our nation!"

But Caiaphas (KAY-ah-fuss), who was the high priest that year, said to them, "You don't know a thing! You don't see that it's better to have one man die for the people than to let the whole nation be destroyed." Caiaphas didn't think of this all by himself, but, as the high priest that year, he was telling in advance that Jesus was going to die for the Jewish people. And Jesus would die not only for them, but also to bring together into one group all the children of God who were living in many places.

From that day on the leaders of the Jews made plans to kill Jesus. For this reason Jesus no longer traveled openly among the Jews, but went from there to a town called Ephraim (EE-frah-im). It was near the desert [where no people lived]. There Jesus stayed with his disciples.

11:45-54

Hosanna to King Jesus

Six days before the Passover holiday began, Jesus came to Bethany, where Lazarus lived. He was the man Jesus had raised from death. Some friends prepared a dinner there in Jesus' honor. Martha helped serve it. Lazarus was one of the guests who sat at the table with Jesus.

During the dinner Mary took a jar of very expensive perfume and poured it on Jesus' feet. Then she dried his feet with her hair. The whole house was filled with the odor of the perfume.

Judas Iscariot (JEW-dahs Is-CARE-ee-ot), one of the disciples of Jesus, the one who was about to turn Jesus in to the leaders of the country, said, "Why wasn't this perfume sold . . . and the money given to the poor?" He said this, not because he cared about the poor, but because he was a greedy thief. He carried the money bag and used to take some of it for himself.

Jesus said, "Let her alone. She did this in advance of the day of my burial. You will always have poor people around you, but you will not always have me."

When a large crowd of people heard that Jesus was in Bethany, they came. They wanted not only to see Jesus but also Lazarus, whom Jesus had raised from death back to life. Because of Lazarus many Jews were leaving their own religion and were believing in Jesus.

The next day a big crowd of people was in Jerusalem for the Passover celebration. When they heard that Jesus was coming to the city, they took branches from palm trees and went out to meet him. "Hosanna (Hoh-ZAH-nah)," * they shouted. "Great and good is he who comes in the name of the Lord. He is the king of the Jews!"

Jesus found a young donkey and sat on it, just as the Scriptures said he would! "Don't be afraid, people of Jerusalem; your king is coming, sitting on a young donkey!" His disciples did not understand this at first. But later, when Jesus had been raised to glory, they remembered that these things were written about him.

The crowd that had been with Jesus when he called Lazarus out of the grave and made him alive again had reported what had happened. That was the reason why the crowd in Jerusalem had gone out to meet Jesus. When the Pharisees saw this, they said to one another, "You see, we are getting nowhere. The whole world is following him."

12:1-19

At the Last Supper

On the evening of the Passover holiday, Jesus knew the time had come for him to leave this world and go to the Father. . . . During his last supper with his disciples, . . . Jesus, knowing that he had come from God and was going back to God, got up from the supper table and took off his coat. Then he tied a towel around himself, poured some water into a bowl, and began to wash the disciples' feet. He also dried their feet with the towel he had tied around himself.

When he came to Simon Peter, Peter said to him, "Lord you shouldn't be washing my feet!" Jesus answered, "What I am doing you don't understand now, but you will later." Peter said to him, "I will never let you wash my feet!" Jesus said to him, "If I don't wash you, you will not be a part of me." Then Simon Peter said to him, "Lord, [in that case] don't just wash my feet, but wash my hands and my head too." . . .

Jesus washed their feet and put his robe back on. Then he sat down again and said to them, "Do you understand what I have done to you?" You call me teacher and Lord, and you're right, because that's what I am. If I, then, your Lord and teacher, have washed your feet, you also ought to wash one another's feet. I have given you an example, so that you would do what I have done to you. I tell you the truth, no servant is greater than his master; nor is a person who is sent greater than the one who sent him. Now that you know these things, you'll be happy if you'll do them." . . .

After Jesus had said this, he was very upset and said, "I tell you the truth, one of you is going to betray me." The disciples looked at one another, not sure they knew whom he meant.

One of his disciples, whom Jesus loved, was sitting very close to Jesus. Simon Peter motioned to him and said, "Ask him who it is he's talking about." So being close to Jesus he said to him, "Lord, who is it?" Jesus answered, "It is he to whom I will give this piece of bread after I have dipped it [in the sauce].

So Jesus dipped the piece of bread and gave it to Judas, the son of Simon Iscariot. As soon as Judas took the bread, the devil went into him. Jesus said to him, "What you are going to do, do quickly."

Now, no one at the table knew why Jesus had said this to Judas. Because Judas had the money bag, some thought that Jesus had told him to go and buy what they needed for the Passover supper, or that he should give something to the poor outside. So, after receiving the piece of bread, Judas left at once, and it was night.

After Judas left, Jesus said, . . . "A new commandment I give to you, that you love one another. As I have loved you, so you must love one another. If you will love one another, then everyone will know you are my disciples."

Simon Peter said to Jesus, "Lord, where are you going?" Jesus answered, "You cannot follow me now where I am going, but later you will." Peter said, "Lord, why can't I follow you now? I'm ready to die for you!" Jesus answered, "Are you really ready to die for me? I'm telling you the truth, Peter, before the rooster crows you will say three times that you don't even know me."

13:1-38

The Vine and Its Branches

"I really am the vine and my Father is the gardener," said Jesus. "He breaks off any branch that does not give fruit. And every branch that does bear fruit he cuts and cleans so that it will give more fruit. You already have been made clean by the words I spoke to you."

"Remain connected with me and I will remain united with you. No branch can bear fruit by itself. It has to get life from the vine. In the same way you cannot bear fruit unless you remain with me. I am the vine and you are the branches. Get your life from me and you will bear much fruit. Without me you can do nothing. . . .

"By this my Father is honored: when you bear much fruit and thereby show that you are my disciples. I have loved you the way my Father has loved me. Remain in my love. If you will obey my teachings, you will live in my love, just as I have obeyed my Father's will and live in his love. I have told you these things so that my joy may be in you and your joy may be complete.

"My commandment is this: Love one another the way I have loved you. The greatest love a person can have for his friends is to give his life for them. You are my friends if you do what I tell you. I no longer call you servants, because a servant doesn't know what his master is doing. I have called you friends because I have told you everything I have heard from my Father.

"You didn't choose me," said Jesus; "I chose you. And I selected you in the hope that you would bear fruit and that your fruit would last. The Father will give you whatever you ask him in my name. So this is what I command you: Love one another."

15:1-17

What the Holy Spirit Does

"There are many more things I want to say to you," said Jesus to his disciples, "but you aren't able to understand them yet. When the Holy Spirit will come to you, he will lead you into all the truth. He will not speak just anything, but he will speak what he hears, and he will tell you about things to come. He will honor me and will tell you what is mine. Everything my Father has is mine. That's why I said the Spirit will take what is mine and will tell it to you.

"In a little while," said Jesus, "you won't see me anymore; and then a little while later you will see me again." Some of the disciples said to one another, "What's he trying to tell us by saying, 'In a little while you won't see me anymore, and then a little while later you will see me again'? He also says, 'It's because I am going to the Father.' What does he mean by 'a little while'? We don't understand."

Jesus knew they wanted to ask him, so he said to them, "Are you asking yourselves what I meant by saying, 'In a little while you won't see me anymore, and then a little while later you will see me again'? I tell you the truth, you will cry and be sad, and the world will be happy. You will be sad, but your sadness will turn into joy.

"When a woman is about to have a baby, she is sad because her time of suffering has come. But when the child is born, she is so happy she forgets the pain she had. You are sad now, but I will see you again, and then you will be very happy. And no one will be able to take your joy away from you.

"When that day comes," said Jesus, "you will not ask me for anything. But I tell you the truth, whatever you ask the Father in my name, he will give it to you. Up to now you have not asked for anything in my name. Ask and you will receive, so that your happiness will be complete."

16:12-24

Jesus' Prayer for His Followers

When Jesus had finished saying these things, he looked up to heaven and said, "Father, the time has come. Give glory to your son so that your son can give the glory to you. You gave him the right to rule all people and the power to give eternal life to all those you gave to him.

"And this is the life that lasts forever: knowing you, the only true God, and Jesus Christ, whom you sent," said Jesus. "I honored you on earth. I did the work you gave me to do. And now, Father, give me the glory I had with you before the world was made.

"I do not pray only for these disciples," said Jesus, "but also for those who believe in me through their message. May they all be one, Father, as you are in me and I am in you. May they be in us so that the world will believe that you sent me. The same glory you gave me I have given to them so that they will become completely one. That's so the world will be able to see that you sent me and that you love them as you love me.

"Father," Jesus said as he continued to pray, "I want those you have given to me to be with me where I am. Then they will see my glory, the glory you gave me, because you loved me before the world was made.

John

O holy Father," said Jesus, "the world does not know you, but I know you. And these know that you sent me. I made you known to them. I will continue to do so in order that the love you have for me may be in them and that I also may be in them."

17:1-5, 20-26

Jesus Arrested

When Jesus had finished his prayer, he and his disciples went out across the Kidron (KID-ron) valley. On the other side there was a garden that Jesus and his disciples went to. Judas, who was planning to turn Jesus in to his enemies, also knew the place. Jesus had gone there often with his disciples.

So Judas, after getting a group of soldiers and some officers from the chief priests and the Pharisees, went to the garden with lanterns and torches and swords. Jesus knew everything that was going to happen to him, so he came forward and said to them, "Who are you looking for?" The soldiers answered, "Jesus of Nazareth." Jesus said to them, "I am he."

Judas, who had led the soldiers to Jesus, was standing there with them. When Jesus said to them, "I am he," they stepped back and fell to the ground. Again Jesus asked them, "Who are you looking for?" They said again, "Jesus of Nazareth." He said, "I told you I am Jesus. If you're looking for me, let these men go their way." He did this so that what he had said about not losing any of his men [except Judas] would come true.

Then Simon Peter, who had a sword, drew it. He struck the high priest's servant and cut off his right ear. The man's name was Malchus (MAL-kus). Jesus said to Peter, "Put your sword back where it was. Do you think I won't drink the cup of suffering my Father has given me to drink?"

Then the group of soldiers and their captain and the Jewish officers arrested Jesus and tied him up. First they took him to Annas. He was the father-in-law of Caiaphas (KAY-ah-fus), who was the main priest that year. It was Caiaphas who had told the Jewish leaders it was best that one man should die for the people.

Simon Peter followed Jesus and so did another disciple. This other disciple was well known to the high priest, so he went with Jesus into the courtyard of the high priest. At first Peter stayed outside the gate. But the other disciple spoke to the girl at the gate and brought Peter inside. The girl at the gate said to Peter, "Aren't you one of the disciples of that man?" Peter said, "I am not."

Now, it was cold. So the servants and the guards had built a fire and were standing around it, warming themselves. Peter went over and stood with them, warming himself.

As Peter was standing there and warming himself, others said to him, "Aren't you one of that man's disciples?" Peter denied it, saying, "I am not." But one of the servants of the high priest, a relative of the man whose ear Peter had cut off, asked, "Didn't I see you in the garden with him?" Again Peter said, "No." Right then a rooster crowed.

18:1-18, 25-27

Jesus Before Pilate

It was early in the morning when they took Jesus from the house of Caiaphas to the governor's palace. The Jews themselves did not enter the palace because they thought that would be sinful. So Pilate [the governor] went out to them and asked, "What do you say this man has done wrong?" Their answer was, "We would not have brought him to you if he had not done a crime."

Pilate said to them, "Then take him and give him a trial by your own laws." But the Jewish leaders said to Pilate, "We are not allowed to put anyone to death." This happened as Jesus said it would happen when he told what kind of death he would die.

Then Pilate went back into the palace and called for Jesus. "Are you the king of the Jews?" He asked Jesus. Jesus answered, "Are you yourself asking this or did others say this to you about me?" Pilate said, "Am I a Jew? Your own people and their priests handed you over to me. Why? What have you done?"

Jesus said, "My kingdom is not a part of this world. If my kingdom belonged to this world, then my followers would fight to keep me from being handed over to the Jewish leaders. But my kingdom is not a part of this world." Pilate said to him, "So you are a king?" Jesus answered, "Yes, I am a king. I was born and came into the world for this reason: to speak the truth. All who love truth listen to me." Pilate said to him, "What is truth?"

After he said this, Pilate again went out to the people. He said to them, "I don't find him guilty of any crime. But every year a man in prison is allowed to go free as part of the Passover celebration. Shall I let the king of the Jews go free?" They shouted, "Not this man, but Barabbas (Bah-RAB-bahs)." Barabbas was a robber.

18:28-40

How Jesus Suffered

Then Pilate took Jesus and had him whipped. And the soldiers made a crown of thorny branches and put it on his head. Then they put a purple robe on him and made fun of him by saying, "Long live the king of the Jews." They also hit him with their fists.

When Pilate went out again, he said to the people, "Look, I am bringing him out to you now so you'll see that I find him 'not guilty' of any crime." Then Jesus was brought out, wearing the crown of thorns and the purple robe. Pilate said to the crowd, "Look at the man!"

When the chief priests and the officers saw Jesus, they shouted, "Crucify* him! Crucify him!" Pilate said to them, "You take him and crucify him. I found no

322

reason to do so." The Jewish leaders shouted back, "We have a law that says he ought to die because he called himself the Son of God." When Pilate heard this, he was even more afraid.

So Pilate went back into the palace and asked Jesus, "Where are you from?" But Jesus gave him no answer. Pilate therefore said to him, "You won't speak to me? Don't you realize I have the power to free you or to crucify you?" Jesus answered, "You would have no power over me at all if it were not given to you by God." . . .

When Pilate heard this he tried to find a way to set Jesus free. But the people who wanted Jesus killed shouted back, "If you set this man free, you will not be Caesar's (SEE-zar)* friend. Anyone who claims to be a king is an enemy of Caesar."

When Pilate heard this, he brought Jesus out and . . . said to the crowd, "Here is your king!" They shouted back, "Kill him! Kill him! Crucify him!" Pilate said to them, "Do you want me to crucify your king?" The chief priests answered, "We have no king except Caesar." So Pilate handed Jesus over to the mob to be crucified.

19:1-16

Jesus Nailed to a Cross

The leaders took Jesus to the place called *The Place of the Skull*. In Hebrew it is called *Golgotha* (GUHL-gah-thah). There they crucified him. And with him two others, one on each side and Jesus between them. Pilate wrote a sign and had it put on the cross. It said, "Jesus of Nazareth, the king of the Jews."

Many of the Jews read this sign, for the place where Jesus was crucified was near the city. The sign was written in Hebrew, Latin, and Greek. The chief priests of the Jews said to Pilate, "Don't write, 'The king of the Jews,' but 'This man *said* I am the king of the Jews.'" Pilate answered, "What I have written I have written."

When the soldiers had finished nailing Jesus to a cross, they took his clothes and divided them into four parts, one part for each soldier. They also took the robe, but it was made of one piece, without a seam. So they said to one another, "Let's not tear it; let's throw dice to see who may have it." This happened so that what the Scripture says would come true: "They divided my clothes among themselves, and for my robe they gambled." This is what the soldiers did.

Standing near the cross of Jesus were his mother, and his mother's sister Mary, the wife of Clopas (KLO-pahs), and Mary Magdalene (MAG-dah-leen). When Jesus saw his mother and the disciple he loved standing near, he said to his mother, "Woman, there is your son!" Then he said to the disciple, "There is your mother!" From that time on that disciple took her to live in his home.

19:17-27

The Death of Jesus

After this Jesus knew that everything was about over. In order to make the Scripture come true, he said, "I'm thirsty." Now, there was a bowl of cheap wine there, so someone soaked a sponge in the wine, put it on a stick, and held it to his mouth. When Jesus had tasted it, he said, "It is finished." Then he bowed his head and died. . . .

After this a man named Joseph from the town of Arimathea asked Pilate if he could take Jesus' body. Joseph was a secret disciple of Jesus because he was afraid of the Jewish leaders. Pilate told him he could have the body, so Joseph went and took the body down from the cross. Nicodemus (Nick-o-DEE-mus), who had gone to see Jesus at night, also came with Joseph and brought 100 pounds of spices.

The two men took Jesus' body and wrapped it in linen cloths with the spices. That was the way the Jews prepared a body for burial in those days. Near the place where Jesus had been put to death there was a garden.

In the garden there was a new grave in which no one had ever been buried. Because it was the day before the Sabbath and the grave was close by, they laid the body of Jesus there.

19:28-30, 38-42

Jesus Appears Alive

On the first day of the week [Sunday morning] Mary Magdalene went to the grave early, while it was still dark. There she saw that the stone had been taken away from the door of the grave. So she ran and went to Simon Peter and the other disciple, the one Jesus loved, and said to them, "They have taken the Lord out of the grave and we don't know where they have put him."

Peter and the other disciple left at once and went to the tomb. They both ran, but the other disciple ran faster than Peter and reached the grave first. He bent over to look in and saw the linen cloths lying there, but he didn't go in. Then Simon Peter came along and went into the grave. He saw the linen cloths lying there and the cloth that had been wrapped around Jesus' head. It wasn't lying with the other cloths, but was rolled up by itself.

Then the other disciple who had reached the grave first also went in. He saw and believed, even though they did not yet understand the Scripture that said the Savior would rise from death. Then the two disciples went back to their homes.

But Mary stood crying outside the grave. As she was crying, she bent over and looked into the grave. Inside she saw two angels dressed in white clothes, sitting where the body of Jesus had been. One was at the head and the other at the feet.

The angels said to her, "Woman, why are you crying?" She said to them, "Because they have taken away my Lord, and I don't know where they have put him." As she said this, she turned around and saw Jesus standing there. But she didn't know it was Jesus.

Jesus said to her, "Woman, why are you crying?

Who are you looking for?" Mary thought he was the gardener, so she said to him, "If you took him away, sir, tell me where you put him and I will go and get him." Jesus said to her, "Mary!" She quickly turned and said to him, "Rabboni (Ra-BO-nigh)!" This means *teacher* in Hebrew. Jesus said to Mary, "Don't try to hold on to me, because I have not yet gone back to my Father. But go to my brothers and tell them for me, 'I am going to my Father and your Father, to my God and your God.'" So Mary Magdalene went and said to the disciples, "I have seen the Lord." And she told them he had said these things to her.

20:1-18

Jesus and Thomas

On that Sunday evening the disciples were meeting together behind locked doors because they were afraid of the leaders of the Jews. All at once Jesus appeared and stood among them. "Peace be with you," he said to them. Then he showed them his hands and his side, and the disciples were very glad when they saw it was their Lord.

Then Jesus said to them again, "May you have peace. As my Father sent me, so I send you." Then he said, "Receive the Holy Spirit. When you forgive anybody's sins, they are forgiven. When you do not forgive them, they are not forgiven."

Thomas, one of the 12 disciples, the one called the Twin, was not with them when Jesus came. So the other disciples told him, "We have seen the Lord." But he said to them, "Unless I see the holes the nails made in his hands and can put my finger on those holes and put my hand in his side, I will not believe."

Eight days later the disciples were together again in that house. This time Thomas was with them. The doors were locked, but Jesus came again and stood among them. "Peace to you," he said. Then he said to Thomas, "Put your finger here and look at my hands. Then put your hand in my side. Stop your doubting and believe." Thomas said, "My Lord and my God!" But Jesus said to him, "Do you believe because you see me? Those people who believe without seeing me are the most blessed."

Jesus did many other wonderful works that his disciples saw. They are not all written in this book. But these have been written so that you will believe that Jesus is the Messiah, the Son of God, and that by believing you will receive life in his name.

20:19-31

THE
Acts
OF THE FIRST CHRISTIANS

In the first book, dear Theophilus (Thee-AHF-ill-us), I wrote about all the things Jesus did and taught, from the beginning until the day he was taken to heaven. Before he went to heaven, he gave instructions through the Holy Spirit to the men he had chosen to be his apostles (ah-PAH-suhls). After his great suffering he showed himself alive to them in many ways. For 40 days he appeared to them and talked with them about the kingdom of God.

While meeting with them Jesus ordered them not to leave Jerusalem. "Wait for what my Father promised and what I told you about," he said. "John baptized with water, but in a few days you will be baptized with the Holy Spirit."

Those who were meeting with Jesus asked, "Lord, is this the time when you will give this country back to the Jews?" Jesus answered, "It is not for you to know the times that my Father alone decides. But you will receive power when the Holy Spirit will come into your life, and you will tell about me in Jerusalem, all over Judea (Jew-DEE-ah),* and Samaria (Sah-MER-ee-ah),* and to the ends of the earth.

When Jesus had said this and while they were watching, he was lifted up into the sky. And a cloud came and took him out of their sight. While they were still looking up at him leaving them, all at once two men in white robes stood beside them. They said, "You men from Galilee, why do you stand looking up into heaven? This Jesus who was taken from you into heaven will return in the same way you saw him go into heaven."

Then the followers of Jesus returned to Jerusalem from the hill called Olivet (Ahl-i-VET). It's about a half mile away from the city. When they entered the city, they went to the room where they were staying: Peter and John and James and Andrew, Philip and Thomas, Bartholomew (Bar-THAHL-ah-meeoo) and Matthew (MATH-yoo), James the son of Alphaeus (AL-fee-us), Simon the Patriot (PAY-tree-ot), and Judas, the son of James. All of these often met and prayed together as a group, along with the women disciples of Jesus and Mary, the mother of Jesus, and his brothers.

1:1-14

The Coming of the Spirit

When the day of Pentecost arrived, all the believers in Jesus were together in one place. Suddenly a noise that sounded like a strong wind came from the sky. It filled the whole house where they were sitting. Then the disciples saw what looked like tongues of fire coming down on each one of them, and they were filled with the Holy Spirit. Then they began to speak in languages they didn't know. The Holy Spirit gave them the power to do this.

Now, at that time many religious Jews from other countries of the world were in Jerusalem. Hearing the noise, a large crowd came running to see what was happening. When each one heard the disciples of Jesus speaking in his own language, they were very surprised. They said, "Aren't these men who are talking Galileans (Gal-i-LEE-ans)*? How is it, then, that . . . all of us hear them telling in our own language the great things God has done?"

Surprised and puzzled, some of the people kept asking each other, "What does this mean?" But others made fun of the disciples, saying, "These men are full of new wine."

Then Peter, standing up with the 11 disciples, spoke to the crowd in a loud voice. "People of Judea and all you who live in Jerusalem, listen to me and understand this. These men are not drunk, as you suppose. It is only nine o'clock in the morning. But what is happening is exactly what the prophet Joel (JO-el) said would happen. . . . All the people of Israel are to know that God has made this Jesus, whom you nailed to a cross, both your Lord and Messiah."

When the people heard this, they were very worried. They said to Peter and the other disciples, "What should we do, brothers?" Peter said to them, "Turn away from your sins and be baptized, every one of you, in the name of Jesus Christ for the forgiveness of your sins. Then you will receive the Holy Spirit as a gift from God. For God's promise of this gift was made to you and to your children and to all people everywhere. It is a promise the Lord our God makes to everyone he calls to himself."

Peter also said many other things to the people. He urged them to save themselves from the sinful people around them. Those who believed what he said were baptized. About 3,000 people were added to the group that day. And they all continued to meet together to learn the teachings of the apostles, to be with one another, and to eat the Lord's Supper and pray together.

2:1-8, 12-16, 36-42

The Church in Jerusalem

One day, about three o'clock, Peter and John went

to the temple. It was the time for prayer. At the gate called Beautiful there was a man who had been born lame. Everyday he was carried to this gate to beg for money from the people who went into the temple.

As Peter and John were about to enter, the beggar asked them to give him something. Peter looked at him, as did John, and said, "Look at us!" So the lame man looked at them, expecting to get some money.

Peter said, "I have no money, but I'll give you what I have: In the name of Jesus Christ of Nazareth, get up and walk!" Then he took him by the right hand and pulled him up. At once the man's feet and ankles became strong. He jumped on his feet and walked and went into the temple with them.

As the man enjoyed walking for the first time in his life, he went jumping along and thanking God. The people who saw him knew he was the one who usually sat begging at the Beautiful Gate of the temple. So they were very surprised at seeing him and wondered what had happened to him.

The man held on to Peter and John, so all the people came running to them in the place called Solomon's (SAHL-ah-mahn)* Porch. They were really wondering about it all.

When Peter saw this, he spoke to the people. "People of Israel," he said, "why do you wonder about this and why do you stare at us? Do you think it was by our own power or holy lives that we made this man walk? The God of Abraham, Isaac, and Jacob, the God of our ancestors (AN-sess-ters),* gave his servant Jesus glory. . . .

"He was holy and good," Peter said, "but you asked Pilate to free a murderer and killed the one who gives people life. This Jesus God raised from the dead. We saw him alive. And this man whom you see and know has been made strong by the power of Jesus' name and faith in his name. It was faith in Jesus that gave this man the perfect health you all see he has." . . .

3:1-16

Peter and John on Trial

As Peter and John were still talking to the people, the priests and the captain of the temple guards came to them. They were angry because the two disciples were teaching the people that Jesus had risen from the dead and that therefore dead people can come back to life.

So they arrested the two disciples of Jesus and put them in jail until the next day, since it was already evening. But many who had heard Peter's message believed, and the number was about 5,000 men.

The next day the leaders of the Jews, the rulers of the temple, and the teachers of the Jewish religion met together in Jerusalem. They met with Annas, the top religious leader. Caiaphas and others who were in his family were there too. They had Peter and John brought before them. "By what power or in whose name did you do this?" they asked them.

Then Peter, full of the Holy Spirit, said to them, "Rulers of the people and of the temple, if we are being questioned about the good deed done to the lame man and how he was made well, then you and all the people of Israel should know that it was by the power of Jesus Christ of Nazareth that this man is standing before you well. This Jesus you crucified, but God raised him from the dead. . . . And there is no one else in all the world who can save us."

When the members of the court saw how bravely Peter and John spoke and knew that they were ordinary men without an education, they were impressed. They realized that Peter and John had been with Jesus, but they couldn't argue with them because the man who was healed was standing there with them.

So they told Peter and John to leave the room and then talked among themselves. "What can we do with these men?" they asked. "All the people living in Jerusalem know that a wonderful deed has been done by them, and we cannot say it didn't happen. But to keep this matter from spreading any farther, let's warn these men not to speak any more to anyone in the name of Jesus."

When they called Peter and John back into the room, they told them not to speak or teach any more in the name of Jesus. But Peter and John said to them, "You must decide whether God thinks it is right to obey you rather than him. We cannot stop talking about what we have seen and heard."

So the leaders warned the two disciples even more strongly and then let them go. They couldn't find any reason for punishing them, and the people were all praising God for what had happened. The man who had been healed was over 40 years old.

As soon as Peter and John were free, they went to their friends and reported what the chief priests and temple rulers had said to them. When their friends heard what had happened, they all joined together in a prayer to God.

"Lord God," they said, "you made the heaven and the earth and the sea and everything in them. You spoke through our ancestor David, your servant, by means of the Holy Spirit when he said, . . . 'The kings of the earth stand ready, and the leaders get together against the Lord and against his chosen Messiah.' Herod and Pontius Pilate both met here with others in this city against Jesus, your holy servant, whom you chose to be the Messiah. They met to do everything you had already decided would take place."

"And now, Lord," they said, "note the threats they made and give your servants courage to speak your message while you heal and do other wonderful works through the name of your holy servant Jesus." When they had finished praying, the place where they were meeting shook. And all the people there became filled with the Holy Spirit and spoke the Word of God without fear of what might happen to them.

4:1-31

More Trouble Begins

Many miracles and wonderful things were done for

the people by the apostles. Every day the believers met together in a group at Solomon's Porch. Nobody outside the group dared to join them even though the people spoke very well of them. But more and more believers joined the group, a large number of men and women.

Soon sick people were carried out into the streets and were put on beds and mats. People did this so that when Peter would walk by, at least his shadow might fall on some of them. Crowds of people also came from the towns around Jerusalem. They brought their sick and those who had bad spirits that were making them sick. All were healed.

Then the high priests and his friends, people who didn't believe anyone lived after dying, became very jealous of the disciples. So they had them arrested and put into a jail. But that night an angel of God opened the prison gates and brought the disciples out. The angel said to them, "Go back to where you were in the temple, and tell the people all about this new life." The apostles did as they were told. Early the next morning they went back to the temple and started teaching.

The high priest and his friends called a meeting of the city council and all the rulers of the Jews. They sent orders to the prison to have the disciples brought to them. But when the officers arrived, they didn't find the disciples in prison. So they returned. "When we arrived at the jail," they reported, "we found it locked up tight and the guards on duty. But when we opened the gates, we found no one inside."

When the captain of the temple guards and the priests heard this report, they wondered what had happened and what might happen next. Then someone came and told them that the men they had put into prison were standing in the temple and were teaching the people. So the captain went with his men and brought the disciples to the meeting. But they didn't use any force because they were afraid the people might stone them. *5:12-26*

Peter and John Warned

At their meeting they made the disciples stand in front of the council. The high priest questioned them. "We gave you strict orders not to teach in the name of this man," he said. "But still you have spread your teaching all over Jerusalem. And you are making it look as though we killed this man," he said.

To that Peter and the other apostles answered, "We must obey God rather than men! The God of our fathers raised Jesus from death after you people killed him by nailing him to a cross. God made him his leader and savior, to give the people of Israel a chance to repent and have their sins forgiven. We have seen these things and are telling about them, and so is the Holy Spirit whom God gives to those who obey him."

When the men of the council heard this, they became very angry. They wanted to kill the disciples. But one of them, a Pharisee named Gamaliel (Gah-MAY-lee-el), a teacher who was very respected by all the people, stood up and asked that the prisoners be taken out of the room.

Then he said to the council, "Men of Israel, be careful what you do to these men. Some time ago a man appeared and claimed that he was somebody great. About 400 men joined him. But he was killed and all his followers were scattered, and his teachings came to nothing. After him came a certain Judas from the country of Galilee. He gathered some followers, but he too was killed and all his followers were scattered.

"And so in the present case I tell you," he said, "let these men alone. If this teaching and work of theirs is their own plan, it will disappear. But if it is God's plan, you will not be able to stop it. You may even find yourselves fighting against God!"

So the council took Gamaliel's advice. When they called the disciples back to their meeting, they just had them whipped and ordered them never again to speak about or for Jesus. Then they set the men free.

The disciples left the council meeting feeling happy. They were happy they could suffer shame for the sake of Jesus' name. And every day they kept on teaching and preaching about Jesus Christ—in the temple and in people's homes.

5:27-42

Seven Helpers

In those days, when the number of disciples kept growing, the Greek-speaking Jewish Christians grumbled about the other Jewish Christians. The Greek-speaking Christians said their widows* were not being taken care of when the food was given out each day.

So the 12 apostles called a meeting of all the disciples and said, "It's not right that we should have to give up preaching the Word of God in order to hand out food. So then, brothers, choose seven men from among you, men who are respected and wise. We will have them take care of this work. Then we can spend our time in praying and doing the work of preaching and teaching.

What the apostles said pleased the whole group; so they chose Stephen, who was a man full of faith and full of the Holy Spirit. They also chose six other men. These men were presented to the apostles, who then prayed and placed their hands on them and made them their helpers.

And so the Word of God was spread, and the number of disciples increased greatly in Jerusalem. Also a great number of Jewish priests became Christians.

6:1-7

Stephen Is Killed

Stephen, a man full of faith and power, did many great things among the people. But some men from a group called the Free Men came and argued with Stephen. The Holy Spirit gave Stephen such wisdom that they couldn't win their arguments. So they secretly got some other men to say, "We heard this Stephen speak against Moses and against God."

When the people were stirred up against Stephen, the leaders and the teachers came and captured him and brought him to trial. They got false witnesses to say, "This man is always talking against our temple and our laws. We heard him say that this Jesus of Nazareth will tear down the temple and will change what Moses taught us."

All those sitting in the court looked at Stephen and saw that his face looked like the face of an angel. Then the high priest asked Stephen, "Is this so?" Stephen answered, "Brothers and fathers, listen to me! . . . You always resist the Holy Spirit. Was there any prophet that your ancestors did not mistreat? And they killed God's messengers who announced the coming of his holy servant. And you have killed him. You are the ones who received the laws of God delivered by angels but did not keep them."

When the members of the council heard Stephen say these things, they were furious. They bit their teeth in anger. But he, full of the Holy Spirit, looked up to heaven and saw God's glory. He also saw Jesus standing at the right side of God. "Look!" he said. "I see the heavens open and the Son of Man standing at the right side of God."

Well, when the Jewish leaders heard this, they screamed at him and covered their ears with their hands. Then they all rushed to him and took him out of the city and stoned him.

The men who did this left their coats in charge of a young man named Saul. As they were stoning Stephen, he prayed, "Lord Jesus, receive my spirit." Then he knelt down and shouted, "Lord, do not hold this sin against them." When he had said this, he died. Saul was pleased that Stephen was dead.

6:7-15; 7:1, 51-60; 8:1

The Church Suffers but Grows

The day that Stephen was killed the church in Jerusalem began to be treated very badly. All the believers in Jesus, except the apostles, left the city. They went to different parts of the countries of Judea and Samaria.

Some good men buried Stephen in a grave, and were very sad. But Saul tried to destroy the church. Going from house to house, he took men and women he thought were Christians and put them into prison.

Those Christians who had to go to other places to be safe preached the good news about Jesus wherever they went. Philip went to a city in Samaria and told the people there that their Messiah had come. The crowds paid close attention to what Philip said because they also saw the miracles he did. Evil spirits came out of many people, and many crippled people were healed. So there was much joy in that city.

A man named Simon lived in that city. For many years he had done magic and had led the people of Samaria to think he was somebody great. Many said, "He has the great power of God." So they paid attention to him because he fooled them with his magic.

But now, when the people believed Philip's message about the kingdom of God and the name of Jesus Christ, they were baptized, both men and women. Also Simon believed. And after being baptized, Simon hung around Philip and was surprised at the great miracles Philip was able to do.

When the apostles in Jerusalem heard that people in Samaria had received the Word of God, they sent Peter and John to them. When they arrived, they prayed that the believers might receive the Holy Spirit. The Holy Spirit had not yet come to them. They had only been baptized in the name of the Lord Jesus. So Peter and John laid their hands on the people and then they received the Holy Spirit.

When Simon saw that the Spirit of God was given

to people when they placed their hands on them, he said to Peter and John, "Give this power to me too, so that anyone on whom I put my hands will receive the Holy Spirit." He offered them money if they would give him this power.

But Peter said to Simon, "May your money die with you because you thought you could buy God's gifts with money! You can't take part or share in our work because your heart isn't right in God's sight. Turn away from this very wrong thinking of yours and ask the Lord to forgive you for thinking such a thing as this. For I see that you are full of envy and are tied up by your sin." Simon said, "Please pray to the Lord for me, so that none of the things you said will happen to me."

After Peter and John had finished telling what they knew and believed about Jesus and his teachings, they went back to Jerusalem. On their way they preached the good news in many towns of Samaria.

8:2-25

Philip and the Ethiopian (Ee-thee-O-pee-ahn)*

But as for Philip, an angel of the Lord said to him, "Get ready and go down to the road that goes from Jerusalem to Gaza (GAY-zah)." This road went through a desert where nobody lived, but Philip went anyway.

Soon a man from the country of Ethiopia (Ee-thee-O-pee-ah) who had come to Jerusalem to worship [the God of the Jews] came down that road. He was on his way home in his chariot (CHAIR-ee-ot).* This man was an important person in charge of the money that belonged to the queen of Ethiopia.

As the man rode along in his chariot, he was reading the book of the prophet Isaiah. The Holy Spirit said to Philip, "Go over to that chariot." So Philip ran up to it and heard the man reading from the Book of Isaiah. "Do you understand what you are reading?" asked Philip. The man answered, "How can I unless someone will help me?" Then he invited Philip to climb up and sit and talk with him.

The passage in the Bible that the man was reading was this: "Like a sheep that is taken to be killed or a lamb that makes no sound when its wool is cut off, so he remained silent. He was put to shame and no one cared. Who will be able to describe the people of his time? For his life on earth was taken."

The man said to Philip, "Please tell me, about whom did the prophet say this, about himself or someone else?" Philip then began to explain. Starting with this passage, he told the man the good news about Jesus.

As they went down the road, they came to a place where there was some water. The man said, "Look, here is some water! What is to keep me from being baptized?" Philip said to him, "If you believe with all your heart, you may be baptized." He answered, "I believe that Jesus Christ is the Son of God."

Then the man from Ethiopia ordered his driver to stop the chariot, and he and Philip went down into the water. There Philip baptized the man. And when they came back out of the water, the Spirit of the Lord took Philip away and the man saw him no more. So the man continued on his way very happy. But Philip found himself at a place called Azotus (A-ZO-tus). From there he went and preached the good news about Jesus in all the towns along the way to Caesarea (Sez-ah-REE-ah).*

8:26-40

Saul Becomes a Christian

But Saul kept on talking about killing the disciples of Jesus. He went to the high priest and asked for letters that would introduce him to the Jewish church leaders in Damascus (Dah-MAS-kus).* The letters gave him permission to arrest and bring back followers of Jesus he might find there.

Now, as Saul came near the city of Damascus, all at

once a light from the sky flashed around him. He fell to the ground, and then he heard a voice say to him, "Saul, Saul, why are you working against me?" "Who are you, Lord?" Saul asked. The voice answered, "I am Jesus, the one you are working against. Get up and go into the city. There you will be told what to do."

The men who were traveling with Saul were standing there, not knowing what to say. They heard the voice but saw no one. When Saul got up from the ground, his eyes were open but he couldn't see anything. So the others took him by the hand and led him to the city of Damascus. For three days Saul wasn't able to see at all. During that time he didn't eat or drink anything.

In Damascus there was a disciple whose name was Ananias (An-ah-NIGH-us). The Lord said to him in his mind, "Ananias!" And he answered, "Here I am, Lord." Then the Lord told him, "Go to the street called Straight Street and at the house of Judas ask for a man named Saul. He is praying there. In his mind he has seen a man named Ananias come and place his hands on him so he could see again."

Ananias answered, "Lord, I have heard about this man from many people, how he has done many terrible things to your people in Jerusalem. And here he has permission from the chief priests to arrest all who call on your name." But the Lord said to Ananias, "Go, because I have chosen him to serve me, to make my name known to Gentiles (JEN-tighles)* and kings and to the people of Israel. And I myself will show him how much he must suffer for my sake."

So Ananias went and entered the house [where Saul was staying]. And laying his hands on him he said, "Brother Saul, the Lord Jesus sent me. He is the one who appeared to you on the road as you were coming here. He sent me so that you might be able to see again and become filled with the Holy Spirit." At once something like fish scales fell from Saul's eyes, and he could see again. He got up and was baptized before he did anything else. Then he ate some food [for the first time in days], and his strength began to come back.

For several days Saul stayed with the disciples in Damascus. He went straight to the synagogues and began to preach about Jesus. "He is the Son of God," said Saul. And all who heard Saul were surprised. "Isn't this the man who caused so much trouble for the followers of Jesus in Jerusalem? And didn't he come here to arrest such people and take them in chains to the chief priests?"

But Saul's preaching became more and more powerful, and the Jews in Damascus couldn't deny his proofs that Jesus was the Messiah. So after a number of days the Jewish leaders met and made plans to kill Saul. But Saul was told what their plans were. Day and night they were watching the city gates to kill him [as he left]. So one night his followers let him down over the wall in a basket.

When Saul came to Jerusalem, he tried to join the disciples of Jesus there. But they were all afraid of him. They didn't believe he really had become a disciple.

So Barnabas took Saul to the apostles and told them how Saul had seen the Lord on the road to Damascus and how the Lord had spoken to Saul. Barnabas also told them how Saul had preached fearlessly in the name of Jesus in Damascus. So Saul lived with them in Jerusalem for a time and went all over Jerusalem, preaching boldly in the name of the Lord.

9:1-29

Peter and Dorcas

In the city of Joppa (JAH-pah) there lived a woman believer whose name was Tabitha (TA-bi-tha). Her name in Greek is Dorcas (DOOR-kus), which means a deer. Dorcas did many good things and helped the poor a lot.

One day she got sick and died. Her friends washed

her body and laid it in an upstairs room. When the disciples of Jesus heard that Peter was at Lydda (LID-dah), a town not far from Joppa, they sent two men to Peter with a message. It said, "Please come to us right away."

So Peter got ready and went with them. When he arrived, he was taken to the upstairs room [where the body of Dorcas was being kept]. All the widows she had helped crowded around him, crying and showing him the clothes Dorcas had made for them while she was alive.

But Peter put them all out of the room and knelt down and prayed. Then he turned to the dead body and said, "Tabitha, get up!" Slowly she opened her eyes, and when she saw Peter, she sat up. Peter reached over and helped her get up. Then he called the believers and the widows and presented Dorcas alive to them.

The news about this soon spread all over Joppa, and many more people believed in the Lord. Peter stayed in Joppa for a while with a man named Simon, a man who made leather.

9:36-43

The Story of Cornelius (Kor-NEEL-ee-uhs)

In the city of Caesarea (Sez-ah-REE-ah) there lived a man named Cornelius. He was a captain in the Roman army and a religious man. He and his whole family worshiped God. He gave a lot to the poor people, and he prayed to God all the time.

One afternoon about three o'clock he somehow saw an angel of God coming to him. The angel said to him, "Cornelius." Cornelius was afraid as he stared at the angel. "What is it, Lord?" he asked. The angel answered, "God has seen and remembered your prayers and your gifts. Now send some men to Joppa and have them bring a man named Simon Peter to you. He is staying with a leathermaker named Simon. His house is by the sea."

When the angel who spoke to him went away,

Cornelius called two of his servants and a soldier who took care of him. After telling them what had happened, he sent them off to Joppa.

The next day, as they were on their way and getting near the city, Peter went up on the roof of his house to pray. It was about noon. On the roof he became hungry and wanted something to eat.

While the food was being prepared, Peter fell asleep and had a dream. He saw the sky open up and something like a big white sheet being let down to the earth by its four corners. On the cloth were all kinds of animals and snakes and birds. Then a voice came to him that said, "Get up, Peter, and kill anything on the cloth and eat it."

But Peter said, "No, Lord; I have never eaten anything that our religious laws forbid." Then the voice spoke to him again, saying, "Do not call anything unclean that God has made clean." This happened three times. Then the cloth with the animals was taken back up into heaven.

While Peter was wondering about the meaning of what he had seen, the men sent by Cornelius learned where Simon's house was. Standing in front of the gate, they called out and asked whether a man called Simon Peter was staying there.

Peter was still thinking about the dream when the Holy Spirit said to him, "Listen!" These men are looking for you. Get up, go down, and go with them. Don't hesitate to go with them because I sent them to you."

So Peter went down and said to the men, "I'm the one you are looking for. Why have you come?" They answered, "Cornelius, an army captain, a good man who worships God and is very well respected by the Jewish people, he sent us. He was directed by one of God's angels to send for you to come to his house. He wants to hear what you have to say." So Peter invited them in to first spend the night there.

The next day Peter went with them, and some of the

believers in Jesus living in Joppa went along. On the following day they arrived at Caesarea. Cornelius was expecting them and had called together his relatives and close friends. When Peter arrived, Cornelius met him, knelt down at his feet, and worshiped him. But Peter made him get up. "Stand up," he said. "I too am only a man."

As Peter spoke with Cornelius, he went into the house and found many people waiting to meet him. He said to them, "You know it is against our law for a Jew to visit with or have anything to do with a Gentile. But God has shown me that I must not call any person common or unclean. So I came as soon as I was sent for. Now tell me what you want."

Cornelius said, "Four days ago, about this time, I was praying in my house, and suddenly a man dressed in shiny clothes stood in front of me. He said, 'Cornelius, God has heard your prayer and remembers your gifts of love. Send someone to Joppa to call for a man whose name is Simon Peter. He is staying in the house of Simon, a leatherworker who lives by the sea.' So I sent for you at once, and you have been good enough to come. Now we are all here in the presence of God to hear anything the Lord has told you to say."

Then Peter spoke and said, "I now see that God plays no favorites, but that in any country whoever worships him and does what is right pleases him. You know the message he sent to the people of Israel. It announced the good news of peace through Jesus Christ, who is the Lord of all. This word was preached throughout all Judea. . . . And we are witnesses to all that Jesus did in the country of the Jews and in Jerusalem. They put him to death by hanging him on a cross, but God raised him on the third day and made him visible. . . .

"And Jesus commanded us to preach to people and to tell them that he is the one chosen by God to judge the living and the dead. All the prophets spoke about him, saying that everyone who believes in him will receive forgiveness of sins through the power of his name."

While Peter was still speaking, the Holy Spirit came to all who were listening to the message. And the Jewish believers who had come from Joppa with Peter were surprised that God gave the Holy Spirit to Gentiles also. For they heard them speaking in strange languages and praising God.

Then Peter said, "These people have received the Holy Spirit just as we did. Does anyone therefore have the right to stop them from being baptized with water?" So he ordered that they be baptized in the name of Jesus Christ. After they were baptized, Cornelius and his friends asked Peter to stay with them for a while, which he did.

10:1-48

Peter Freed from Prison

The Christians who moved from Jerusalem when trouble started went to such distant places as Cyprus (SIGH-prus).* But they told the message of Jesus only to Jews. Later some of the believers from Cyprus and Cyrene (Sigh-REEN)* went to a city called Antioch (AN-tee-awk) and spoke about the Lord Jesus also to the Greek people there. The Lord gave them power, and a great number of people believed and turned to the Lord. . . .

About that time some prophets came from Jerusalem to Antioch. The Spirit of God caused one of them, Agabus (AG-ah-bus), to stand up [in the meeting] and say that there would soon be a great shortage of food all over the world. This later happened when Claudius (KLAW-dee-us) became the ruler of the country. So the disciples decided that each one would send as much money as he could to help the Christians who lived in Judea. They did this and sent the money with Barnabas and Saul to the church leaders in Jerusalem.

At that time King Herod began to use his power

against some members of the church of Jesus in Jerusalem. He had James, the brother of John, put to death with a sword. And when he saw that this pleased the leaders of the Jews, he went ahead and had Peter arrested. This was done during the Passover celebration.

After his arrest Peter was put in jail. Four groups of four soldiers each were told to guard him around the clock. Herod planned to put Peter on public trial after the Passover. So Peter was kept in prison. But the people of the church prayed hard to God for him.

The night before Herod was going to bring Peter to trial before the people, Peter was sleeping between two guards. He was tied with two chains and soldiers at the gates were guarding the prison. All at once an angel of the Lord appeared and a light shone in the prison cell where Peter was.

The angel hit Peter on his side and woke him up. "Get up quickly," said the angel, and the chains fell off Peter's hands. Then the angel said to him, "Get dressed and put on your sandals." Peter did this at once.

Then the angel said to Peter, "Wrap your coat around you and come with me." When he went out, Peter followed him. At first Peter wasn't sure that what was happening was really happening; he thought it was all a dream.

When they passed by the first guard and then the second, they came to the iron gate that opened to the city. The gate opened for them by itself. When they went up one street, the angel disappeared. As Peter began to realize what had happened, he said to himself, "Now I'm sure the Lord sent his angel. He saved me from Herod's power and from all the things the people wanted him to do to me."

After he realized what had happened, Peter went to the home of Mary, the mother of John Mark. Many Christians had come together there to pray for Peter. When Peter knocked at the outside door, a girl named Rhoda (RO-dah) came to see who it was.

Rhoda knew at once that it was Peter's voice, but in her happy excitement she ran back into the house without opening the door. "Peter is standing outside the gate," she told the group. "You're out of your mind," they told her. But she said he really was there so they said, "It must be his angel."

Peter kept on knocking, so at last they opened the door. When they saw Peter, they were very surprised. He motioned to them to be quiet and then explained to them how the Lord had brought him out of the jail. "Tell this to James and the rest of the brothers," he said. Then he left and went somewhere else.

The next morning there was big excitement among the soldiers over what had happened to Peter. Herod gave orders to search for him. But they couldn't find him. So Herod questioned the guards and then ordered them to be killed.

11:19-30; 12:1-19

Paul on a Mission

One night [as Paul and a young man named Timothy were traveling about and telling the good news of God's love], Paul had a dream. In that dream a man from Macedonia (Ma-sah-DOH-nee-ah)* was standing and calling to Paul. He was saying, "Come over to Macedonia and help us." After this, we [Luke and Paul and others in his group] tried to go to Macedonia. We decided that God had called us to preach the gospel to the people there.

So, leaving by ship from Troas (TRO-as), we sailed straight to a city called Samothracia (Sam-o-THRAY-see-ah). The next day we went to the city of Neapolis (Nee-AP-o-lis). From there we went to Philippi (Fil-IP-igh), which is the main city of Macedonia. . . . We stayed there for several days.

On the sabbath day we went outside the gate of the city to the riverside. We thought people might come together there for prayer. Some women came, and we sat down and talked to them.

One of the women who listened to us was Lydia (LID-ee-ah), a seller of purple cloth. She was a worshiper of God, and the Lord made her willing to listen to what Paul said. So when she and her whole family were baptized, she said to us, "If you have decided I am a true believer in the Lord, come and stay in my house." Because she kept on asking us, we went and stayed with her.

One day as we were going to the place for prayer, we were met by a slave* girl. This girl had the power to tell what was going to happen in the future. By telling fortunes she earned a lot of money for her owners. For many days she followed us, shouting, "These men are servants of the Most High God. They tell you how you can be saved!"

Finally Paul became bothered by her. He turned around and said to the bad spirit in her, "In the name of Jesus Christ I order you to come out of her." At once the spirit went out of her.

But when her owners saw that their way of making money was now gone, they grabbed Paul and Silas (SIGH-las)* and took them to the market place, where the rulers of the city sat and ruled. They said to the rulers, "These men are Jews and are causing trouble in our city. They are teaching a religion that we Romans cannot accept and practice."

The crowd joined in attacking Paul and Silas. So the leaders tore off their clothes and had them whipped. After Paul and Silas were hit many times with sticks, they were thrown into jail. The jailer was told to keep them locked up tightly. So the jailer put then into an inside room and locked their feet in heavy blocks of wood.

About midnight Paul and Silas were praying and singing hymns to God. The prisoners were listening to them. All at once there was a big earthquake. It shook the prison from top to bottom and all the doors flew open. Also the chains fell off of all the prisoners. When the jailer woke up and saw that the prison doors were open, he took his sword and was about to kill himself. He thought the prisoners had all escaped.

But Paul shouted to him at the top of his voice, "Don't hurt yourself! We are all here!" Then the jailer called for a light and ran in. Shaking with fear, he knelt down in front of Paul and Silas and said, "Sirs, what must I do to be saved?" They said, "Believe in the Lord Jesus, and you will be saved—you and all your family."

Then Paul and Silas spoke the Word of God to him and to all who lived in his house. That night the jailer washed their wounds, and he and all his family were baptized. Then he took Paul and Silas into his house and gave them some food to eat. He and his family were very happy that now they believed in God.

The next morning the Roman leaders sent police officers with the order, "Let those men go." So the jailer reported to Paul, "The leaders have sent an order to let you go. You may leave and go in peace." But Paul said to the police, "We were beaten in front of many people without a trial. And we who are Roman citizens were put into prison. Now they want to send us away secretly? Oh, no! They must come here and take us out themselves."

Well, the police reported to the rulers of the city what Paul had said. When they heard that Paul and Silas were Roman citizens, they were frightened. So they came and told Paul and Silas they were sorry about what had happened. Then they themselves took Paul and Silas out of the prison and asked them to leave their city.

After Paul and Silas left the prison, they first went to Lydia's house. There they met with the believers in Jesus and urged them to remain true to Jesus. Then they left.

16:9-40

The People of Ephesus (EH-feh-sus)

After all these happenings, Paul decided to travel through Macedonia and Greece and go to Jerusalem.

349

"After I've been there," he said, "I must also see Rome." Then he sent Timothy and Erastus, two of his helpers, to Macedonia while he stayed in Asia a while longer.

About that time there was a lot of excitement [in Ephesus] over the Christian way. A man named Demetrius (De-MEE-tree-uss) was making little silver models of the temple in which a Greek goddess called Diana was worshiped. His business brought the workers a lot of money.

One day he called all his workers together, along with others who did the same kind of work. He said to them, "Men, you know that our money comes from our work. And you can see and hear for yourselves what this fellow Paul is doing not only in Ephesus but almost all over Asia. He is saying that gods made by human hands are not gods at all, and he has convinced many people. So there is danger that this business of ours will get a bad reputation.

"Not only that," he continued, "the temple of the great goddess Diana may come to mean nothing to people, and her greatness may be destroyed—she who is worshiped by everyone in Asia and throughout the world!"

When the men heard this, they became angry and shouted, "Great is Diana of Ephesus!" Soon the whole city was in an uproar. The mob grabbed two men who had been traveling with Paul and dragged them into a theater nearby. Paul wanted to go in and try to talk to the crowd, but his disciples wouldn't let him. . . . Some of the Jews in the crowd pushed Alexander to the front. He held up his hand to speak. But when the people saw he was a Jew, they all shouted together for about two hours, "Great is Diana of Ephesus!"

Finally one of the city officials stopped the noise. He said, "Men of Ephesus, who doesn't know that the city of Ephesus is the keeper of the great Diana's temple and has the sacred stone that fell down from heaven? Since this is true, you ought to calm down and not do anything foolish. The men you brought here have not said or done anything against our goddess. If Demetrius and the workers with him have something against anyone, there are courts and there are lawyers. Let them fight each other in court. But if there is something more that you want, it will have to be settled in a regular meeting." . . . When he had said this, he sent the people home.

After the excitement had died down, Paul sent for the disciples and urged them to remain faithful. Then he said good-bye and went to Macedonia. . . . At a place called Miletus [on the way back] Paul sent a message to Ephesus. In it he asked the elders of the church to meet him.

When the church officers came, he said to them, "You know how I lived among you . . . and how I did not keep from telling you anything I thought would be of help to you as I taught you in public and in your homes. To both Jews and Greeks I spoke about believing in our Lord Jesus Christ. And now I am going to Jerusalem. The Holy Spirit is making me go. I don't know what will happen to me there. I only know that in every city the Holy Spirit has warned me that prison and trouble are waiting for me.

"But I do not consider my life to be worth anything to me. I only want to finish the task that I received from the Lord Jesus. That work is to tell the good news of the grace* of God. . . . And now I turn you over to God and leave you with the message of his grace. He is able to build you up and give you the blessings he gives to all his people." . . .

When Paul had finished speaking, he knelt down with them all and prayed. As they hugged him and kissed him good-bye, they were all crying. They were sad most of all because he had said they would never see him again. Then they went with him to a ship that was waiting. . . .

19:21—20:38

351

Paul's Return to Jerusalem

When we got to Jerusalem, the Christians there were glad to see us. The next day Paul went with us to see James. All the leaders of the church came too. After greeting them, Paul told them the things God had done for Gentiles (JEN-tighles)* through his work. When they heard this, they thanked the Lord. . . .

21:17-20

PAUL'S LETTER TO THE
Romans

From Paul, a servant of Jesus Christ, . . . to all of you in Rome whom God loves and has called to be his holy people: May you receive grace and peace from God our Father and from the Lord Jesus Christ.

First I thank my God, through Jesus Christ, for all of you because your faith is being talked about all over the world. God, whom I serve with all my heart by preaching the good news about his son, knows that I always mention you in my prayers.

I keep asking that somehow by God's will I might finally be able to come and visit you. For I very much want to see you in order to give you a spiritual blessing that will make you stronger. What I mean is that we need to be helped by each other's faith, you by my faith and I by yours.

1:1-12

Why Everybody Needs the Gospel

I want you to know, my brothers [and sisters], that I often planned to visit you, but until now something has always kept me from doing so. I want to see some good results among you just as I have among other Gentiles. For I have a duty to help all people, so I am eager to preach the good news also to you who are in Rome.

I am not ashamed of the gospel. It is God's power for saving everyone who believes, first the Jews and then also the Gentiles. For the gospel tells how God makes people all right in his eyes. It is through faith [in Jesus]. As the Scripture says, "A person who is right with God through faith will live."

But God in heaven shows his anger against all sin and evil of people whose sinfulness keeps the truth from being known. What can be known about God is plain to them. God himself has shown it to them. Ever since God created the world, people could see what God is like through the things he has made. These show his everlasting power and show that he is God. So they have no excuse.

But even though they know God, they do not give him the honor that belongs to him, nor do they thank him. Instead, they think only foolish things and their empty minds become dark. They say they are wise but they become fools. They give God's honor (God doesn't die) to statues made to look like people [who die] and to birds and animals and snakes.

Because people trade the truth about God for a lie and worship and serve what God has made instead of the creator, God lets them do the rotten desires of their sinful hearts. God is the one who is to receive honor and thanks forever. Amen.

1:13-25

Saved by Faith

Now we know that what the laws of God say speaks to those who live by laws. That's in order to stop all human excuses and to make the whole world guilty in the sight of God. No human being ever becomes right in God's sight by doing what laws command. God's laws only help us to see that we have sinned.

But now God has shown us his way of putting

people right with himself, and it has nothing to do with laws. . . . God makes people all right through their faith in Jesus Christ. God does this to all who believe in Jesus Christ because there is no difference in people; all have sinned and fail to have the glory of God. They are made right with God through the gift of his grace. They are saved by Jesus Christ, who bought them with his blood and made them free from their sins. People receive all this through faith.

All this shows how right God is. In the past God was patient and often overlooked sins. But now God shows that he is the only one who has no sin and that he puts everyone who believes in Jesus right with him.

What then can we brag about? Nothing! Why not? Is it because we obey God's laws? No, but because we believe. And this is what we believe: that a person becomes right with God only through faith and not by doing what laws command.

3:19-28

The Spirit Gives Life

The Spirit of God raised Jesus from the dead. If the same Spirit lives in you, God will also give life to your bodies through his Spirit living in you.

So then, Christian brothers [and sisters], we ought not do what our sinful old selves want us to do. If you do what your sinful old selves want you to do, you will die. But if, with the power of the Holy Spirit, you put to death the sinful actions of your body, you will live.

All who are directed by the Spirit of God are children of God. . . . When we say to him, "Abba," meaning Father, it is the Holy Spirit telling our spirit that we are children of God.

If we are God's children, then we will receive what he has promised us. We will share with Christ all the things God has given to him. But we must share his suffering in order to share his glory.

8:11-17

Loving by Living

So then I beg you, my Christian brothers and sisters, to give your bodies to God because of his kindness to us. Give them as a holy and pleasing gift to God. This is real worship. Do not act like the sinful people in this world, but let God change you by giving you a new way of thinking. Then you will know what God wants you to do and what is good and pleasing to him and perfect. . . .

Be sure your love is real; [don't just pretend to love]. Hate what is sinful; hold on to what is good. Love one another like brothers and sisters. Be eager to honor other people more than they honor you. Never stop caring, be alive and happy, serve the Lord. Let your hope keep you happy. Don't give up when troubles come. And keep on praying.

Give to your fellow Christians who need help, especially meals and a place to stay. Pray for those who make trouble for you; wish them well instead of cursing them. Be happy with people who are happy and be sad with those who are sad.

Live in peace with one another. Don't be proud, but enjoy the company of ordinary persons. And don't think you know everything! And when someone does something bad to you, don't pay him back with something bad. Think of doing what everybody knows is the good thing to do.

As much as it's possible, live in peace with everybody. Never take revenge, my dear friends, but let God's anger take care of the matter for you. The Scriptures say, "Revenge is mine; I will pay back to people what they should get," says the Lord.

No, if your enemy is hungry, feed him; if he is thirsty, give him a drink. By doing this you will put burning* coals on his head. Don't let evil rule you, but win over evil by doing good. . . .

Owe no one anything except love. Whoever loves his fellowman does all that God's laws command. The commandments, "Do not commit adultery; do not murder; do not steal; do not covet"—these and any other commandments are summed up in this one sentence, "Love your neighbor as yourself." Anyone who loves his neighbor will do him no harm. Therefore by loving we keep all laws of God.

12:1-21; 13:8-10

The grace of our Lord Jesus Christ be with you all. Amen.

16:20

THE FIRST LETTER OF PAUL TO THE
Corinthians

[This letter is] from Paul, who was chosen by God to be a missionary of Jesus Christ. [It is] also from Sosthenes (SAHS-teh-nees), our Christian brother. [The letter is] to the church of God in Corinth, to those who have been made holy by Christ Jesus and have been called to be God's people together with all who call on the name of our Lord Jesus Christ, their Lord and ours. May God our Father and the Lord Jesus Christ give you love and peace.

I thank God all the time for you. I am thankful for the loving favor God has given to you through Christ Jesus. He has made your lives richer in every way—in everything you know and say. This shows that what I said about Christ is true. You have all the spiritual gifts you need while waiting for our Lord Jesus Christ to appear. He will keep you alive and strong and without blame until he comes again. God, who called you into a life with his son Jesus Christ, our Lord, keeps his promises.

Trouble in the Church

I beg you, Christian brothers and sisters, in the name of our Lord Jesus Christ, to agree among yourselves and not to divide into little groups. Be united by having the same thought and purposes. For some people from Chloe's (KLO-ee's) family have told me, my dear brothers and sisters, that there is quarreling among you.

What I mean is that some of you are saying, "I'm with Paul," or "I belong to Apollos (Ah-PAHL-uhs)," or "I'm with Peter," or "I belong to Christ." Is Christ divided? Was it Paul who died on a cross for you? Were you baptized as Paul's disciples?

I'm glad I didn't baptize any of you except Crispus (KRIS-puhs) and Gaius (GAY-uhs). So none of you can say that you were baptized as my followers. [Oh yes, I also baptized Stephanas (STEHF-ah-nuhs) and his family, but I don't remember whether I baptized anyone else.]

Christ did not send me to baptize. He sent me to preach the gospel. And I did not use fancy language when I preached so that the power of Christ's death on the cross would not be lost.

For the message about Christ's death on a cross sounds like nonsense to the people who are dying in sin, but to us who are being saved [from sin] it is the power of God.

1:1-18

God's Partners

So then, what is Apollos? What is Paul? They are only servants of God who helped you to believe. I planted the seed, Apollos watered the plant, but it was God who made the plant grow. Neither the one who plants or the one who waters is the important person. Only God, who makes the plant grow, really matters.

The one who plants and the one who waters are equal in what they do, and each one will receive his wages [from God] according to the work he does. For we are partners in working together for God, and you are God's field.

You are also God's building. With the gifts God gave me, I laid the foundation like an expert builder would, and another man is building on that foundation. But each person must be careful how he builds. For God has made Jesus Christ the one and only foundation, and no one can make any other kind of foundation.

Now some will build on that foundation with gold, silver, or precious stones; others with wood, hay, or straw. But the kind of work each man does will become known. There will come a day when it will be tested by fire. The fire will show what kind of work each person has done. If the work a person has done on the foundation will last, he will receive a reward. But if a person's work easily burns up, he will lose it. He himself will be saved, but like a person escaping through a fire.

Don't you know that you are God's temple and that God's spirit lives in you? If anyone destroys God's temple, God will destroy him. For God's temple is holy, and you are such a temple.

3:5-17

The Gifts of the Spirit

Now, Christian brothers and sisters, I want you to know about the gifts of the Holy Spirit. [First of all] you know that before you were Christians you were led to worship false gods. Therefore I want you to understand that no one who is led to speak by God's Spirit ever would say he hates Jesus. And no one can say "Jesus is Lord" [and really mean it] unless he is directed by the Holy Spirit.

Now, there are different kinds of gifts, but the same Spirit gives them. There are different kinds of services that are done, but it's the same Lord who is served. And people do these services in different ways, but it is the same God who makes them all able and willing to do the services.

What the Spirit does for each person is for the good of all. To one the Spirit gives the ability to speak wisely; to another the Spirit gives faith; to another, the power to heal or to work miracles; to another, the power to speak and teach God's word; to another, the ability to tell the difference between the Holy Spirit and other spirits; to another, the ability to speak with special sounds or to explain them. It is the one same Spirit who gives all of these gifts, and he gives to each individual as he pleases.

The body of Christ is like our body, which has many parts, and all the parts together are only one body. By one Spirit we were all baptized into one body—Jews and Gentiles, slaves and free people—and we have all been given the one Spirit.

The body does not have only one part but many parts. And if the foot would say, "Because I am not a hand I do not belong to the body," that would not make the saying true. And if the ear would say, "Because I am not an eye, I do not belong to the body," that would not make it stop being a part of the body.

If the whole body were just an eye, how could it hear? And if the whole body were only an ear, how could it smell? But as it is, God arranged the parts of the body, each one of them, just as he wished.

If all the parts were only one part, there would not be a body. As it is, there are many parts and one body. So then, the eye must not say to the hand, "I don't need you!" Nor can the head say to the feet, "I don't need you!" No, we need especially the parts of the body that seem to be the least important.

And those parts of our body that we think shouldn't be shown get more care than those parts that are seen. God has so made the body that more care is given to the parts that need it the most. This keeps the body united and all the different parts caring for each other. When one part of the body suffers, all the other parts suffer with it. When one part is honored, all the parts are glad.

Now here is what I am trying to say: All of you are the body of Christ, and each one of you separately is a part of it. And God has given each some special gift to use in his church. . . . Set your heart on the best gifts. And now I will show you the best gift of all.

12:1-31

The Gift of Love

Even if I speak the languages of other people and of angels, if I have no love in me, my words will sound like a lot of noise. And if I have the gift of preaching and teaching and understand all mysteries and know everything, and if I have all the faith I need to move mountains but I don't have love [in my heart], I am nothing. If I gave away everything that I have and even let my body be burned, it would do me no good if I didn't love.

Love is patient and kind. Love is never jealous and doesn't brag. It isn't proud or rude. Love does not insist on its own way. It does not get angry easily or remember being hurt. Love is not happy over wrong things, but is happy over what's right. Love takes everything that comes along, believes all things, keeps on hoping and keeps on loving, no matter what.

Love never ends. [It goes on forever.] . . . There are three things that last—faith, hope, love. These are the great gifts of God's Spirit. But the greatest of these is love.

13:1-8, 13

PAUL'S SECOND LETTER TO THE
Corinthians

From Paul, an apostle of Jesus Christ by God's will, and from our brother Timothy, to the church of God in

Corinth and to all the Christians in Greece: May you have love and peace from God our Father and the Lord Jesus Christ.

Paul Thanks God

We thank and praise the God and Father of our Lord Jesus Christ. He is a merciful father and the God who always gives comfort (KUHM-furt).* He comforts us in all our troubles so that we are able to comfort others in any kind of trouble. We can give the same kind of comfort God gives to us. As we share Christ's sufferings, so through him we also share his comfort.

When we suffer, it is for your good. If we are helped, then you too are helped. You too will receive the strength not to give up when you have the troubles we have had. So our hope for you remains steady, for we know that as you share our sufferings you also will share in the help we receive.

We want you to know, Christian brothers and sisters, of the troubles we had in Asia. The problems were so great that we didn't think we could keep going. At times we thought we were going to die. But all this happened so that we wouldn't rely on ourselves but only on God, who raises the dead.

God saved us from what looked like certain death, and he will keep on saving us. We trust that he will save us also in the future. You too must help us by praying for us. Then, when the many prayers for us will be answered, many people will give thanks to God for the blessings he gave us in answer to these prayers.

1:1-11

A New Life from Christ

Christ died for everyone so that those who live would no longer live for themselves, but for him who died for them and was raised back to life. . . . When anyone becomes a Christian, he becomes a new person. What he was disappears; it's amazing, a new life has

361

started. All this is done by God, who brought us together with him through what Christ did and gave us the work of bringing others to a happy and peaceful life with him also.

God was in Christ, bringing the whole world into peace with him by not holding people's sins against them. And he has given us the message of his forgiveness and love to tell to others. So we are speaking for Christ, and God is speaking to you through us.

Speaking for Christ we beg you to change from enemies to friends of God. Christ never sinned, but for our sake God let him suffer for our sins so that by joining him we could receive the holiness of God.

5:15-21

On Giving to Others

We want you to know, brothers and sisters, what God's love has done in the churches of Macedonia (Ma-sah-DOH-nee-ah).* They were put to a test by much trouble, but they have much joy. And even though they are very poor, they have given much. They gave as much as they could and more because they wanted to. They begged us to let them help the Christians in Jerusalem. It was more than we could have expected. First they gave themselves to the Lord and then, by God's will, they gave themselves to us as well.

So we have urged Titus (TIGH-tus), who began this work, to continue it and to help you complete this service of love. You are leaders in so many things—in faith, in preaching, in learning, in seriousness, and in your love for us. Now I want you to be leaders also in this matter of giving.

I am not saying this as a command, but by showing you how eager others have been to help, I am trying to find out how real also your love is. You know the love of our Lord Jesus Christ. Though he was rich, for your sake he became poor, so that by his being poor you could become rich.

And this is my opinion in this matter: you ought to finish what you started a year ago. You wanted to do it. Now finish doing it with the same strong desire you had when you started. If a person is ready to give, he ought to give from what he has and not from what he does not have. . . .

Remember this: the person who plants only a few seeds will have a small crop; the one who plants a lot of seeds will have a large crop. Each one should give as he has decided in his heart. He ought not give while wishing he could keep it or because he feels he has to give. God loves the person who gives gladly. And God can give you everything you need and more, so that you will always have enough of everything and more than enough to give to others.

It's as the Scriptures say, "The godly person gives much to the poor, and his kindness lasts forever." And God, who provides the seeds for the man who plants and bread for food, will also give and multiply what you need and will produce a bigger harvest by your kindness. He will make you rich enough to be generous, and this will lead others to give thanks to God.

These gifts you give will not only help people of God in need, but will also result in many thanks to God. By this act of love you will prove what you are, and many others will praise God for this proof of your loyalty to the gospel of Christ. And so they will pray for you with deep affection because of the great love of God in you. Thank God for his gift that is too wonderful for words.

8:1-12; 9:6-15

THE LETTER OF PAUL TO THE
Galatians

[This letter is] from Paul, a missionary who was not sent by people or by any one man, but by Jesus Christ and God the Father, who raised Jesus from the dead. All the Christians who are with me join me in sending greetings to the churches of Galatia (Guh-LAY-shee-ah).* May God, our Father, and our Lord Jesus Christ give you grace and peace.

In order to save us from this sinful world, Christ gave his life for our sins. This was the will of our God and Father. To him be the glory forever and ever. Amen.

Paul's Only Gospel

I am very surprised that you are so quickly leaving the one who taught you the love of Christ and are turning to another gospel. There really isn't any other gospel, but I say this because there are some people who are upsetting you by wanting to change the gospel of Christ.

But even if we or an angel from heaven preached to you a gospel that is different from the one we preached to you, let him be cursed. As we said before and now say again, if anyone is preaching to you a gospel that is different from the one you received from me, let him be cursed.

Does this sound as though I'm trying to get the favor of people or of God? Or am I trying to please people? If I were still trying to please people, I would not be a servant of Christ.

I want you to know, Christian brothers and sisters, that the good news I preached to you was not something dreamed up by a human being. I did not receive it from any man, and I wasn't taught it. I received it from Jesus Christ, who showed it to me.

You heard of my former life when I practiced the Jewish religion—how I fought without mercy the church of God and tried to destroy it. I was ahead of most Jews of my age in what I knew of the Jewish religion, and I had a strong desire to follow the ways of my ancestors.

But God chose me before I was born and in love called me to work for him. And when he revealed his son to me so that I could preach him to the Gentiles, I didn't go to anyone for advice. Nor did I go to Jerusalem to see those who were apostles before me. But I went away into Arabia (Ah-RAY-bee-ah)* and then I returned to Damascus (Dah-MAS-kus).*

It was three years later when I went to Jerusalem to visit Peter, and I remained with him just 15 days. I didn't see any other apostles except James, the Lord's brother. I am writing the truth. God knows I am not lying.

Then I went to places in Syria (SEER-ee-ah) and Silicia (Sigh-LISH-ee-ah). At that time the people in the Christian churches in Judea (Jew-DEE-ah) didn't know me by sight. They knew only that others said, "The man who used to fight us is now preaching the faith he once tried to destroy." So they praised God for what they heard about me.

1:1-24

Law or Faith?

All who depend on doing what the laws of God demand live under a curse. For it is written, "Everyone who does not do everything that is written in the books of the law is under God's curse." But it's clear that no one gets right with God by obeying laws, because the Scripture says, "He who gets right with God through *faith* will live." Laws do not depend on faith because the Scripture says, "Only the person who does *everything* the laws require will live by them."

Christ saved us from the curse of laws by becoming a curse for us. As the Scripture says, "Cursed is anyone who is hanged on a tree." Christ did this in order that the blessing God gave Abraham could be given to the Gentiles (JEN-tighls),* and so that we all would receive the Spirit of God through faith [instead of by keeping laws].

3:10-14

The Life of Freedom

Brothers and sisters, you were called [by God] to [a life of] freedom. But do not use your freedom as a chance to sin. Instead live this free life by loving and serving one another. For all the laws of God are summed up in one commandment: "Love your neighbor as you love yourself." But if you bite and hurt each other, watch out or you may be completely destroyed by one another.

What I say to you is this: let the Holy Spirit direct every step of your lives and do not try to satisfy the desires of your old sinful selves. For your sinful desires are the opposite of what the Holy Spirit wants, and what the Holy Spirit wants does not agree with what our old sinful self wants. The two fight against each other, and this keeps you from doing what you want to do. But if the Holy Spirit leads you, you are not living under any laws.

Now, the things your old sinful self wants to do are plain: sex sins, dirty behavior and wild living, the worship of false gods, witchcraft, hating and fighting, jealousy, anger, selfishness, arguing, separating into little groups, coveting, getting drunk, wild parties, and such things as these. I warn you now as I have before: those who do such things will not get to live in the kingdom of God.

But the fruit that comes from having the Holy Spirit in us is love, joy, peace, patience, kindness, goodness, and being faithful, gentle, and in control of one's self. Against such things there is no law. And those people who belong to Christ Jesus have nailed their old sinful selves and their sinful desires on his cross. So if the Holy Spirit is living in us, let us also have him direct every step of our lives.

5:13-23

Help Others

Brothers and sisters, when persons are caught doing any kind of wrong, those of you who are stronger Christians ought to gently help them come back to God's ways. And watch out for yourself so that you too won't be tempted [to do wrong]. Help each other in your problems and in this way keep the law of Christ.

If anyone thinks he is something when he is nothing, he is fooling himself. Every person ought to test what he himself does. If it is good, then he can be proud of what he himself has done instead of comparing himself with others. For everyone must carry his own load.

The person who is taught the word [of God] ought to share the good things he has with his teacher. Do not fool yourselves; no one can make a fool of God. A person will get back whatever he plants. If he does things to please his old sinful self, he will get nothing but bad results from this. If he does things to please the Holy Spirit, he will get eternal life from the Holy Spirit.

So let us never become tired of doing good; for if we do not give up, in time we will get a harvest of blessings. So then, whenever we have the chance, let us do good to everyone and especially to our Christian brothers and sisters. . . .

May the love of our Lord Jesus Christ be in your spirit, Christian brothers and sisters. Amen.

6:1-10, 18

THE LETTER OF PAUL TO THE
Ephesians

From Paul, a missionary for Jesus Christ by the will of God, to God's people who are faithful to Christ Jesus.

May God our Father and the Lord Jesus Christ give you grace and peace.

Thanks for Christ's Blessings

We thank the God and Father of our Lord Jesus Christ. In our being united with Jesus he has blessed us by giving us every spiritual blessing in heavenly places. Before the beginning of the world God chose us to be his people through Christ, so that we would be holy and without faults in his sight. In love God planned to make us his children through Jesus Christ. That was his plan and purpose. We praise the glorious grace he freely gave to us through his dear son.

By the blood [meaning death] of Jesus we are set free from sin; that is, our sins are forgiven. How wonderful is the grace that God gave us so generously! With wisdom and understanding he has told us the secret of what he has planned to do through Christ—to someday bring together all things in heaven and on earth under the rulership of Christ. . . .

Because I have heard of your faith in the Lord Jesus and your love toward all of his people, I never stop giving thanks to God for you. I remember you in my prayers and ask the God of our Lord Jesus Christ, the great and glorious Father, to give you his Spirit. He will make you wise and will reveal God to you so that you will know him.

May you know the hope to which God has called you, how rich are the wonderful blessings he has

368

promised to his people, and how very great is his power in us who believe. This power in us is the same as the mighty power he used when he raised Jesus Christ from the dead and put him at his right side in the world of heaven.

Christ rules there above all other rulers and powers and lords in this world and in that which is to come. God has put all things under Christ's feet and has made him the head over all things for the good of his church, which is his body.

1:1-10, 15-23

How God Saved Us

God is rich in mercy and loved us with a very great love. Even when we were spiritually dead in sins he made us alive together with Christ. By grace you have been saved. He raised us up with Christ to rule with him in heavenly places. He did this to show, for all time to come, the great riches of his grace in his kindness toward us through Jesus Christ.

For it is by grace that you have been saved through faith, and this is not your own doing. It is a gift of God, and not because of something you have done. So it is not something to brag about. We are God's work. He united us to Christ Jesus for a life of good works that he prepared for us to do.

So then, you Gentiles no longer are foreigners and strangers, but you are fellow citizens in God's kingdom and members of the family of God's people. You are built on the foundation laid by the apostles and prophets. The cornerstone is Christ Jesus himself. He holds the whole building together and makes it grow into a holy temple of the Lord. By being connected with Jesus you also are being made a part of this house where God lives through his Spirit.

2:4-10, 19-22

Paul's Prayers and Praises

For this reason I get down on my knees and pray to

the Father from whom every family in heaven and on earth receives its name. I ask that from the riches of his glory he will give you strength and power in your inner selves through his Spirit.

I also pray that Christ will live in your hearts through faith so that you will have your roots in love. May you, together with all God's people, have the power to understand how broad and long and high and deep is Christ's love. It is beyond anything we can ever understand fully. But may you be filled with the fullness of God.

Now, by the power at work in us God is able to do much more than we will ever ask or think. So to God be glory in the church and in Christ Jesus for ever and ever. Amen.

3:14-21

Live a Christian Life

I, who am a prisoner for serving the Lord, beg you to live the kind of life anyone who is called by God ought to live. Be humble and gentle and always patient. In love tolerate one another's faults. Be eager to keep the peace and oneness that the Holy Spirit gives.

We all belong to one body and we have the same Spirit, just as we have all been given the one same hope. There is one Lord, one faith, one baptism, one God and Father of all people. He is above all and works through all and is in all. . . .

Therefore stop lying to each other. Everyone ought to speak the truth because we all are parts of one another. If you become angry, don't sin. Don't let the sun go down with you still angry, and don't give the devil a chance to rule you.

The person who has been stealing ought to work instead of stealing, using his hands for earning an honest living so he can give to others who need help. Never let any harmful talk come out of your mouths. Say only what is good and helpful to those you are talking to, so that what you say will give a blessing to those who hear you.

And do not make God's Spirit sad [by the way you live], because God has marked you with his Spirit for the day when you will be free from all sin. So stop being bitter, mean, and angry. No more shouting, hurtful talk, and hateful feelings. Instead, be kind to one another, feel kind, and forgive one another as God in Christ has forgiven you.

4:1-6, 25-32

THE LETTER OF PAUL TO THE
Philippians *

From Paul and Timothy, servants of Jesus Christ, to all the Christians who are living in Philippi and to the church leaders and their helpers: May God our Father and the Lord Jesus Christ give you grace and peace.

I thank my God every time I think of you. Every time I pray for all of you, I pray with joy. I am thankful for your help in the work of the gospel from the very first day until now. And I'm sure that he who began this good work in you will keep on doing it until the day that Jesus Christ will come again. . . .

1:1-6

Paul in Prison

I want you to know, Christian brothers and sisters, that what has happened to me has really helped spread the good news. The palace guards and all the others around here know that I am in prison because I serve Jesus Christ. And my being in prison has made most of my Christian brothers stronger in their faith and much bolder in speaking the word of God to others.

Some people, of course, preach Christ because they

371

are jealous or want to make trouble, but others are doing it with good will. Those who mean well do it out of love, knowing that I have been put here to prove that the gospel is true. Others preach about Christ for selfish reasons, not sincerely. They want to cause me suffering while I am in prison.

Whatever their reasons, whether they pretend or mean what they say, Christ is preached, and I am happy about that!

1:12-18

The Christian Life

So if there is such a thing as Christians encouraging each other or helping one another in love or having the same Spirit and feeling kindness and sympathy, make me completely happy by agreeing in what you think and do. Have the same love and reasons in what you do.

Don't do anything for selfish reasons or because of pride. Be humble and consider others better than you are. Don't always be thinking only about what is best for you, but also about the good of others.

Think the way Jesus Christ thought. Even though he was like God, he didn't think that being equal with God was what was most important. No, he gave it all up and became a servant. He was born a man, and as a human being he humbled himself even more by willingly dying on a cross.

That is why God highly honored Jesus and gave him a name that is greater than any other name. He did this so that when the name of Jesus is mentioned, everyone in heaven or on earth or under the earth will bow and everyone will say that Jesus Christ is Lord. In that way God the Father will receive glory. . . .

Do everything without grumbling or arguing. Then no one will be able to criticize you, and you will be perfect children of God living in a world of sinful people. And you will shine among them as lights in the world. Hold on to God's message of life, so that when

Jesus Christ comes again I can be proud that all my effort and work was worthwhile.

2:1-11; 14-16

Timothy

If the Lord Jesus is willing, I will send Timothy to you soon so that he can bring me some cheerful news about you. I have no one else who is as interested in you as Timothy is. Everyone else thinks about himself instead of about the work of Jesus Christ.

You know how Timothy proved his worth. He was like a son helping his father when he worked with me in preaching the gospel. I therefore hope to send him to you as soon as I see how things are going to turn out for me. I hope that by the help of the Lord I myself can come soon too.

2:19-24

Paul's Instructions

Brothers and sisters, imitate me. And watch those who live as I have taught you to live. There are many, as I have often told you before and now tell you again with tears, who live as enemies of Christ's death on the cross. In the end they will all be destroyed. Their god is their stomach, and they are proud of things they should be ashamed of.

But we are citizens of the kingdom of heaven and we wait for our Savior, the Lord Jesus Christ, to come from heaven. He will change our poor bodies and make them like his marvelous body. He will do this with the power that he has for ruling all things.

3:17-21

Be happy always in your life with the Lord. Again I'll say it: be happy. Let everyone see how gentle you are. The Lord is coming again soon. Don't worry about anything, but in everything give thanks to God as you ask him for whatever you need. And God's peace, which is greater than we can understand, will keep your hearts and minds with Christ Jesus.

Finally, Christian brothers and sisters, keep thinking about such things as these: whatever is true, whatever is respectable, whatever is right, whatever is decent, whatever is lovely, whatever is kind. If there is anything good and worth praising, think about these things too. Do the things you learned from me, the things you heard from me and saw me do. The God who gives peace will be with you.

4:4-9

PAUL'S LETTER TO THE
Colossians*

From Paul, a missionary God wanted for Jesus Christ, and from our brother Timothy, to God's people and our faithful Christian brothers and sisters in Colossae: May our Father [in heaven] give you grace and peace.

Prayer of Thanks

We always thank God, the Father of our Lord Jesus Christ, when we pray for you because we have heard of your faith in Jesus and your love for all God's people. We know your love comes from what you are looking forward to in heaven. [Remember that] you heard about this hope in the good news that has come to you. It is the truth.

This gospel is producing results and spreading all over the world, just as it has among you ever since the day you heard of the grace of God and really understood it. You learned it from Epaphras (EH-pa-fras), a dear fellow servant who is a faithful minister for Christ and worked for you. He told us about the love God's Spirit has given you.

For this reason we have never stopped praying for you since the day we heard about you. We ask God to fill you with the wisdom and understanding that the Holy Spirit gives so that you will know what he wants you to do. Then you will be able to live as the Lord wants you to live, always pleasing him. You will do every kind of good work, and you will grow in your knowledge of God.

May you become strong with the power that comes from God's great power so that you will be able to endure everything patiently and happily. Always give thanks to the Father. He has given you a share of what he has promised to his people who live in light. He saved us from a life in darkness and has put us into the kingdom of his dear son. By him we have been set free; that is, our sins are forgiven.

1:1-14

Paul's Work for the Church

I want you to know how hard I've worked for you, and for the people in Laodicea (Lay-o-di-SEE-ah), and for many others who have never seen me. I want them to be full of courage and tied together by love. May they also have the rich blessings of a sure understanding of God's secret, which is Jesus Christ. In him are hidden all the treasures of God's wisdom and knowledge.

I tell you this so that no one will fool you with sweet talk. Though my body is far away from you, my spirit is with you. I am glad to see your strong faith in Christ. Since you accepted Christ Jesus as the Lord, live united with him. Have your roots deep in him and grow in him. Let him make you strong in the faith you have been taught. And give thanks to him often.

2:1-7

Living with Christ

If you have been raised with Christ, look for the things that are in heaven. That's where Christ sits on his throne at the right side of God. Keep your minds thinking about things in heaven, not about things here on earth. For you have died, and your [new] life is now hidden with Christ in God. When Christ, who is our life, will appear, then you also will appear with him and will share his glory.*

Put to death, therefore, what is sinful in you: sex sins, indecent behavior, wrong and shameful desires, and coveting, which is idol worship. Because of such things God's anger comes down on people. At one time you yourselves used to do such things when you lived that kind of life.

But now get rid of all these things too: anger, bad temper, hateful feelings, dirty talk, and lies against others. Never lie to one another because you have put out of your life your old ways and have put on a new self. This new person God, its creator, is continually making more like him. . . .

Because you have been chosen by God to be his people and are loved and made holy by him, practice mercy and kindness toward others. Be humble, gentle, patient, and helpful to one another. Whenever you have a complaint against another person, forgive him. You must forgive the way the Lord has forgiven you.

And to all these add love, which ties everything together and makes all these things perfect. And let the peace of Christ rule in your hearts, for this peace is what God has called you to enjoy as a part of his body. And be thankful.

Let the teachings of Christ keep on living in you richly. Teach and remind each other of all his wisdom. Sing psalms, hymns, and godly and unworldly songs with hearts full of thanks to God. Whatever you do or say, do it all in the name of the Lord Jesus and give thanks to God the Father through him.

3:1-17

The New Life

Wives, obey your husbands. This is what you ought to do as Christians. Husbands, love your wives and never treat them meanly. Children, always obey your parents, for that pleases the Lord. Fathers, don't scold your children so much that they become discouraged. Servants, obey those who are your human masters; and don't do it just to please them only when they are watching you; but do it sincerely because you worship the Lord.

Whatever you do, work at it with all your heart as though you were working for the Lord and not just for people. Remember that from the Lord you will receive as your reward what he has promised to give to his people. You are serving the Lord Jesus. And the wrongdoer will suffer for the wrong he does. God doesn't play favorites. . . .

I, Paul, write this greeting with my own hand: May you continue to receive God's grace. Don't forget my [prison] chains.

3:18-25; 4:18

THE FIRST LETTER OF PAUL TO THE
Thessalonians*

From Paul, Silvanus (Sil-VAY-nuhs), and Timothy, to the church of the Thessalonians who belong to God the Father and the Lord Jesus Christ: Grace and peace to you.

Examples of Christian Believers

We thank God for all of you all the time and always mention you in our prayers. For while praying to God our Father, we remember your acts of faith, your works of love, and your steady hope in our Lord Jesus Christ.

Christian brothers and sisters, we know God loves you and that he has chosen you [to be his people]. For we brought the gospel to you not only with words, but also with power and the Holy Spirit, and you were fully convinced it was true. You also know what kind of men we were when we lived among you for your good. And you became imitators of us and of the Lord.

And even though you suffered much, you received the message with the joy that comes from the Holy Spirit. So you became an example to all the believers in Macedonia (Ma-sah-DOH-nee-ah)* and Greece. For not only the message about the Lord went from you to Macedonia and Greece, but also the news of your faith in God has gone everywhere.

So there is nothing we need to say. People themselves tell us how you welcomed us when we visited you and how you turned away from idols to God and now serve a true and living God. They also tell us how you are waiting for his Son to come from heaven, his Son Jesus, whom God raised from the dead. He will save us from the anger of God that is coming.

1:1-10

Paul's Work

We also thank God continually for this: When you heard the Word of God from us, you received it not just as a message from some men, but as the Word of God, which is what it is. The Word is now at work in you who believe.

You, Christian brothers and sisters, became just like the Christian churches of God in the country of Judea. You suffered the same things from the people in your country that those churches had to suffer from the Jews, who killed the Lord Jesus and the prophets. They also drove us away. They displease God and are against people when they try to stop us from preaching to the Gentiles the message that would save them.

2:13-16

Finally, brothers and sisters, you learned from us how you ought to live in order to please God, and you have been living that way. But we beg and urge you, in the name of the Lord Jesus, to do so even more. For you know the instructions we gave you by the directions of the Lord Jesus. This is God's will: he wants you to be holy and to keep away from sex sins. Each one of you should know how to rule his body properly, keeping it holy and respecting it. Do not please your own desires like the people who do not know God.

No person ought to do wrong to his Christian brother or sister. The Lord will punish those who do such wrongs, as we strongly warned you before. For God did not call us to a life of uncleanness but of holiness. So then, whoever fails to keep this in mind is not disobeying men but God, who gives his Holy Spirit to you.

But there is no need for anyone to write to you about loving your fellow believers in Jesus. You yourselves have been taught by God to love one another. And you do love all the Christians all over Macedonia (Ma-sah-DOH-nee-ah).* But we beg you, brothers and sisters, to do so more and more. Try to live a quiet life, mind your own business, and earn your own living, as we told you before. Then you will be respected by those who are not Christians, and you will not have to depend on anyone for what you need.

4:1-12

Some Advice from Paul

But we beg you, brothers, to respect those who work with and for you, especially those whom the Lord has placed over you and are your teachers. Think much of them and love them because of the work they do. And live in peace among yourselves.

And we urge you, Christian brothers, to warn the lazy, encourage the timid, help the weak, be patient with them all. See that no one pays back a wrong with a wrong, but always try to do good to one another and to all people. Always be happy, never stop praying, and be thankful no matter what happens. This is what God wants you to do as followers of Christ Jesus.

Do not prevent the Holy Spirit from burning in you, and do not fail to listen to those who teach. Test everything, hold on to what is good, and avoid everything that looks like evil.

May the God who gives peace make you complete-ly holy, and may he keep your spirit, soul, and body healthy and free from any faults at the coming of our Lord Jesus Christ.

5:12-24

THE SECOND LETTER OF PAUL TO THE
Thessalonians*

From Paul, Silvanus, and Timothy, to the church of the Thessalonians who belong to God our Father and the Lord Jesus Christ: Grace and peace to you from God the Father and the Lord Jesus Christ.

We thank God always for you, Christian brothers. It is right for us to do this because your faith is growing so well and your love for each other is becoming greater. That is why we also boast about you in the churches of God. We tell how your faith stays strong even when people make your life very hard for you and make you suffer.

1:1-4

Saved by the Truth

Concerning the coming of our Lord Jesus Christ and our meeting together to be with him: we beg you, brothers, not to be easily mixed up or excited by reports that the Lord has come back. People may say that I wrote this in a letter or that a spirit told them. Don't let anyone fool you.

That day of the Lord will not come until many people turn against God and the leader of all who break God's laws will come. He is the man of sin who works against and puts himself above every kind of god that is worshiped. He will take his seat in the house of God and will say that he himself is God. . . .

But we always thank God for you, brothers. You

are loved by the Lord. God chose you from the beginning to be saved. He chose to make you holy by the Holy Spirit and gives you faith in the truth. God called you to this faith through the good news we preached to you. He invited you to receive the glory of our Lord Jesus Christ.

So then, brothers, keep a strong hold on what we have taught you, both by our preaching and by our letter. May our Lord Jesus Christ himself and God our Father fill your hearts with peace and give you the strength to do and say every good thing. He loved us, and through his grace he gives us comfort and good hope that never ends. *2:1-4; 13-17*

The Duty to Work

Finally, brothers, pray for us. Pray that the Lord's message may continue to spread rapidly and succeed as it did among you. And pray that God will rescue us from sinful and evil people, for not all believe [the gospel].

But the Lord is faithful. He will make you strong and keep you safe from the devil. And the Lord gives us faith in you. We believe you are doing and will keep on doing the things we told you. May the Lord direct your hearts to the love of God and to the faithfulness of Christ.

And we command you, brothers, in the name of the Lord Jesus Christ, to keep away from any Christian who is living a lazy life and isn't doing what we taught you. You know you should follow the way we lived when we were with you. We worked hard when we were with you. We didn't eat anyone's food without paying for it.

We worked hard night and day so none of you would have to give us anything. It wasn't because we didn't have the right [to ask you for food], but we did not so that you would follow our way of living. For when we were with you we told you that whoever isn't willing to work shouldn't be allowed to eat.

We hear that there are some people among you who are lazy, not doing any work and spending their time talking about what others are doing. In the name of the Lord Jesus Christ we command and urge such persons to do their work quietly and earn their own living.

If anyone refuses to obey what we have said in this letter, remember who he is and have nothing to do with him so he will be ashamed. Do not treat him as an enemy, but warn him as a brother.

3:1-15

Closing Words

Now may the Lord himself, the source of peace, give you peace at all times and in all ways. The Lord be with you all. I, Paul, write this greeting with my own hand. This is the way I sign every letter; this is the way I write. May the grace of our Lord Jesus Christ be with you all.

3:16-18

PAUL'S FIRST LETTER TO
Timothy

From Paul, an apostle of Christ Jesus by order of God, our Savior, and Christ Jesus, who is our hope, to Timothy, a real son to me in the [Christian] faith. May God the Father and Christ Jesus our Lord give you grace, mercy, and peace. . . .

Paul Thanks God

I thank Christ Jesus our Lord, who has given me strength for my work. I thank him because he trusted me and gave me a chance to serve him, even though in the past I spoke against him and hunted down his people and insulted him.

God was kind to me because I did not believe and therefore did not understand what I was doing. The

Lord gave me the grace and faith and love that are in Jesus Christ.

This is a true saying that deserves to be completely believed. Christ Jesus came into the world to save sinners [from their sins]. And I am the worst of them. But I received mercy so that Jesus Christ could show his perfect patience for an example to those who would later believe in him in order to receive eternal life. To the king who is eternal, who never dies but is invisible, to him let us give honor and glory forever and ever! Amen.

1:1-2, 12-17

Pray and Give Thanks

First of all, then, I urge you to pray and give thanks for all people, for kings and all others who are in positions of power. Pray so we may live quiet and peaceful lives; godlike and respected in every way. This is good, and it pleases God, our Savior, who wants all people to be saved and to come to know the truth.

There is one God, and there is one person standing between God and all people, bringing them together. That man is Christ Jesus. He gave his life to free all from the power of sin. And God made this known to the world at the right time.

This is why I was chosen to be a teacher and missionary. I am to teach faith and truth to the people who do not know God. I am telling the truth; I am not lying. . . .

I hope to come and see you soon. But I am writing this letter so that if I'm delayed, you will know how to act among people in God's family. They are the church of the living God, the pillar and support of the truth.

Great is the secret of our religion. It is that God appeared on earth as a man, had a right spirit, was seen by angels, was preached to many nations, was believed by people in the world, and was taken into heaven.

2:1-7; 3:14-16

The Good Servant of Jesus

The Holy Spirit tells us plainly that in later times some people will leave their faith. They will listen to lying spirits and teachings about devils. Those who teach this pretend it is the truth when they know it is a lie. They do this so much that their consciences no longer tell them it's wrong.

These false teachers also teach that it is wrong to marry and to eat certain foods. But God created these foods to be eaten with thanks by those who know and believe the truth. Everything created by God is good, and nothing he has made is to be put aside if it can be used with thanks. It is made holy by the Word of God and prayer.

If you will tell these things to our Christian brothers and sisters, you will be a good minister of Christ Jesus. You will also feed your own spirit through these words of faith and the good teaching you have followed.

But keep away from godless and foolish stories. Train yourself for a godly life. Physical exercise has some value, but exercise in godly living has far more value. It promises life both now and for the future. This saying is true and deserves to be completely accepted.

We work hard and do our best because we have placed our hope in the living God, who is the Savior of all human beings, especially of those who believe.

Tell people that this is what they must do. Don't let anyone look down on you because you are young. Set an example for other believers by your talk and by what you do—by your love, your faith, and your clean living. Until I come, give time and effort to the public reading of Scripture, to preaching, and to teaching.

Be sure to use the gift that the church council leaders saw in you when they laid their hands on you [and told you what to do for Jesus]. Practice these things so that everyone will see that you are growing as a Christian. Watch yourself in how you act and in what you teach. Keep on doing this, for by doing so, you will save both yourself and those who hear you.

4:1-16

Other Instructions

Teach and preach these things. Others may teach something else and may not agree with the true teachings of our Lord Jesus Christ and with teachings that lead to godly living. But such people are full of pride and know nothing.

They want to argue and quarrel about words, and this causes jealousy and fighting and hurtful talk and unkind suspicions. Such men, whose minds are twisted by sin, don't know how to tell the truth. They think that religion is a way to make money.

A godly life makes a contented person very rich. We brought nothing into the world, and we cannot take anything out of the world. So if we have food and clothing, that ought to satisfy us. Those who desire to be rich fall into temptation and into a trap of many foolish and harmful desires. These drag people into sins that destroy them.

For the love of money is a source of all kinds of evil. Some people have wandered away from faith in Jesus because of their love for money. By doing so they have given themselves many heartaches and pains.

But you, man of God, avoid all of these things. Aim at being right with God, living a godly life and having faith, love, loyalty, and gentleness. Fight the good fight of faith. Take hold of the life that lasts forever. It is to this you were called. . . .

6:3-12

Timothy

From Paul, an apostle of Christ Jesus chosen by God and sent to tell the life that God has promised through Christ Jesus, to my dear son Timothy.

May God the Father and Christ Jesus, our Lord, give you grace, mercy, and peace.

I thank God, whom I serve with a good conscience as my ancestors did. When I remember you, as I always do, in my prayers and I remember your tears [as we parted], I very much desire to see you. That would fill me with joy. I remember your very real faith, the faith your grandmother Lois and your mother Eunice (YOO-niss) had. I'm sure you now have it too.

For this reason I remind you to keep alive the gift of God that is in you, the spirit you received when I laid my hands on your head [and prayed that God would use you]. For God did not give us a spirit of fear. He gave us a spirit of power and love and self-control.

1:1-7

The Soldier of Jesus Christ

You, my son, be strong with the strength Christ Jesus has. And what you heard me preach to many people give to others, to others who then will be able to teach others.

Take your share of suffering as a good soldier of Jesus Christ. No soldier in active service gets mixed up in the affairs of ordinary life because he is busy trying to please his commanding officer.

An athlete does not win the prize unless he plays according to the rules. The farmer who does the hard work ought to get the first share of the crops. Think about what I am saying, because the Lord will help you understand it all.

Remember Jesus Christ, who was raised from death. He was a descendant of David, as I told you in my gospel, the gospel for which I am suffering and wearing chains like a criminal.

But the Word of God is not chained. That is why I suffer everything. I do it for the sake of the people God has chosen to be saved by Christ Jesus. They will receive his everlasting glory.

This is a true saying: If we have died with him, we will also live with him. If we remain true to him, we will also rule with him. If we say we don't know him, he will say he doesn't know us. [But even] when we are not true to him, he remains true to us because he cannot be anything but what he is.

2:1-13

A Good Worker

In a big house there are not only things made of gold and silver. There are also things made of wood and clay. Some are for special occasions; others for everyday use. If a person stays away from sin, he will be like one of the very best dishes in the house, saved and used by the master of the house for his best purposes.

So run away from the sinful desires that young people often have and go after what is right. Desire faith, love, and peace along with those people who really love the Lord. Have nothing to do with foolish and stupid arguments; you know that they cause quarrels.

The Lord's servant should not be a troublemaker. He must be kind to everyone, a good teacher, willing to suffer a lot, and a person who is gentle when he corrects people who are against him. God may change their hearts so that they will come to know the truth. In that way they may escape from the devil's trap after they have been captured by him to do what he wants them to do.

2:20-26

Teach the Truth

Now, you know my teachings, how I live, what I try to do, my faith, my patience, my love, and how I keep on working for God even though I have had troubles and suffering. You know all the things that happened to me, . . . the terrible things I had to suffer. But the Lord rescued me from them all.

Yes, all who want to live a godly life with Christ Jesus will be treated badly [by people, as he was], while sinful people and false teachers will go from bad to worse. They will lead others into wrong ways and will be misled themselves.

But as for you, continue in what you have learned and have believed. You know from whom you learned it. Ever since you were a child you have known the Holy Scriptures. They are able to teach you how to be saved though faith in Christ Jesus.

All Scripture is inspired by God and is useful for teaching, for correcting faults and errors, and for training people in right living. It gives the person who serves God everything he needs for doing every kind of good work.

3:10-17

Closing Words

The Lord will rescue me from all evil and will save me for his heavenly kingdom. To him be the glory forever and ever! Amen. . . .

May the Lord Jesus be with your spirit, and may God's grace [his loving favor] continue to be with you.

4:18, 22

THE LETTER OF PAUL TO
Titus

From Paul, a servant of God and an apostle of Jesus Christ, . . . to Titus, my true son in the faith we both have: may you receive grace and peace from God the Father and Christ Jesus our Savior.

I left you in Crete (KREET)* so that you would do what needed doing. I asked you to choose church leaders in every town. [But remember] they must be men others can't talk against. A church leader must have only one wife, and his children must be believers [in Jesus] and not have the reputation of being wild or disobedient.

Because a church leader is in charge of God's work, he must be someone people can't say bad things about. He must not be proud or get angry easily. He cannot be a drunkard or someone who fights a lot or is greedy. He must be friendly and love what is good.

He must be able to rule himself well, do all things in a right way, live a holy life, and control himself. He must hold on to the message he was taught, so that he can teach others the true teaching and also show those who disagree with them where they are wrong.

1:1-9

What to Teach

As for you, teach what is right and true. Ask the older men to be sober, serious, and sensible. Their faith and love are to be healthy and steady.

Also ask the older women to be careful how they act. They are not to go around talking about other people or be slaves to drinking. They are to teach what is good.

The older women are to teach the younger to love

their husbands and children, to be sensible and decent, and to be good housewives who are kind and who obey their husbands. If this is done, no one will be able to say anything bad about the Word of God.

Also teach the young men to control themselves. In all things be an example of good deeds. Be sincere and serious in your teaching and use words that cannot be criticized. Then people who are against you will be ashamed because they will not be able to say anything bad about you. . . .

2:1-8

Christian Behavior

Remind people to obey the leaders of their country and to be ready to do any good thing. Tell them not to speak bad about anyone, to be peaceful and gentle, and to be kind to all people. For there was a time when we too were foolish and disobeyed [God] and went wrong. Sinful desires and pleasures ruled us. Our lives were full of coveting and anger. People hated us and we hated them.

But when the goodness and loving kindness of God, our Savior, appeared, he saved us. It was not because of things we did to be right with God. It was because of his mercy [that he saved us] through the washing by which the Holy Spirit gives us new life.

God gave the Holy Spirit to us richly through Jesus Christ, our Savior, so that we could become right with God by his gracious love. That is how we receive the everlasting life we hope for. What I have told you is true. . . .

All who are with me send greetings to you. Give our greetings to our Christian friends there. God's grace be with you all.

3:1-7, 15

THE LETTER OF PAUL TO
Philemon

From Paul, a prisoner for the sake of Christ Jesus, and from our brother Timothy, to Philemon, our dear fellow worker [for Christ], our sister Apphia (AF-fee-ah), our fellow soldier Archippus (Ar-KIP-suhs), and to the church in your house: may God our Father and the Lord Jesus Christ give you grace and peace.

I always thank my God when I speak of you [Philemon] in my prayers, because I hear of your love toward all God's people and the faith you have in the Lord Jesus. My prayer is that your sharing of your faith will spread the knowledge of all the good things that are ours in Jesus Christ.

Your love, my Christian brother, has given me much joy and comfort, because you have cheered the hearts of God's people.

A Request

So now, through Christ I am bold enough to tell you what you ought to do. But because I love you I prefer to ask you instead of ordering you. I, Paul, an ambassador (am-BASS-ah-dawr)* and now also a prisoner for Christ Jesus, make this request to you for my son Onesimus (O-NEZ-ee-muhs). I have become his father while I have been in prison here. At one time he was of no use to you, but now he is useful to both you and me.

I am sending him back to you, and with him goes my heart. I would like to keep him here with me so that he could help me in your place while I am in prison for the sake of the gospel. But I do not want to do such a thing without you agreeing so that your kindness will not be forced but willing.

Perhaps Onesimus was away from you for a while so that you could have him back for good. Now he is no longer just a slave. He is a dear brother, especially to me. And how much more he will also mean to you now, both as a person and as a brother in the Lord!

So if you think of me as your partner, welcome him back as you would welcome me. If he has done anything wrong to you or owes you anything, charge it to me. I, Paul, guarantee this by writing it with my own hand: "I will pay you back." And don't forget you owe me your very life.

Yes, brother, I want some benefit from your being a Christian, so cheer up my heart as a brother in Christ [by doing what I've asked you to do]. I'm sure, as I write to you, that you will do what I ask and much more. At the same time get a room ready for me because I am hoping God will answer your prayers that I be given back to you. . . .

May the grace of the Lord Jesus Christ be in your spirit.

1-22, 25

THE LETTER OF PAUL TO THE
Hebrews

Long ago God spoke to our ancestors through the prophets in many different ways. But now in these days he has spoken to us through his Son. He is the one to whom God has given everything and through whom he made the world. He shines with the glory of God and is exactly like God.

1:1-3

A Warning

Be careful, Christian brothers and sisters, that none of you will have a bad, unbelieving heart that will lead you away from the living God. Help one another every day while you still can, so that none of you will become stubborn and fooled by sin. For we are all partners with Christ if we keep on trusting him to the end the way we trusted him at the beginning.

3:12-15

Jesus, the High Priest

We have a great high priest (PREEST),* Jesus, the Son of God, who has gone through the heavens. So let us hang on to the faith we have. Our high priest is a person who is able to understand how weak we are. He was tempted in every way we are tempted, but he didn't sin. Let us go with complete trust to where God rules with love, so that we will receive mercy and find loving-kindness when we need help.

4:14-16

They Lived by Faith

Now, faith is being sure we're going to get the things we hope for. It is being sure of the things we cannot see. It was by faith that people long ago received God's approval.

Through faith we understand that the world was made by the Word of God, that what we see was made out of what cannot be seen.

By faith Abel (AY-bel) offered to God a better gift in worship than Cain offered. Through his faith Abel received God's favor as a good man. God showed this by accepting Abel's gift. Even though Abel died, through his faith he is still speaking to us.

Because Enoch (EE-nahk) had faith, he was taken to God without dying. He couldn't be found because God had taken him. The Scriptures tell how he pleased God before he was taken. No one can please God without faith. Whoever wants to come near to God must believe that God exists and that he rewards those who look for him.

It was faith that made Noah build a large boat for the saving of his family. God had told him what was going to happen. By building the boat Noah showed the world how sinful it was. Noah became right with God through his faith in God.

Because Abraham had faith, he obeyed God when God told him to leave his home and go to a promised land. He left his home without knowing where he was going. By faith he kept living in the country God had promised to him, even though it was like a foreign land. Isaac and Jacob also received the same promise. They all lived in tents because Abraham was looking for a city whose builder and maker is God.

By faith Sarah became able to have a baby long after she was past the age of having children. She believed that God would do what he had promised. And from Abraham, who also was too old to have children, came a family with as many children as stars in the sky and grains of sand on the seashore.

All these persons died having faith in God. They didn't receive what God had promised them. But from a long way off they could see coming what God had promised and they looked forward to it. They admitted they were strangers and foreigners on earth. And people who say such things show that they are looking for a country of their own.

Of course, they weren't thinking about the country they had come from. If they had, they could have gone back. But they wanted a better country. That is why God is not ashamed to be called their God. He has prepared a city for them.

11:1-16

Looking to Jesus

Since we have around us such a large crowd of people who have had faith in God, let us get rid of everything that weighs us down, especially sin that holds on to us tightly. Let us keep on running the race God has planned for us and keep our eyes on Jesus. He is the pioneer and perfecter of our faith. He didn't stop believing in God when he had to suffer shame and die on a cross. He knew the joy that would later be his. Now he is sitting at the right side of God's throne [and ruling God's kingdom].

12:1-2

Christian Living

Keep on loving one another as Christian brothers and sisters. Don't forget to be friendly to strangers. Some people have invited angels into their homes without knowing it. Remember those in prison. Think of them as though you were in prison with them. And think of those people who are being mistreated because you are a part of the same body [of Christ].

Marriage ought to be respected by everyone, and husbands and wives must be faithful to each other. God will judge those who commit adultery.

Keep your lives free from the love of money, and be satisfied with what you have. God has said, "I will never let you down or leave you." That is why we can say with confidence, "The Lord is my helper. I will not be afraid. What can anyone do to me?"

Remember your leaders who spoke the Word of God to you. Think of how they lived and imitate their faith. Jesus Christ is the same yesterday, today, and forever.

13:1-8

THE LETTER BY
James

From James, a servant of God and of the Lord Jesus Christ, to God's people scattered all over the world: Greetings.

If any of you lacks wisdom, ask God for it. He will give it to you. He is always willing to give it to anyone—generously and without question. But you must have faith [when you ask], and you must not doubt that he will give you what you ask.

Anyone who doubts is pushed and tossed by the wind. Such a person, uncertain in all that he does, must not think that he will receive anything from the Lord. . . .

And know this, my dear brothers and sisters: Everyone ought to be quick to listen, but be slow to speak and slow in getting angry. A person's anger does not help him to be right with God.

Also put out of your life all that is dirty and wrong and receive willingly the Word that is taught to you. It has the power to save you. But be doers of the Word, and don't foolishly think it will do you any good if you only listen to it.

1:1, 5-8, 19-22

Faith and Works

My Christian brothers and sisters, since you have faith in our Lord Jesus Christ, who is the Lord of glory, you must never treat one person better than another. Suppose a rich man wearing gold rings and fine clothing comes into your meeting and a poor man in ragged clothes also comes in. If you pay more attention to the well-dressed man and you say to him, "Have a seat here, please," but you say to the poor man, "Stand over there," or "You may sit down here on the floor by my feet," are you not thinking that one is more important than another? This kind of thinking is sinful.

2:1-4

You do a good thing when you obey the great law of God in the Scriptures that says, "You shall love your neighbor as yourself." But if you treat one person differently than another, you sin, and that law of God says you are a lawbreaker.

And whoever keeps all the laws of God but breaks one becomes guilty of breaking them all. For he who said, "Do not commit adultery," also said, "Do not kill." Even if you do not commit adultery, you become a lawbreaker if you kill.

So speak and act as people who will be judged by a law that sets people free [the law of love]. For God will not show mercy when he judges people who have shown no mercy. But still his mercy can win over anyone who shows no mercy.

2:8-13

What good does it do, my Christian brothers and sisters, if you say you have faith but do not do the things that prove you have faith? Can that kind of faith save you? Suppose a brother or a sister needs clothes and doesn't have enough to eat. What good does it do to say to them, "God bless you! Keep warm and eat well!" if you don't give them the things they need? So it is with faith. A faith that does not do things is a dead faith.

2:14-17

Being Friends of God

What starts wars and fights among you? Is it not your desires that are fighting inside you? You want things you don't have, so you are ready to kill to get them. And because you strongly desire things you cannot get, you quarrel and fight.

You do not have because you do not ask God for what you want. And when you ask you don't receive it because you ask wrongly. You ask for things for your own pleasure. Unfaithful people! Don't you know that loving the sinful things of the world puts you against God? . . .

Stand up against the devil, and he will run away from you. Come close to God, and he will come close to you.

4:1-8

THE FIRST LETTER FROM
Peter

From Peter, an apostle of Jesus Christ; . . . May you enjoy a growing amount of grace and peace.

The Hope of God's People

Let us thank the God and Father of our Lord Jesus Christ! Because of his great mercy he gave us a new life and a new hope by raising Jesus Christ from the dead. And we look forward to blessings that last forever and do not spoil or fade away. They are kept in heaven for us. . . .

So you can be glad about this, even though you may have to suffer all kinds of tests for a little while. These tests are to see how real your faith is. Even gold, which can be destroyed, is tested by fire. So your faith, which is worth much more than gold, must also be tested. By passing the tests it brings you praise and honor and glory at the appearing of Jesus Christ.

You love him even though you have never seen him. Though you do not see him now, you believe in him and have a joy so great that words can't describe it. And through your faith your lives will be saved.

1:1-9

Suffering for Doing Good

When someone does something bad to you, don't do the same to him. If someone talks about you, don't talk about him. Instead, bless the person [wish him well], because that's what God wants you to do so that you will receive a blessing.

For "whoever wants to enjoy life and have good days must keep his tongue from speaking bad things and his lips from talking bad about others. He must turn away from what is sinful and do what is good. He must look for peace and go after it. For the Lord watches over those who do right and listens to their prayers, but he is against those who sin" [Psalm 34:12-16].

Who will harm you if you are eager to do what is right? But even if you have to suffer for doing what is right, you will be blessed. Don't be afraid of people or worry about them, but simply worship Christ as your Lord.

Always be ready to give an answer to anyone who asks you to explain the hope you have, but do it gently and with respect. Keep your conscience clear, so that when you are mistreated, those who make fun of your good behavior as a follower of Christ will become ashamed of what they say.

It is better to suffer for doing right, if that should happen to be God's will for you, than to suffer for doing wrong. Christ also suffered for sins, once and for all. He was a good man suffering for us who have sinned in order to lead us to God. His body was killed but his spirit was made alive.

3:9-18

Follow Christ While Suffering

The end of the world is near. Therefore stay thoughtful and alert so you can pray. Most important of all, keep steady your love for one another, because love covers up many many sins.

Cheerfully share your home with others. God has given each of you a special gift. As good managers of God's different kinds of gifts, use yours for the good of one another.

Whoever preaches ought to preach God's Word. Whoever serves ought to do it with the strength God gives him. In that way God will be honored through Jesus Christ. To him belong glory and power forever and ever. Amen. . . .

4:7-11

God Cares for You

Throw all your cares and worries on God because he cares for you. Be alert and watchful. Your enemy, the devil, prowls around like a hungry lion, looking for someone to eat. Be strong in your faith and stand up to him. Remember that other Christians all over the world are suffering the same experiences that you are suffering.

The God of all grace has called you to share his everlasting glory in Christ. After you have suffered for a little while, God himself will pick you up, put you back on your feet, and make you stronger than you were. May he rule forever and ever. Amen.

5:7-11

THE SECOND LETTER FROM
Peter

From Simon Peter, a servant and missionary of Jesus Christ, to those who have received the same faith we have. It is a faith in the goodness of our God and Savior Jesus Christ. May you have more and more of his love and peace as you get to know God and our Lord Jesus better.

1:1-2

A Shining Lamp

We did not follow cleverly made-up stories when we told you about the power and coming of our Lord Jesus Christ. We saw his greatness with our own eyes. For when he received honor and glory from God the Father, we were with him on the holy mountain. When God said to him, "This is my dear son, with whom I am well pleased," we ourselves heard this voice coming from heaven.

400

So we are sure that what the prophets said is true. And you will do well to pay attention to what they said. It is like a lamp that was shining in a dark place until the [new] day dawned and the light of the morning star [Jesus] shone into our hearts.

Above everything else, however, you must understand this: that no teaching of Scripture is simply a matter of someone's own opinion. No prophet's message ever came just by someone wanting to write. But men spoke a message that came from God when the Holy Spirit directed them.

1:16-21

The Coming of the Lord

This is now the second letter I have written to you, my dear friends. In both letters I have tried to get you to remember the holy prophets' messages and the command from the Lord and Savior given to you by your apostles.

First of all you must understand that in the last days [of the world] people will laugh at the truth. They will follow their own sinful desires and will say, "He promised to come again. Where is he? Ever since the first human beings died everything has continued as it was since the creation of the world."

But don't forget this, my dear friends, that for the Lord one day is like 1,000 years, and 1,000 years are like a day. The Lord is not slow about keeping his promise [to come again] in the way some people figure slowness. No, he is being patient with you, because he doesn't want any person to die. He wants all to turn away from their sins.

But the day of the Lord's coming will come like a robber: On that day the heavens will disappear with a loud noise. The sun, moon, and stars will burn up. And the earth and all that is in it will be burned up. . . . Therefore, my dear friends, since you are waiting for these things to happen, do all you can to be found free from sin and at peace [with God, yourself, and other people]. And consider our Lord's patience [in not coming] as part of his plan to save people. . . .

Grow in the grace and knowledge of our Lord and Savior Jesus Christ. To him be the glory both now and forever! Amen.

3:1-15, 18

THE FIRST LETTER FROM
John

My dear children, I am writing this to you so that you will not sin. But if anyone does sin, we have a friend who will plead for us with [God] the Father. This friend is Jesus Christ, who is right with God. And he is the one who takes away our sins, and not only ours, but also the sins of the whole world.

By this we can be sure that we know him: If we do his teachings. Anyone who says, "I know him," but does not do his teachings is a liar. There is no truth in him. But whoever does what God has said is a person whose love for God has really become perfect.

This is how we can be sure that we are living in God: Whoever says that he is living in God ought to live in the same way Jesus Christ lived.

2:1-6

God's Children

See what great love the Father has given us. We are called children of God, and so we are! The reason the world doesn't know us [that is, doesn't realize that we are God's children] is that it doesn't know him.

Dear friends, we are God's children already now, but it isn't clear just what we will be. But we know that when Jesus Christ will appear, we will be like him, because we will see him as he really is. And everyone who has this hope in Jesus will keep himself pure because Christ is pure. . . .

This is the message you have heard from the very beginning: We must love one another and not be like Cain, who was a child of the devil and killed his own brother. And why did Cain murder him? Because he did what was sinful and his brother did what was right.

Don't be surprised, Christian brothers and sisters, when the people of the world hate you. We know we have left death and have gone over into life because we love our brothers and sisters. A person who does not love has not gone from death to life. Whoever hates his brother is a murderer, and you know that a murderer does not have eternal life in him.

We know what love is because Christ gave his life for us. So we ought to give our lives for our brothers and sisters. But if a person has enough to live on and sees that his brother needs food and clothing, how can God's love be in him if he doesn't help his brother?

My children, let us not love only with words or talk. Let us really love and show it in actions.

3:1-3; 11-18

God Is Love

Dear friends, let us love one another, because love comes from God. The person who loves is a child of God and knows God. Whoever does not love does not know God, because God is love.

God showed his love for us by sending his only son into the world so that we could have life through him. This is love: It is not that we have loved God, but that he loved us and sent his son to pay for our sins.

Dear friends, if God loved us that much, then we also ought to love one another. No one has ever seen God. When we love one another, God lives in us and his love grows ever more perfect in us. . . .

We love because God first loved us. If a person says, "I love God," but hates a fellow human being, he is a liar. For anyone who doesn't love his brother [or sister] whom he has seen cannot love God, whom he

403

has not seen. This, then, is the command we have from Jesus: He who loves God must love his brother [and sister] also.

4:7-12; 19-21

THE SECOND LETTER BY
John

From John, the leader of the church, to one of God's chosen women and her children, whom I truly love. And I'm not the only one. All who are in the church love you because of the truth that is in us all and will be forever.

Grace, mercy, and peace from God the Father and from Jesus Christ, the Father's son, will be with us all. May they be truly ours in love.

1:1-3

Love One Another

I was very happy to find some of your children believing and living in the truth [of the gospel of Jesus Christ], just as the Father has commanded us. And now I beg you, dear lady, that we all love one another. This is no new commandment I write you, but the one we have had from the outset.

This love requires that we follow God's word and ways. As you heard from the beginning, God's will is that we all follow [live in and do] love. For many false teachers are in the world. They do not admit that Jesus Christ came as a human being. Such a person does not tell the truth and is an enemy of Christ. . . .

Anyone who does not stay with the teaching of Christ does not have God. Whoever stays with the teaching has both the Father and the Son [in his heart and life]. If anyone comes to you with some other kind of teaching, do not take him into your home.

The children of your sister who also was chosen by God send you their greetings.

1:4-7, 9-11, 13

THE THIRD LETTER BY
John

From John, the elder [of the church], to my dear Gaius (GAY-uhs), whom I love as a fellow Christian.

My dear friend, I pray that everything is going well with you and that you are in good health. I know that your spirit is well, for I was very happy when some Christians came by and told me how you are living the gospel. Nothing can make me happier than hearing that my children are following the truth.

My dear friend, you are very loyal by what you are doing for other Christians, especially also for strangers. They have told the church here about your love. As a service to God please help them continue on their trip. For they are traveling in God's service and have accepted nothing from people who do not know God. So we ought to help such men. In that way we can be working with them as they teach others the truth [about God].

I wrote a letter to the church, but Diotrephes (Dee-AHT-reh-fees), who wants to be the leader, will not pay any attention to what I say. So when I come, I will tell what he is doing—the awful things he is saying against me. Not only that, he refuses to welcome fellow Christians. He also stops those who want to welcome them and puts them out of the church.

Dear friends, do not follow what is sinful; follow what is good. The person who does good belongs to God; whoever does what is evil has not seen God. . . . May you have peace. All your friends send you their greetings. Greet all our friends, every one of them.

THE LETTER BY
Jude

From Jude, a servant of Jesus Christ and a brother of James, to those who have been called by God, who live in the love of God the Father, and who are being kept for Jesus Christ. May you receive more and more of God's mercy, peace, and love. . . .

You must remember, dear friends, what the missionaries of our Lord Jesus Christ said would happen. They said to you, "In the last days [before the coming again of Jesus] there will be people who will make fun of what you believe. They will prefer to follow their own godless desires."

These are men and women who cause people to divide into little groups against one another. They love things in the world and do not have the Holy Spirit.

But you, dear friends, keep on building yourselves up [and become strong] in your most holy faith. Let the Holy Spirit direct your praying. Keep yourselves in the love of God and wait for our Lord Jesus Christ to give you everlasting life through his mercy.

Try to convince people who doubt. Save some by snatching them out of the fires [of hell]. Be kind and forgiving to others [who are sinners]. But be afraid of their sins. Hate even the clothes they wear.

Give glory, honor, and power to him who is able to keep you from falling [away from your faith]. The only God, our Savior through Jesus Christ our Lord, will bring you happily to his wonderful self without sin. He had glory and power before the world began, he has it now, and will have it forever. Amen.

1-2, 17-25

406

THE
Revelation
GIVEN TO JOHN

This book tells what God revealed* to Jesus Christ so he could show his servants what will happen soon. And Christ made these things known by sending his angel to his servant John. John here reports the Word of God and the teachings of Jesus Christ and all that he saw.

The person who reads this book and listens to it being read and does what it says will be happy. For all these things will happen very soon.

"See!" [said the Lord Jesus], "I stand at the door and knock. When anyone hears my voice and opens the door, I will come in to him, and we will eat together. I will allow the person who wins to sit beside me on my throne, just as I sat by my Father on his throne when I won my victory."

1:1-3; 3:20-21

Pictures of Heaven

After this I [John] looked and saw an open door in heaven. And a voice that I had heard speaking to me like a trumpet said, "Come up here and I will show you what must happen after this."

At once I was under the control of the Holy Spirit, and I saw a throne in heaven with someone sitting on the throne. And the one who sat there appeared like jasper (JAS-pur),* and all around the throne was a rainbow that looked like the colors of an emerald (EM-er-ald).* Around the throne were 24 other thrones. Seated on the thrones were 24 church leaders dressed in white clothes and wearing gold crowns. . . .

After this I looked and saw a large crowd of people—so many that no one could count them. They were from every nation and race and language. They were standing in front of the throne and were dressed in white robes and were holding palm branches. They shouted, "We are saved by our God, who sits upon the throne." . . .

And all the angels stood around the throne . . . and lay down on their faces in front of the throne and worshiped God. They said, "Amen! Praise and glory and wisdom and thanks and honor and power and might belong to our God forever and ever! Amen."

4:1-4; 7:9-12

A New Heaven and Earth

Then I saw a new heaven and a new earth. The first heaven and the first earth had passed away, and there was no more sea.

I also saw the holy city, the new Jerusalem (Je-ROO-sah-lem) coming down out of heaven from God. It was ready like a bride is dressed and waiting for her husband.

And I heard a loud voice saying from the throne, "See! God's home is with people. He will live with them, and they will be his people. God himself will be with them, and he will wipe away all tears from their eyes. There will be no more death, and there will be no more sadness and crying or pain. The old things will have disappeared."

And he who sat upon the throne said, "See! I make all things new! . . . I, Jesus, have sent my angel to you with this message for the churches: I am both the root and a descendant of King David. I am the bright morning star."

The Spirit and the bride [the church of Jesus] say, "Come." And everyone who hears this should say, "Come." And anyone who is thirsty may come. And whoever wants the water of life may take it. It's a free gift. . . .

The one who tells these things says, "Yes, I am coming soon!" So be it. Come, Lord Jesus.

May all of God's people have the grace of the Lord Jesus. Amen.

21:1-5, 22:16-21

Glossary

Note: The words with an asterisk are in the glossary.

A

Aaron (AIR-on): The brother of Moses

Abba (AH-bah): The Hebrew word for father

Absalom (AB-suh-luhm): David's favorite son

adultery (uh-DUHL-tur-ree): Sex sins

ambassador (am-BASS-ah-dawr): A representative and messenger

ancestor (AN-sess-ter): Person way back in a family, like great-great-grandfather

anoint (ah-NOYNT): Appoint

apostles (ah-PAH-suhls): Messengers, missionaries, "those sent"

Arabia (Ah-RAY-bee-ah): A desert country south of Palestine

ark (AHRK): A large boat or ship

ark of the covenant (KUHV-eh-nuhnt): A box in which the Ten Commandments and some other holy items were kept

B

baal (BAY-ahl): Statue of the god Baal, who sometimes was worshiped by the people of Israel

barley (BAHR-lee): A seed or grain

Bethany (BETH-ah-nee): A town where Lazarus, Mary, and Martha lived; near Jerusalem in the country of Judea

blessed (BLEH-sed): Well off and happy

burning coals on the head: An expression for shame

C

Caesar (SEE-zar): The ruler of the Roman empire

Caesarea (Sez-ah-REE-ah): A city not far from Jerusalem

Canaan (KAY-nahn): The country that is now Palestine

Chaldeans (Kal-DEE-uhns): A name for the people of Babylon

chariot (CHAIR-ee-ot): A two-wheeled horse-drawn wagon or cart

chronicler (KRON-ik-ler): A teller of what happened

Colossians (Ko-LAH-shuhns): People who lived in Colossae (Ko-LAH-see)

comfort (KUHM-furt): Something that helps and cheers a person in trouble

countenance (KOWN-teh-nehns): Look and facial expression

covenant (KUHV-eh-nuhnt): An agreement with God; also the promise God made to love his people

Crete (KREET): An island near Greece

crucify (KREW-si-figh): Nail to a cross

cymbals (SIM-bahls): Brass plates that make a clashing sound when struck together or with a drumstick

Cyprus (SIGH-prus): A large island in the northeast part of the Mediterranean Sea

Cyrene (Sigh-REEN): A city on the north coast of Africa

D

Damascus (Dah-MAS-kus): A city north of Jerusalem to which Christians had fled

Darius (Dah-RIGH-uhs): A king of Persia

descendants (dee-SEN-dents): Children and children's children

Deuteronomy (Doo-ter-ON-an-mee): "Second law" because it presents the Ten Commandments a second time.

disciples: Pupils and followers of a teacher

Dothan (DO-thahn): A little town near Samaria

E

Ecclesiastes (Ay-klee-zee-AS-tees): A book by a preacher.

El-Elohe-Israel (EL-el-O-ay-IS-rah-ail): God, the God of Israel

Elijah (Ee-LIGH-jah): An Old Testament prophet

emerald (EM-er-ald): A bright green stone

Ephesians (Eh-FEE-shuhns): The Christians in the city of Ephesus (EH-feh-sus)

410

eternal (ee-TER-nal): Everlasting, never-ending; life that never ends

Ethiopian: (Ee-thee-O-pee-ahn): A man from Ethiopia, a country in northern Africa

exiles (EG-zighls): Persons taken away from their native country

Exodus (EX-uh-duhs): Going out, referring to the going out of the Israelites from Egypt

F

famine (FAM-in): A time of great food shortage

fast: Not to eat

fruit of our lips: Words of praise

G

Galatia (Guh-LAY-shee-ah): A part of the country that is now Turkey

Galileans (Gal-i-LEE-ans): People from Galilee, in northern Palestine

gallows (GAL-ohs): A platform built for hanging people

Gaza (GAY-za): One of five cities in which Philistines (Fil-ISS-tins) lived

Genesis (JEN-eh-sis): Beginnings

Gentiles (JEN-tighles): All people who are not Jews

glory: Shining greatness

go the way of all things: To die

grace of God: God's unearned and undeserved love

H

heathen (HEE-then): People who do not know the true God

Hebrews (HEE-broos): Another name for the people of Israel

Hebron (HEE-bruhn): A city south of Bethlehem in the mountains of Judah

heir (AIR): One who inherits; that is, receives possessions from another

herbs (ERBS): Plants used for seasoning foods and medicine

hosanna (hoh-ZAH-nah): A word like "hurrah," meaning praise

I

image (IM-age): An imitation or likeness of a person or thing

Israel (IS-rah-ail): Another name for Jacob and all Jews

J

Jahweh (YAH-way): One of the names by which the people of Israel knew God

jaspar (JAS-pur): A valuable, colorful stone

Jeroboam (Jair-o-BO-uhm): A young man who fled to Egypt because Solomon was afraid he might become king

Jesse (JES-see): The father of King David

Joab (JO-ab): The general of David's army

Judea (Jew-DEE-ah): The country around Jerusalem, a part of Palestine

Judges (JUHD-jehz): An Old Testament book that gives the history of rulers who were called judges

L

Lamentations (La-men-TAY-shuhns): Songs of sadness over what happened to Jerusalem

leper (LEP-er): A man with a serious skin disease called leprosy

Levi (LEE-vigh): One of the sons of Jacob

Levites (LEE-vights): Men in the family or tribe of Levi

Leviticus (Leh-VIT-ee-kuhs): A book of directions for the Levite men who served in the tent church and those who worked as priests

lice (LIGHS): Small insects

lizard (LIZ-urd): A four-legged, snake-like little animal

locust (LO-kuhst): A kind of grasshopper

lord: The ruler

lots, draw: Little stones with names on them were put into a box and one was then taken out without looking

M

Macedonia (Ma-sah-DOH-nee-ah): The area north of Greece

412

manger (MAYN-ger): A box that holds food for cattle

manna (MAN-nah): Flaky food that God gave the Israelites during their 40 years of wandering in the desert

Messiah (Meh-SIGH-ah): The Christ, the promised Savior of God's people

Miriam (MEER-ee-am): The sister of Moses

Moses (MO-zehs): The baby drawn out of the water, who later became a great leader of God's people

mountain of the Lord: Mount Zion, the hill in Jerusalem on which the temple was built

N

Nathan: A prophet during King David's reign

Numbers (NUHM-bers): An Old Testament book that reports the counting, numbering, and travels of the people of Israel

P

papyrus (pah-PIGH-ruhs): A tall water plant in the Nile valley

parable (PER-ah-buhl): A story with a lesson

Passover (PASS-over): The festival of remembering how God saved his people from slavery and death in Egypt

Persia (PUR-shah): The name of the country where the people of Judah were captives

Peter: The disciple Simon, also called Peter, meaning "like a rock"

Pharisees (FAIR-i-sees): A group of religious Jews who were usually strict and proud

Pharoah (FER-ah-oh): The king of Egypt

Philippians (Fill-IP-pee-uhns): The people who lived in the city of Philippi (Fill-IP-igh)

Pilate (PIGH-luht), Pontius (PON-shus): The Roman governor who condemned Jesus to death on a cross

plagues (PLAYGS): Something that causes great suffering

priest (PREEST): A religious leader

prophet (PRAH-fet): A person who speaks for God

Proverbs (PRAH-vurbs): Sayings that give advice

Q

quails (KWAYLS): Birds good for eating

R

rabbi (RAB-igh): A Jewish teacher

Rameses (RAM-zees): A town and area in Egypt

repent (ree-PENT): Turn from sinning to living with God

Reuben (ROO-ben): The oldest of the 12* sons of Jacob

revealed: Made known

rod and staff: Walking sticks that could also be used for guarding and defending a flock of sheep

roots of Jesse: A name for the Messiah who was to come from the family tree of Jesse and King David

S

sabbath (SA-bahth): A day for rest and worship; in the Old Testament it was the seventh day of the week

Sabeans (Sah-BEE-uhns): A wandering tribe of raiders

sackcloth, put on: To wear course clothing to show sorrow over something

sacrifice (SACK-ri-fighs): To give up something

salvation (sal-VAY-shun): A person or power that frees and saves

salvation (sal-VAY-shun), God's: God's way of saving people

Samaria (Sah-MER-ee-ah): The land between Galilee and Judea in Palestine

Samaritan (Sah-MER-i-tahn): A man or woman from Samaria

Samuel (SAM-yoo-el): A great leader of the Jewish people about 1,100 years before Jesus lived on earth

Satan (SAY-tun): Another name for the chief of devils or evil spirits

scorpions (SCOR-pee-ons): A large stinging bee; also a whip that stings because of sharp pieces of metal on the ends

seraphim (SER-ah-fim): Special angels

shield (SHEELD): Protection against injury

Silas (SIGH-las): A man who worked with Paul

slave: A person owned by another person

Solomon (SAHL-ah-mahn): The wise and very rich king of Israel who built the first temple in Jerusalem

Son of Man: Jesus

sower (SO-er): A farmer who, in Bible times, planted seeds by throwing them by hand

steward (STOO-werd): A person who manages a business or household for someone else

Succoth (SUCK-oth): A place near the Red Sea

Syria (SEER-ee-ah): A country north of Israel

T

tabernacle (TAB-er-nack-l): A tent church

temple: A house of God, a place where God agreed to meet with his people

Thessalonians (Thess-ah-LON-ee-uhns): Christians who lived in Thessalonica (Thess-ah-lo-NIGH-kah), a city in Greece

tongs (TAWNGS): A tool used for lifting and holding

twelve sons, the sons of Jacob: Reuben, Simeon, Levi, Judah, Issachar, Zebulun, Dan, Naphtali, Gad, Asher, Joseph, and Benjamin

V

visions (VIZH-uhns): Mental pictures or dreams, sometimes of the future

W

widow (WI-doh): A woman whose husband is dead

wilderness (WIL-der-ness): An area uninhabited by human beings

Word: A message from God

Z

Zerub-babel (Ze-RUB-bah-bel): A chief priest in the Old Testament

Zion (ZIGH-on): A name for the people of Jerusalem and for the entire kingdom of Judah; also a hill in Jerusalem on which the temple was built